KOREA
NORTH AND SOUTH

KOREA
NORTH AND SOUTH

The Deepening Crisis

Edited by Gavan McCormack
and Mark Selden

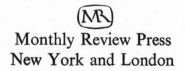

Monthly Review Press
New York and London

Library of Congress Cataloging in Publication Data
Main entry under title:
Korea, North and South.
    A rev. and expanded version of Crisis in
Korea, edited by G. McCormack and J. Gittings.
    Bibliography: p.235.
    1. Korea — Politics and government — 1960–
2. Korea (Democratic People's Republic) — Politics
and government. 3. Korean reunification question
(1945–   ) I. McCormack, Gavan. II. Selden,
Mark. III. Crisis in Korea.
DS922.26.K67   951.9'04   78–4503
ISBN 0–85345–448–5

Monthly Review Press
62 West 14th Street, New York, N.Y. 10011
47 Red Lion Street, London WC1R 4PF

Manufactured in the United States of America

10 9 8 7 6 5 4 3 2 1

Contents

Explanatory Notes

1. *Names.* In accordance with East Asian practise, Korean and Japanese names are written with the surname first, except where the Westernised form has become standard or better known — e.g., Syngman Rhee, John Chang, Channing Liem.
2. All references to $ are to US dollars at current exchange rates.
3. References to the *Guardian* are to the London, UK, daily.
4. Figures for US troops and nuclear weapons in Korea may vary slightly in the texts; in the period prior to completion of the manuscript troop levels fluctuated between 40 and 42,000, and the number of nuclear weapons is not officially revealed. The figure for South Korea's total debt is also uncertain since official Seoul statistics are unreliable.

Preface

The problems of divided Korea have been disregarded or misunderstood for over thirty years in the West. In 1945 the Korean people regained their independence from Japan, only to have their country cut in half by foreign intervention. In 1950 a civil war broke out, only to be internationalised and conducted (under the flag of the 'United Nations') with all the brutality that would later accompany American aggression in Vietnam — but without any of the publicity or protest. The ending of the war restored the artificially imposed *status quo* of division. Over the two decades since then there has developed a self-reliant, socialist but hard-to-understand North Korea (Democratic People's Republic of Korea, or DPRK), and a dependent, capitalist and repressive South Korea (Republic of Korea, or ROK).

The policy of the United States, Japan and other external powers who have directly shaped Korea's recent history is to perpetuate this *status quo* — to permanently divide Korea. While the North has successfully asserted its independence the South, precisely as a function of its high rate of growth, is increasingly locked into a subordinate relationship with the international capitalist world which seeks to perpetuate this division. In this book we show first that this relationship runs counter to the fundamental demand of the Korean people for national independence, and second that unification between North and South — which is frustrated by the external powers — is also a basic goal for the Korean people.

These twin imperatives in the Korean situation — for freedom from foreign interference and for ultimate re-unification — are not difficult to understand in the case of other countries subjugated by foreign powers and/or divided. But we must recognise the fact that Korea somehow seems different to many in the West.

Why is this so, and why is Korea the odd country out, a country about whose problems many people would just prefer to forget? In this volume we try to face up squarely to the reasons for Korea's international neglect, and we have identified the following myths which must be dispelled if support is to be forthcoming for legitimate Korean aspirations for self-determination and re-unification.

1. The myths of Cold War history, as applied to Korea and above all to the Korean War, were set with exceptional solidity in the early 1950s, when the United States was at the peak of its post-war power and influence and Western opinion generally was much less critical than in the 1960s and 1970s. Portraying the division of Korea as necessary, and the war as proof of northern perfidy, these myths sought to present the Korean case as somehow so 'different' that the normal demands for self-determination and for unification need not apply.

We show instead with abundant evidence (a) that by intervening in 1945 and forcing the division of Korea, the United States frustrated the country's liberation by popular, democratic and pro-socialist forces *who were Koreans*; and (b) that the Korean War was essentially a civil war in character, that the accepted truths in the West about its origins, about the conduct of the American side of the war, about the negotiations and the position of the North and of China, were always suspect and often demonstrably false.

2. The myth of the 'economic miracle' in South Korea continues to divert attention from the sufferings of the people of the South and to rationalise the division of Korea. South Korea under Pak Chung Hee has been transformed into a Mecca for multi-national business operations, but the gulf that separates this state from that of true economic development is wide. Precisely as a consequence of its spiraling GNP growth, literally millions of people have been driven off the land to lead a marginal existence in the slums of Seoul; police-state methods have pressed wages to rock bottom; the country is riddled by foreign debt and its leading economic sectors are controlled by Japanese and US capital. Since 1972 even the façade of democ-

racy has been abandoned and the jails have been filled with students, Christians, workers and many former government leaders who remain committed to democracy, social justice, national integrity and eventual re-unification. Increasingly the economic outlook is for growing debt and dependency. Particularly galling for Koreans in the South is the re-establishment of a high degree of influence and control by the colonial power whose depredations are so vividly remembered — Japan.

3. The myths about the DPRK — the North — arise from the barrier of ignorance and misunderstanding by which it is hemmed in. To a large extent this is the result of bias and hostility in the West, but certain features of the DPRK's political culture are disturbing, and its own propaganda is extremely counter-productive. We hope that the achievements of socialism in the North will prove far more enduring than these negative aspects. We discuss both, critically but with a fundamental sympathy for the attempt to build socialism in a hostile international environment.

The issue of a divided Korea can no longer be ignored. With the victory of liberation movements throughout Indo-China and changing configurations of international power in Asia, the Korean CIA's extension of Pak Chung Hee's system of repression and corruption from South Korea to the United States, Japan and Europe, President Carter's twin policies emphasising human rights and withdrawal of US ground forces in Korea, and a series of initiatives in the United Nations and other international forums, the question of Korea has again surfaced as a critical international test of principles of national self-determination. After twenty-five years in which conditions of a divided Korea were frozen and the barriers to re-unification strengthened, the issue of Korea again emerges at the centre of conflict and of human aspiration in Asia, and as an explosive issue in Japanese and American politics.

This book is very much a collective effort initiated by members of the Korea Committee (UK), 6 Endsleigh Street, London WC1. The Committee has been supported in this work by the Socialism Project of the Transnational Institute (Washington, DC, and Amsterdam), by the Association for Radical East Asian Studies (London) and the Committee of Concerned

Asian Scholars (North America). The Committee was set up in December 1975 to work towards the independence and re-unification of Korea. Apart from those whose names are attached to the various chapters, we gratefully acknowledge assistance of various kinds from Herbert Bix, Bruce Cumings, Paul Clifford, Pharis Harvey, Sato Masato and Takemoto Machiko.

The present publication revises and expands *Crisis in Korea* (London; Spokesman Books, 1977), with some chapters revised slightly and with the addition of new chapters on 'Korea and the Middle East,' 'The United States and Korea at the Crossroads,' 'The South Korean Economy,' and 'Britain, Europe and Korea,' as well as the Introduction.

Introduction

The United States and Korea at the Crossroads

Mark Selden

In 1945 Korea stood on the verge of emerging as a free and united nation from the long night of Japanese colonialism. American intervention denied it that prize, and has been the main factor in its being withheld from the Korean people ever since. The country remains divided, tense with the threat of war and the promise of renewed foreign involvement. As the 'Korean problem' becomes more difficult to contain, it is time to move beyond containment and to think of solution.

With the American defeat in Indo-China, Korea re-emerged as a focal point of conflict, immediately in 1975 with defence Secretary James Schlesinger's brandishing of nuclear weapons against the North, and persistently with conflict over troop withdrawal and ROK-US scandals. Analysis of three inter-related problems at the core of public debate in the United States — the Carter administration's troop withdrawal policy, the elaborate web of US-Korean scandal known as Koreagate, and the co-ordinated campaign praising the ROK economic 'miracle' — underlines the necessity for fundamental policy changes by the US and its allies to pave the way for a just and lasting solution to the problems of a divided and occupied Korea. This requires nothing less than reassessment of premises formulated in the 1950s and unquestioned since concerning US policies directed towards permanent division of the Korean peninsula and defining Korea's role in the world system.

I. The Carter Administration and US-Korea Policy in Regional Perspective
'I believe it will be possible to withdraw our ground forces

In preparing this essay I have benefited from the assistance and critical acumen of Herbert Bix, Pharis Harvey, Michael Klare, John Roberts and Suehiro Akira.

11

from Korea on a phased basis over a time span to be determined after consultation with both South Korea and Japan. At the same time, it should be made clear to the South Korean government that its internal oppression is repugnant to our people and undermines the support for our commitment there.'
Jimmy Carter, June 23, 1976.

In the major foreign policy address of his presidential drive, Jimmy Carter linked the issues of troop withdrawal and human rights, and introduced the Japan factor in US-Korea policy.

Important elements of the Carter troop withdrawal proposal reaffirm strategic premises of the Kissinger-Nixon diplomacy which inaugurated far-reaching adjustments in the post-Second World War order in Asia. The goal of stabilising a divided Korea, with the southern region in the American orbit, is unchanged. So, too, the dual strategy of ROK-US-Japan regional integration and of the realignment of US military forces to the island periphery of Asia. Thus, coinciding with the beginning of troop withdrawal from Vietnam, in 1970 the US announced and in 1971 completed without significant public discussion the reduction of 20,000 of its 64,000 troops in Korea, coupled with a $1.5 billion ROK force-modernisation programme designed to permit full withdrawal of US ground forces.[1]

Nevertheless, significant new elements in US-Korea policy, particularly the 1977 linkage of the troop withdrawal proposal with human rights diplomacy, and persistent hints of US diplomatic overtures to the DPRK, have precipitated sharp conflict in the US as well as in Japan and Korea.

Human rights as a rallying point for American foreign policy can best be understood in terms of the Carter administration's response to mounting challenge to the US global position and to certain glaring failures of the Kissinger diplomacy. The human rights issue provided the administration with a weapon of counter-attack against a wave of domestic and international criticisms of US policy which reached a peak in the final years of the Vietnam War but which continues and assumes new forms in the final years of the 1970s. From the Third World came denunciation of the US rôle in repressing national independence movements in Vietnam, Laos, Cambodia, Southern Africa and the Middle East. Moreover, the call for a new international economic order centred on US manipulation of North-South issues which perpetuated global poverty and inequality at the expense of Third World nations. The Kissinger diplomacy, directed towards redefining the relationship between the great powers and typified by the opening of a new phase in US-China relations, slighted not only issues of morality in favour of power politics but generally ignored the problems of the Third World. The appointment of Andrew Young, a black former civil rights activist, as Ambassador to the United Nations, and his emergence as the most visible (and controversial) spokesperson for US policy is one manifestation of the greater Carter sensitivity to North-South issues in general and to Africa in particular.

In the US, the breakdown of the anti-communist rationale, undermined both by the Vietnam War and the opening to China and the Soviet Union, enabled critics to raise human rights issues as a challenge to premises of American global policy. Thus the Nixon and Ford administration had been forced repeatedly to resort to subterfuge to elude Congressional restrictions on aid to strategic dictatorial régimes.

The human rights offensive attempted to turn the tables by placing both the Soviet Union and Third World nations on the defensive; thrusting aside the image of the American desecration of Vietnam, the United States sallied forth as the global champion of human rights. Human rights issues could be employed to attack the major US rival, the Soviet Union. They could also be used to pressure dictatorial client states to clean up their repressive images, to liberalise their policies in order to foster increased internal stability, and above all, to provide leverage to insure the maximum operational latitude for American capital. While the Carter administration quickly discovered serious pitfalls in human rights diplomacy, particularly the awkward necessity to repeatedly defend American policy with reference to human rights considerations, the goal clearly was to deflect criticism against the US and to extend US latitude in international affairs.

In the case of Korea, the administration quickly downplayed human rights rhetoric while calling for a military re-alignment. The issue of a complete US military withdrawal from the peninsula — the critical precondition for Korean independence and re-unification — is the crux of the matter. The persistence of the conflict manifested in the policy debate and the continuing Koreagate scandal reveals that powerful interests oppose attempts to transcend current policies despite the fact that these have become increasingly untenable. They include important corporate, military and intelligence interests, US as well as Japanese and Korean, with significant and often utterly corrupt stakes in the old order.

The issue of US troop withdrawal from Korea was debated during the Nixon administration in the course of the agonising re-appraisal of the post-Vietnam US military posture. Advocates of full ground troop withdrawal, including Defence Secretary Melvin Laird, were defeated. Kissinger's voice was decisive and the phased withdrawal co-ordinated with ROK force modernisation was abandoned, according to Laird's retrospective account.[2]

At the outset of his campaign for the presidency Jimmy Carter advocated a complete US troop pull-out from Korea. US forces, the last remaining on the Asian mainland, were, in Carter's view, hostages in an exposed and static position and subject to the whims of an erratic Pak Chung Hee administration. Drawing a major lesson from Vietnam, Carter recognised that their presence threatened US involvement in another protracted Asian land war, with the potential for spilling over into global conflict. Vietnam had, moreover, underlined the liability of reliance on foreign troops which constantly affront nationalist aspirations and may provide a rallying point in a national liberation struggle. Far more effective, at a fraction of the risk, classical naval doctrine held, were air and naval forces stationed off-shore. At the same time, the presence of US troops, the single most powerful symbol of unconditional support for the Pak régime, underlined the contradiction between professed US concern for human rights and the blatant repression practised by the dictatorship. US forces could, moreover, be withdrawn with confidence in the context of expanded military capacities both of the ROK and Japan, and rapid US deployment capabilities. The latter was demonstrated in 1976 in response to the Poplar Tree incident in which two American soldiers died in a clash with the DPRK in the demilitarised zone separating North and South:

'An F-4 squadron from Kadena AFB, Okinawa deployed to Korea the day after the 18 August incident. Within 15 hours of the execute decision, one squadron of F-111s arrived in Korea from Mountain Home AFB, Idaho, having been supported by KC-135 refueling aircraft from the Strategic Air Command and strategic airlift from the Military Airlift Command. These augmenting forces were reinforced by the aircraft carrier Midway and its Task Group which arrived on station in the Korean Strait before . . . 21 August 1976.'[3]

With the withdrawal of the Second Division from Korea, presently scheduled for the early 1980s, US forces in East Asia will consist of 115,000 men, approximately one-half pre-Vietnam War levels. This will include two-thirds of a division on Okinawa, nine tactical fighter squadrons, two carrier task forces, three naval patrol squadrons, and amphibious "lift" sufficient for two battalions.[4]

In the course of the sharp public debate and even fiercer political infighting over his initial troop withdrawal proposal, Carter quickly scaled down his plans, agreeing to retain two of the three brigades of ground forces and nuclear weapons beyond the 1980 presidential election. He had, moreover, prior to the election, determined to preserve indefinitely US air and naval power in Korea. The end result is a policy of continued (gradually reduced) US ground forces within the framework of long-range commitment of US airpower and predicated on all-round strengthening of the US-Japan-ROK military complex. While troop withdrawal proposals have dominated public discussion, the US is fueling the arms race in the Korean peninsula through encouraging and extensively financing accelerated ROK military build-up and the extension of Japanese military power in the region. We are witnessing the emergence of a new stage in a trans-pacific military complex in which dominant American power relies increasingly on Japanese and ROK contributions to preservation of the *status quo*.[5] The discussion which follows charts first the ROK military build-up and then the expansion of Japanese military power as components of a US strategic design for North-east Asia. This strategy, to be sure, coincides with the goals of the dominant interests in the ROK and Japan, while imposing a heavy price on the people of the region.

Secretary of Defence Harold Brown concisely summed up the essential logic of the Carter strategy for North-east Asia as follows:

'The ground forces of South Korea are comparable in numbers and capability to those of the north and should be able to hold defensive positions north of Seoul. However, they might require logistic and tactical air support to insure a successful forward defense and hence an assured deterrent. . . . It probably makes sense to continue approximately our current deployments in the Western Pacific, and with them, our ability to react swiftly to any aggressive moves by North Korea. A case can also be made for Japan to share more of the burden of protecting the sea lines of communication in Northeast Asia.'[6]

In short, the US will gradually withdraw ground forces from the Korean peninsula (at the rate of just 6,000 a year in 1978 and 1979) in favour of greater reliance on US air and naval power and expanded military contributions by the ROK and Japan. And, as Brown pointed out in July, 1977, 'The Republic of Korea is and will continue to be protected by a U.S. nuclear umbrella.'[7] The US is, moreover, preparing a third comprehensive multi-billion dollar military assistance programme supplementing the 1970 Modernisation and 1975 Force Improvement programmes, designed to provide the ROK the basis for military independence which was explicitly promised in each of the two previous programmes.

Attacks on the Carter policy, nevertheless, came quickly, first in the form of General John Singlaub's public warning of the inevitability of war if the troops were withdrawn, forcing Carter to relieve him of his post in Korea. Subsequently, General George Brown, in publicly (but with unmistakable ambivalence) supporting the withdrawal, revealed that the administration had rejected the Joint Chiefs of Staff recommendation to withdraw just 7,000 of the 33,000 ground troops over five years.[8] Frank Gibney, writing in *Foreign Affairs*, and Donald Zagoria in *The New York Times Magazine*, in influential critiques of Carter policy, denounced the troop withdrawal as undermining US credibility and increasing the danger of war.[9] Yet their conclusions remain subjective. Neither enters into serious discussion of the balance of forces in the region.

The ROK Military Build-up

Analysis of the military posture of the two Koreas conclusively shows ROK forces more than adequate to the task of defence and well on the way to building a dangerous offensive capability. When integrated US-Japan-ROK forces are viewed in a larger regional perspective, the balance overwhelmingly favours the US side, *regardless of the presence of US ground or air forces stationed in Korea.* As a 1977 military study by the US Congressional Budget Office correctly notes, the inescapable conclusion is that the real function of the US troops is not to repel attack from the North but to prop up the Pak dictatorship from the challenge of democratic forces in the ROK and to stifle pressures for re-unification.[10]

In the West the debate over military balance in the Korean peninsula has been addressed almost exclusively in terms of the northern threat to South Korea. Yet the South has twice the population and a GNP substantially larger than the North's. It has 300,000 troops with recent combat experience in Vietnam and a military budget that is 80 per cent larger; it has also been the recipient of more than twice the economic and military aid which China and the Soviet Union have accorded the North. Pentagon data reveals that between 1966 and 1975 the South imported $3 billion worth of military hardware, in contrast with $1 billion by the North, and this imbalance has continued.[11] The question of vulnerability to attack must be posed looking in two directions across the DMZ, that is, from the perspective both of the DPRK and the ROK.[12]

South Korea not only has a super-abundance of military power to defend itself against attack, but with its $5 billion five-year Force Improvement Plan, initiated in 1976, it is escalating the already intense arms race in the peninsula. The result is to impose heavier burdens on the people of both North and South, while further destabilising the present balance.

The ROK defence budget has been rising at extraordinary rates; from 300 billion *won* in 1974 it expanded by 50 per cent to 460 billion *won* in 1975 and by another 50 per cent to 740 billion *won* in 1976. In 1977 it reached 950 billion *won* ($1·95 billion). The military budget, 20 per cent of budgetary expenditure in 1975, by 1977 had increased to 35 per cent.[13]

In 1976 the ROK imposed a new 19 per cent defence sales tax and in 1977 it added a value-added tax to finance its current Force Improvement Programme, with US promises to kick in $1·9 billion of the total as partial 'compensation' for troop withdrawal. The proposed ROK military budget for the period 1977 to 1981 is set in the range of $11 to 13 billion.[14] The US, which fought in Korea at the sacrifice of 35,000 American and more than 1 million Korean lives and costs officially estimated at $164 billion, has subsequently maintained its forces in Korea at a cost of $12 billion. It has also provided the ROK with more than $13 billion in military and economic aid, sums substantially greater than those provided to any other nation except Vietnam.[15] It remains intimately involved in current ROK military plans. With the exception of the multi-billion dollar arms deals involving Iran, Saudi Arabia and Israel, in recent years arms sales to the ROK have surpassed all others, reaching a peak of $691 million in FY 1976 and projected at more than $370 million for 1977 and 1978.[16]

1977 assessments of the military balance by the Center for Defence Information, the International Institute for Strategic Studies and the Institute for International Policy, show that the ROK army, fifth largest in the world, enjoys a 140,000-man advantage over the North, favourable terrain for defending against attack, and vastly superior technological capabilities in anti-tank missiles, airpower and anti-aircraft missiles.[17] While DPRK forces have numerical advantages in tanks and aircraft, these are more than compensated for by US-ROK technical advantages, and the latter are increasing. Moreover, a summer 1977 Pentagon study recommended a five-year $8 billion ROK arms sale programme, including 239 jet fighters. In November, the Defence Department formally proposed — subject to presidential approval — sale of 60 F-16 jet fighters to South Korea for $1·2 billion. The F-16, the latest US combat aircraft, is slated as the mainstay of NATO aircraft well into the 1980s. Senator George McGovern has warned that this sale would provide 'the capacity for offensive actions against

North Korea'. The Carter troop withdrawal programme, more-over, calls for the indefinite maintenance of US airpower in South Korea, at present three squadrons of Phantom jets with three times the range and payload of comparable DPRK air-craft.[18]

One ROK response to the Carter troop withdrawal policy has been accelerated domestic defence construction (the North already produces much of its own weaponry), including vigor-ous efforts geared towards production of nuclear weapons. This drive rests fundamentally on US and Japanese military technology, though its ultimate goal is self-sufficiency in basic military hardware. Already in 1975 the ROK purchased a $2 billion Lockheed plant for manufacture of solid fuel missiles. In 1977 it produced 50 per cent of its military equipment, not only M-16 rifles, mines and mine detectors, grenades and 500-pound bombs, but also 500-D helicopters (assembly), patrol boats, M-72 anti-tank rocket launchers, a Korean designed armoured personnel carrier and 155 and 105 mm howitzers. It has also reportedly produced a prototype submarine and de-sign work for a light tank.[19] In short, the emerging phase of the Korean arms race supplements large-scale foreign pur-chases with increasing reliance on imported technology.

The growth of the ROK military industry is integrally linked to the overall strategy of industrialisation fostered by US and Japanese capital. The keystone of the ROK military industries is the Changwon Machine Complex, inaugurated in 1974 and scheduled to house over 100 plants. An $80 million World Bank loan to Hyundai International provided a major stimulus for the $391 million heavy machinery project.[20] Changwon is the site of extensive joint ventures with Japan — 8 of the 11 foreign firms presently building plants in the complex are Japanese — and persistent Japanese press reports have noted the approach of ROK defence firms to their Japanese counter-parts, particularly the Mitsubishi group which dominates Japan's military industry. Korea thus is slated to become the first major export platform for the Japanese military industry, confined to domestic activity since defeat in the Second World War.

The ROK is also pressing hard to attain independent nuclear capability as reflected in the high priority given its nuclear power programme. The Fourth Five Year Plan (1977–81) allocated $110 million to develop nuclear technology. Korea's first nuclear power plant went into trial production in the Spring of 1977 and plans have been announced to complete 5 reactors by 1985 and 25 reactors with total generating capacity of 25,000 megawatts by the year 2000. At that time the $32 billion construction programme is targeted to produce 50 per cent of ROK electric capacity from nuclear reactors. While actively recruiting Korean scientists overseas, the government has also sent 30 specialists to study abroad and is training 90 nuclear engineers in South Korea.[21]

In short, the ROK, with preponderant military and economic power in the peninsula, but with — indeed, precisely in consequence of — grave political weaknesses, is bent on an accelerated military build-up which both reinforces Pak's personal power and adds a further destabilising element to an explosive situation. This US-ROK strategy thus directly negates the aspirations of the Korean people for peaceful reunification as summed up in the July 4, 1972, Joint Communiqué signed by the North and South (see Chapter 12).

The Japanese Military and US Korea Policy

The Carter troop withdrawal proposal is a critical element in US policy pressuring Japan to assume a larger military role in North-east Asia and the Pacific in order to facilitate US cutbacks on costs and direct military commitment while preserving its dominant position in the region. It must be understood in the context of a global strategy, particularly of US-Soviet rivalry and the role of secondary powers.

At first glance, the Carter plan suggests the revival of an historic US policy which may be traced to the Taft-Katsura Agreement of 1905 (encouraging Japanese annexation of Korea to deflect its expansion away from US-controlled Hawaii and the Philippines) and the 1947 policy advanced by General Albert Wedemeyer (calling for withdrawal of all US forces from the peninsula), namely throwing Korea to Japan.[22] The fact that Korea remains, as always for American policy-makers, a pawn in a larger regional and global game — US rivalry with the Soviet Union, China and Japan — constitutes a significant historical continuity. However, both because of Korea's strategic importance in the present conjuncture of US-Soviet rivalry, and because the dynamism of the expansive Korean economy has enhanced the importance of the region, the Carter administration seeks a reduced US military rôle within a US-Japan condominium. Korea is, in short, to be preserved within the US orbit indefinitely, yet perforce the means must change.

Beginning with the Sato-Nixon Joint Communiqué of November, 1969, the US and Japan, with varying shades of emphasis, have repeatedly stated that the defence of South Korea was 'essential' to Japan's own security. Forced by financial and political realities to cut back and rationalise its own Asian military presence, the US has looked to Japan to assume a larger share of military costs and responsibilities in North-east Asia, consistent with its rapidly growing economic stake in the region. In commenting on the 1978 US military budget, for example, Defence Secretary Harold Brown suggested that the Japanese consider placing 'more emphasis on air defence and even more on anti-submarine warfare capability'.[23] And in November, 1977, he indicated publicly for the first time the US intention to gradually reduce its forces in the Pacific, including those in Japan.[24]

Japan, since the late 1960s the world's seventh ranking military power, has steadily extended its military capabilities and sphere of air and naval operations. During the early 1970s, the Japanese enlarged the scope of naval patrols from adjacent sea lanes to 1,000 nautical miles from Japan. As military critic Fujii Haruo has observed of the emerging US-Japan naval division of labour, 'The sea areas to be placed under the MSDF's (Marine Self-Defence Force) control centre on the Tsushima Straits and include both the waters around the Korean peninsula . . . and the most dangerous part of the supply route extending to the US mainland.'[25] This contributes not only to US dominance of the Korean peninsula, but to the major strategic task of blocking the Soviet Union by controlling the three North-west Pacific straits, Soya, Tsugaru and Tsushima, which provide the only Soviet naval access to the Pacific. Despite the increasing ability of the Soviet Union to challenge the US militarily in many parts of the globe, the US bloc retains decisive control of North-east Asia through supremacy on the seas. US control seems assured as long as Soviet preoccupation in the region centres on the Sino-Soviet conflict; similar Chinese pre-occupations have apparently reduced pressures from that quarter for the withdrawal of US forces from the area.

The United States has successfully pressured Japan to increase airpower capabilities with the specific assignment of providing a 'shield in the Pacific' to guard the US fleet against attack launched from the Asian mainland. In August, 1977, the Japanese government announced its intention to purchase 154 US-supplied and licence-built aircraft in FY 1978, including 25 McDonnell-Douglas/Mitsubishi F-15 fighters and, the multi-million dollar Lockheed bribery scandal notwithstanding, 10 Lockheed/Kawasaki P-3C anti-submarine aircraft. The power-packed F-15, which will cost Japan nearly $40 million per plane when fully equipped, modified to SDF specifications, and locally produced, both increases Japan's defence capabilities and expands potential strike power.[26]

There is, in addition, a critical economic dimension to US pressures for a Japanese as well as a South Korean military build-up. In the Fall of 1977 the US forced a 20 per cent plus revaluation of the *yen* and demanded sweeping Japanese measures to reduce the chronic US unfavourable trade balance with Japan. Coming in the midst of Japan's most severe recession since the 1930s — in October, 1977, for example, the closing of 10 blast furnaces left one-third of Japan's 68 steel furnaces idle with real unemployment nationally unofficially estimated at 8 per cent of the work force — US moves which reduced the competitiveness of Japanese exports are being described in Japan as 'undeclared economic war'.[27] Expanded purchases of US military hardware would simultaneously alleviate the balance of payments problem and expand Japan's regional military capability.

If the US is pressing for the modernisation and expansion of the Japanese military, powerful voices within the Japanese establishment have long urged a similar course. For example, Senga Tetsuya, head of the Defence Production Committee of the Japan Federation of Economic Organisations (*Keidanren*), the leading spokesman for military industries, has dramatically warned of the danger that Japan's military 'will turn into bamboo-spear units' in the absence of larger capital spending to insure modernisation.[28]

At the same time, the process continues of chipping away at constitutional restrictions against Japanese military activity. Successive hijackings of Japan Airlines and Lufthansa planes in October, 1977, in which the Japanese government paid a $6 million ransom while West German officials stormed the plane killing the hijackers, prompted strident demands to amend existing laws to permit overseas dispatch of police units in the case of future hijackings.[29] On October 14, 1977, Kurisu Hiroomi, chairman-designate of the Joint Staff Council of the Self-Defence Forces, in a widely publicised news conference, called for full cabinet status and imperial approval for appointment to the post, thus strengthening links between the military and the imperial system.[30] Moreover, pressure for promotion of the arms industry has even come from some quarters in the labour movement, as in the call by the vice-chairman of the Tokyo Electric Union to fight unemployment through expanded military production.[31]

In short, as the US initiated troop withdrawal from Korea, beginning in 1970, Japan expanded its own military capability and powerful pressures exist for further militarisation. ROK-Japan integration, already far advanced in the economic sphere, extends increasingly to the military-strategic realm.[32]

While both Pak Chung Hee and the US government have eagerly wooed Japan to assume a leading economic and military role in Korea, it must be noted that this policy has generated sharp contradictions and public protest within South Korea and among the Korean expatriate community. The November 18, 1977, public statement by former Foreign Minister General Choi Duk Shin, chief negotiator in the Japan-ROK Normalisation Treaty of 1965, is illustrative of mounting criticism of Korea's subordination to its former colonial master, Japan. Denouncing Pak's betrayal of national interests in dropping Korean demands for reparations, Choi describes how, as Ambassador to West Germany, his efforts to find alternatives to complete economic dependence on Japan through a larger German rôle were aborted when in 1967 the Pak régime abducted, jailed and tortured prominent Koreans living in Germany.[33]

The rationalisation of Korea policy in terms of the 'security of Japan', is fraudulent. Even *if* there was a shred of legitimacy to policies by one nation to perpetuate the division and economic subjugation of another, and its former colony at that, Japanese interests of peace and long-term harmonious relationships with neighbours on the peninsula ultimately can only be served by policies fostering the peaceful re-unification of the divided Korean nation. Further Japanese military and economic penetration of the South or build-up of a US-Japan-ROK military nexus will exacerbate tensions in the peninsula and thus run counter to these fundamental interests. Moreover, even in economic terms, Japan's emergence as the leading trading partner of the People's Republic of China suggests that it would establish a long-term economic relationship with an economically viable unified Korean nation.

Toward a New US Korea Policy
The initial Carter linkage of troop withdrawal and human rights touched off a new round in the debate over US-Korea policy without directly posing the core issues of independence and re-unification. In short, the basic framework of US-Korea policy, predicated on perpetuation of the division of the peninsula, has remained unchallenged. The Carter administration has made no attempt, for example, to counter two decades of media and government vilification of the DPRK as an irrational, aggressive power which was designed to justify the long-term US military intervention under United Nations cover. So long as the DPRK remains an international pariah in American consciousness, fundamental US policy is likely to remain trapped in the anachronistic assumptions of the 1950s.

Senator George McGovern has provided the first fundamental critique by a high public official of American Korea policy. In his September, 1977, keynote address to a US-Japan parliamentarians' conference on Korea, McGovern called for breaking the present dangerous impasse through direct negotiations with the DPRK. Observing that 'supporting a régime which is based on fear rather than on positive support runs a high risk of violent upheaval at some point in the future,' McGovern questioned not only the US troop presence but the advisability of escalating military tensions through the arms build-up in the South.[34]

This has opened for public discussion not only the possibility of transcending the isolation of the North, but of a serious dialogue directed towards ending the US military presence and permitting the Korean people to exercise their right of self-determination.

At the same time, however, powerful counter forces are at work. In 1977 a far reaching campaign has unfolded to undermine not only the modest reduction of US forces but to replace the Pak régime's well-earned image of brutality and corruption with the progressive veneer of a modernising nation. Analysis of proponents of conflicting images of Pak's Korea, surfacing simultaneously in the Koreagate scandal and the public relations campaign hailing the ROK economic 'miracle', helps clarify the forces presently contesting the future of US-Korea policy.

II. Koreagate: The Anatomy of US-Korea Corruption

'It is impossible to employ genuinely free men for enslaving others; and conversely, the most brutalized and spineless slaves make the most pitiless and effective despoilers of the liberties of others.' E. Herbert Norman.

The morass of corruption revealed in the Koreagate scandal, like a virulent cancer spreading throughout the body, has tainted every major force and institution shaping the US-ROK relationship: from Presidents Pak and Nixon to the CIA and KCIA, leading US and Japanese multi-national corporations and Korean state capitalist and private enterprises, the US Congress, and the international anti-communist movement embracing the US, Japan and South Korea. In assessing the complex relationships described below, it is important to retain clarity on the central fact that the driving force and dominant partner in every phase of the three decade US-ROK relationship has been the United States.

US Aid and the ROK Political Economy

The roots of US-ROK corruption lie in the absolute imbalance of wealth and power between the US and its dependent ward, as the ROK emerged from a half century of colonialism followed by the devastation of the Korean War. Herbert Bix has described the formation of the Korean mercenary state, shaped militarily, politically and economically in the 1950s to serve US interests.[35] Its origins may be traced in turn to the dual legacies of Japanese colonialism and the division of the nation. Despite the dynamic changes wrought by the Pak régime, the ROK's essential mercenary character remains through the Vietnam War and the advance of Japanese capital in the 1960s, and the era of export-led high speed growth and large-scale induction of private and multilateral capital in the 1970s. Not only the ROK mercenary contribution in Vietnam, but Japan's economic penetration of Korea and high speed ROK economic growth conform to US interests under changing circumstances. (The rapid growth of the 1970s opens the possibility of a more independent ROK role in future; yet so long as this dynamism rests overwhelmingly on foreign capital, technology and trade in a divided Korea, characteristic features of the mercenary state will persist (see Chapter 4).

By 1970, $12·5 billion had been channelled into South Korea in the form of US aid, loans, investment and payment for military forces, dwarfing an economy whose gross investment was approximately $2 billion.[36] From the 1950s the overriding dependence on foreign funds shaped patterns of interaction indicated in Figure 1.

Figure 1.   Capital Flow and Corruption

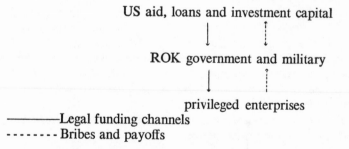

US aid, loans and investment capital

ROK government and military

privileged enterprises
———————Legal funding channels
- - - - - - - Bribes and payoffs

With the state directing major sources of capital since the 1950s, the ROK's characteristic *jaebol* (*zaibatsu*) monopoly form achieved dominance among domestic firms in the context of institutionalised political pay-offs. Those 'political capitalists' or plutocrats who successfully curried favour with the régime monopolised access to scarce capital in return for diverting portions of it for political purposes. A series of major scandals, the largest being the $3 million tungsten–dollar scandal of 1952, involved manipulation of foreign exchange and of monopoly prices on imported grain and fertiliser with the beneficiaries making substantial payments to Rhee's party.[37] Through the maintenance of artificial exchange and interest rates, and, particularly under the Pak régime, with the formation of highly profitable government joint ventures with foreign capital, public officials became enmeshed in a web of corruption and graft. One result was the sharp bifurcation between privileged sectors tied to and serving foreign capital and the state, particularly export-oriented sectors, which grew at the expense of stagnating agriculture and the domestic economy in general.[38] The dynamism of leading sectors was achieved in short by a process of cannibalisation which has accelerated in the 1970s with the inexorable destruction of the countryside to provide urban industry with a labour surplus which would be accommodated in the squatter settlements of Seoul.

Pak's personal military cotérie is at the centre of the political economy of the mercenary state. This pattern, by no means unique — Indonesia and the Philippines, for example, have created their own variants — characterises the particular mode of corruption which has evolved in the ROK. We will consider examples from the vitally important oil industry to illustrate the pattern of the US-Korea economic relationship and the structure of corruption in the mercenary state. All three of Korea's oil companies are 50-50 joint ventures between US multi-national oil and the Pak régime. The largest, Korea Oil Company, a joint venture with Gulf Oil, controls 41 per cent of all oil products sold in Korea and 44 per cent of refining capacity. Its president from 1966–74, General Park Won Suk, a graduate of the Japanese Military Academy, attended the US Air Force College in 1953. After serving as Deputy Director of the KCIA in 1963–64, he became Chief of Staff of the Air Force in 1965–66. His successor was General Yu Chae Hung, likewise a graduate of the Japanese Military Academy, special assistant to President Pak in 1970–71 and Minister of National Defence in 1974 before taking up his post as president of Korea Oil. Pak Chung Hee's power rests heavily on his ability to

forge a network of tight personal relationships linking international capital, the leading sectors of the Korean economy and
his personal followers at the centre of power.[39]

Vietnam and the Korean Mercenary State

The Vietnam War vastly increased the scale and scope of
institutionalised US-ROK corruption. As early as 1950, as
Frank Baldwin has noted, 'The Pentagon's need for an Asian
army in reserve appears to have been a primary factor in US
policy toward Korea'.[40] Syngman Rhee's 1954 offer to provide
troops in Laos was declined by the Pentagon after careful
study, but in 1964 Korea emerged as an international gendarme
in the service of American power. The Vietnam War provided
the first important occasion for dispatch of Korean labour
overseas, perhaps the ultimate corruption in a sordid pattern
of exploitation of the Korean people in the service of a foreign
power and the dictatorship. The ROK has subsequently dis-
patched prostitutes to Japan, children for adoption to the US
and Europe, miners and nurses to West Germany and semi-
militarised construction workers to the Middle East in search
of foreign currency to bolster the power of the dictatorship. In
this way foreign capital is acquired, a safety valve on unemployment provided and the mercenary relationship internationalised.

Eventually more than 312,000 Korean troops served with
notorious brutality in Vietnam. These latter-day Hessians —
covertly paid by the US government which praised their contribution to the cause of freedom — served the Pak dictatorship which controlled the lion's share of payments for their
services. But ultimately, of course, they served the US. In the
end the US paid the Pak régime more than $10 billion for
South Korea's rented troops in Vietnam, including $3·16
billion in military aid between 1966–73, $925 million in over-
seas allowances for two Korean divisions and $546 million
in construction contracts in Vietnam.[41]

The PL 480 Connection, the KCIA and Koreagate

Illicit rice dealings were at the heart of the conglomerate of
extortion, influence-peddling and brutality comprising the US-
ROK relationship in the early 1970s. Under Public Law 480

US government surplus rice flowed to South Korea during the first three years of the Nixon administration in amounts 40 per cent above AID-recommended levels, making Korea second only to India as a recipient of grain.[42] Quantities of rice imported in 1970–73 were nearly four times larger than imports during the 1950s when Korea was recovering from the ravages of war. One result of flooding Korea with surplus rice was to drive down rice prices. For Pak this served the dual purpose of creating large labour reserves by forcing millions off the land and keeping food prices down in the cities. This facilitated the regime's cheap labour, export-oriented development strategy predicated on a large-scale influx of foreign capital. PL 480 held out other attractions as well, in the form of vast rake-offs for Pak and his cronies on the one hand, and for Nixon allies on the other. PL 480 rice provided the most lavish, but by no means the only, sums which Park Tongsun and other ROK agents used for their bribery operations in the US.

The US-Japan-ROK triangle inevitably extends from the military and economic to the realm of corruption. For example, key figures indicted in the Lockheed bribery scandal which brought down the Tanaka cabinet in 1975 are active in Japan's Korea lobby. They include fixer Kodama Yoshio, the recipient of the largest undercover Lockheed funds and doyen of the right wing with experience dating back to opium trading and intelligence in China in the 1930s; and Osano Kenji, Tanaka's principal financial backer, a leading shareholder in Korean Airlines, and owner of vast hotel and real estate holdings in Korea.

The President of Mitsubishi has admitted that four leading trading companies, Mitsubishi, Mitsui, Marubeni and Nissho-Iwai, made rebate payments of $2·5 million between 1971 and 1973 to Korean accounts in American banks. The key intermediary and recipient of the funds in a US bank account was Kim Sung Kon, a leading businessman, government official and chief of the finance committee of Pak's Democratic-Republic Party. The same gentleman successfully extorted $4 million in campaign contributions for Pak from Gulf Oil (see below). These sums, derived from profits on the Seoul Railway, are believed to have been used in KCIA bribery operations in the US. The Japanese scandal directly implicates former Premier

Kishi Shunsuke and Mitsubishi Chairman Fujino Chujiro, both intimates of Pak Chung Hee and the key figures in winning the lucrative railroad construction and equipment contracts for Japan.[43]

The US House Ethics Committee in October, 1977, disclosed that Park Tongsun received $9,204,815 in commissions on his monopoly of US rice sales to Korea between 1969 and January, 1976, including more than $3·5 million each in 1974 and 1975. In conjunction with his other lucrative businesses, co-ordinated under the Pacific Development Corporation, this provided ample funds to bring 120 congressmen and 30 people in the executive branch under the influence of the Pak régime, in the estimate of a September, 1972, KCIA internal report. The KCIA concluded that when US aid to the ROK was under congressional attack, Park Tongsun 'was able to put the persons with influence over the issue of military aid to Korea into his organisation of restoration, including senators and representatives, high-ranking administration officials and White House staffers.'[44] What is certain is the success of efforts not only to block aid cuts to Korea but to produce a significant rise in overall financial commitments in the 1970s.[45]

In November, 1977, the House Committee's Investigation of Korean-American Relations published the 1976 KCIA plan of operations in the United States. Budgeted at approximately $700,000, the detailed plan outlined the use of pay-offs to key congressmen and aids, and for 'implementation of an intelligence network in the White House'. It also mapped out an elaborately funded programme to assure favourable newspaper, magazine and TV coverage and described plans to infiltrate both the church and academic circles, all of which had shown signs of becoming increasingly critical of the Pak régime. The KCIA's psychological warfare bureau took responsibility for these operations. Also targeted for major coercive efforts were the Korean community in the US.[46]

It has been documented, moreover, that Park Tongsun, the central figure in congressional and executive bribery, received direct instructions from ranking officials in the Blue House in Seoul.[47] According to 1974 memos of the KCIA/US chief (code name Catholic Father), receipts for KCIA payoffs for congressional bribes (Operation White Snow) were to be preserved in order to report directly to President Pak Chung Hee (the Chief Priest of Bulkook Buddhist Temple).[48]

The exclusive Georgetown Club, purchased with $3 million in funds provided by the number two KCIA man in the US, Kim Sang Kuen, served as the site for Park's lavish entertainment of US public figures, including then Vice President Gerald Ford and Senate Majority Leader Thomas P. O'Neill.[49]

Large-scale Korean bribery of US officials reached a peak in the early 1970s when the US began its withdrawal from both Vietnam and Korea, and Pak Chung Hee's fears mounted that a complete US troop pull-out and aid cut-off were in the offing. Viewed from the White House, Louisiana and California, the key rice growing states, were essential to Nixon's 1972 electoral and political strategy. Former Democratic Congressman Richard Hanna of California (under indictment) and Otto Passman of Louisiana (until 1976 the powerful Chairman of the House Appropriations Committee, the key congressman in determining foreign aid funding), two key links between the ROK and US rice exporters, are among the major figures implicated in the bribery scandal.[50] In addition, the Korean connection to the executive did not end with Nixon's demise. In 1977 James Howe, husband of Betty Ford's personal assistant, committed suicide during an investigation of a family trip to the Dominican Republic in the company of Park Tongsun.[51]

PL 480 rice exemplifies the two-way impact of the corruption of the ROK-US relationship. US rice undermined Korean agriculture while profiting US-agri-business and key Nixon allies. It also armed the Pak dictatorship with large quantities of sugar-coated bullets which, often in the form of crisp $100 bills stuffed in envelopes for delivery to politicians, returned to undermine the American political process.

The World Anti-Communist League, Moon Sung Myung and the CIA

Among the interstices of US-ROK mutual infiltration is that murky intersection of the world anti-communist movement, evangelical 'Christianity' as practised by Moon Sung Myung and his followers in the Unification Church, and the CIA. Consider the Connecticut Avenue offices in Washington opened in 1964 which link the KCIA, CIA, Asian People's Anti-Communist League and Moon. The APACL (later the World Anti-Communist League), founded under the direction of William Curtin, has principally found its funding and support in reactionary régimes on Taiwan and South Korea and the Taiwan and ROK lobbies in the US and Japan. Here, as well as in analogous Japanese groupings, the China lobby unites with the Korea lobby and international right wing and gangster forces. Army Intelligence officer Curtin served as senior adviser to the Korean Second Army before coming to Washington in 1964. In the same year, Curtin and KCIA Director Kim Jong Pil established the Washington office of the Korean Cultural and Freedom Foundation, whose director was Pak Bo Hi, a major figure in Moon's Unification Church and a KCIA agent. Radio Free Asia launched its anti-communist broadcasting from the same complex. When Radio Free Asia was subject to a Justice Department investigation for failure to register as a foreign agent, it was successfully represented by Robert Amory, former Deputy Director of the CIA and the key government figure singled out by former State Department officer Donald Ranard in blocking the Koreagate investigation in the early 1970s. At this time, Amory represented Corcoran, Foley, Youngman and Rowe, a Washington law firm with long-standing ties both to the oil industry and the CIA.[52] The charges were quietly dropped.

1964 was also the year that Park Tongsun became the President of the newly formed International Youth Federation for Freedom, 'to promote freedom, liberty and democratic principles among the youth of the free world'. American participants included central figures in the ultra-right wing Young Americans for Freedom, many of whom then and subsequently had CIA affiliations and/or were implicated in Watergate. For example, Douglas Caddy, secretary of IYFF, later shared an office with E. Howard Hunt of Watergate notoriety in the public relations firm of Robert R. Mullen and Co., a CIA front in the Far East. A friend of Park at Georgetown from 1956, Caddy was a founder and prominent figure in the YAF. He was cited for contempt and jailed briefly in 1972 in connection with Watergate. Former YAFer Roland Riddell, now a Washington mortgage banker, is the son of a former OSS

officer who later worked for the CIA. Eventually IYFF moved
its lavish offices into Park's Georgetown Club, by which time
it had obtained the fruits of two fund-solicitation mailings of
500,000 each, carrying endorsements by prominent anti-communist figures active in the Taiwan and ROK lobbies, including Senator John Tower, J. Edgar Hoover, Herbert Phil-
brick and Anna Chennault. In 1965 Park returned to Seoul
to sign a 'Declaration of Common Purpose' with the Free
Asia Youth Alliance, proclaiming the intention to 'champion
a worldwide anti-communist campaign . . . to eradicate Communism on earth'. IYFF thus took its place on the eve of full-
scale US involvement in Vietnam, in the ranks of the ultra-
right as a link in the CIA and KCIA-supported Taiwan-ROK
lobby, propounding militant anti-communism.[53]

In the activities of Park Tongsun and the KCIA, subversive
mechanisms initiated by the US to dominate and transform
Korea induced a pattern of reverse penetration culminating in
infiltration of the American political process — much as heroin
from South East Asia came back to haunt the US during the
Vietnam War. Ironically, Moon Sung Myung, with the assistance of the KCIA and perhaps the CIA, reversed a century of
US missionary efforts (Christian and secular) by bringing back
to the US a dynamic 'spiritual' movement in the service of a
foreign power and closely tied to the Nixon administration.
Park Tongsun, whose first associations with the CIA go back
to 1960, applied to American politics methods of bribery and
corruption pioneered by US intelligence agencies and business
interests abroad. It is important to locate this reverse penetration in the perspective of the overall US-ROK relationship.
If the American media has focused on Korean corruption of
US politics, the over-riding fact remains the pervasive distortion
of every aspect of South Korean life by three decades of US
penetration.

Payoffs by Multi-national Corporations

Illicit influence-buying by US-based multi-national corporations in Korea was disclosed in connection with similar illegal
corporate contributions to the Nixon camp. Illegal payments in
Korea, while hardly unique, are, at present, second in size only
to those disclosed in Japan's Lockheed scandal which engulfed

the Liberal Democratic Party. Yet while President Nixon and Premier Tanaka have long since been driven from office in disgrace, Pak Chung Hee retains his position in Korea.

The case of Gulf Oil, the seventh largest US corporation and leading foreign investor in Korea, is instructive. According to testimony by Gulf's Chairman, Bob Dorsey, the company which made more than $4·8 million in illegal political contributions in the US, laundered the following substantial sums to Pak Chung Hee through its Bahamas subsidiary:

— $1 million to Pak's Democratic-Republican Party during 1966.

— $3 million in 1970 for the 1971 election (Pak initially demanded $10 million) in which the leading opposition candidate won 46 per cent of the vote.

— Other contributions, unexplained, which 'do not even remotely approach the magnitude of $4 million'.[54]

In addition, Gulf is alleged to have paid the ROK National Defence Ministry $2·3 million in kick-backs during the years 1971–75, and Park Tongsun has boasted that Gulf paid him $1 million per month for unspecified periods.[55] As Senator Frank Church observed, if other US companies engaged in bribery on a scale comparable for their size to that of Gulf Oil — roughly $200 million in 1975 sales in Korea and world totals of nearly $7 billion — the illicit sums passing to the Pak régime would be in the neighbourhood of $25 to 30 million.

Two other cases of corporate pay-offs have been disclosed. General Motors has acknowledged illicit payments of $250,000 during the South Korean election of 1971 and $229,000 paid to a 'National Defence Fund' in 1974 and 1975.[56] E-Systems, Inc., of Dallas, Texas, a major CIA and Defence Department supplier of secret electronic and radio equipment, including electronic battlefield equipment used in Vietnam, acknowledged in a letter to its shareholders the payment of $1·4 million in 'consultant fees'. Chairman John Dixon explained that the company selected 'certain distinguished Korean citizens' to give E-Systems 'high-level visibility and assistance in the course of our performing the Korean radio contracts. These distinguished individuals elected to call themselves the "Korean Research Institute" in their dealings with us.'[57] E-Systems' cosy relationship with the CIA was further revealed in July,

1977, when the firm purchased the Taiwan-based Air Asia, Ltd, a CIA proprietary, for $1·9 million, just over half its net worth as listed in government documents.[58] In short, business pay-offs involve the giants of American corporate power in the oil and automobile industries, as well as smaller military/CIA-related firms.

The miasma of corruption, portions of which have been exposed in the Koreagate revelations, thus extends from the White to the Blue House, from CIA to KCIA, and embraces the major corporate, government, military and intelligence interests which have defined and distorted US-ROK relations for three decades.

Cover-up and Disclosure

Testimony by former US government officials and the records of Park Tongsun's activities substantiate the fact that KCIA bribery and illegal lobbying activities were widely known in government circles including the State, Justice and Defence Departments as well as the CIA from the 1960s. Park Tongsun himself was the recipient of CIA funds laundered through the Asia Society as early as 1960, was in active contact with CIA agents in connection with the American visit of KCIA director Kim Jong Pil in 1962, and in 1966 presided over the International Youth Federation for Freedom.

It is hardly surprising that investigative efforts to disclose illegal ROK lobbying in the US were repeatedly blocked. Particularly at the height of the Vietnam War, Pak Chung Hee was too valuable to expose, while those directly implicated in the scandal on the American side included not only the CIA and large numbers of congressmen, but the executive branch at the highest levels and leading corporate interests. It was not until Pak's importance had been reduced by the withdrawal of Korean forces from Vietnam that he became an embarrassing liability in the context of draconian repression in South Korea, and when many of his closest American allies came under attack in Watergate the basic facts concerning Koreagate began to surface. This process was accelerated by mounting internal disaffection with the Pak régime, reflected in the defection of many ROK officials, including the former director of the KCIA, Kim Hyung Wook, former Foreign Minister Choi Duk

Shin, and numerous ambassadors and generals who have disclosed diverse elements of the corrupt relationship and brought closer the day of Pak's demise.

Koreagate has focused American anger and contempt on Koreans who subverted the American democratic process. Frequently disregarded in most analysis of this pattern of reverse penetration is the institutionalised corruption of the entire ROK-US relationship, with power and profit concentrated in US hands. Consider again the case of Gulf Oil, which not only controls more than two-fifths of the oil supplies and refineries of the oil-dependent ROK economy, but dominates the petro-chemical industry as sole producer of naptha, its basic ingredient. Gulf owns the largest chain of gasoline stations and supplies a full 62 per cent of the oil requirements of US forces in Korea, worth $39 million in the years 1970–72. In 1974 Gulf's $18·2 billion revenues were approximately 1·5 times the size of Korea's $12·9 billion GNP.[59] The imbalance characteristic of the entire US-ROK relationship is mirrored in the realm of corruption.

Koreagate must also be assessed in the context of the CIA's acknowledged overthrow of legitimate governments in Iran in 1952 (in the service of American oil majors), in Guatemala in 1954 (in support of agri-business), in Chile in 1973 (on behalf of copper and communication interests) and its plots to assassinate Fidel Castro and other foreign leaders. In this global perspective, Pak Chung Hee, Park Tongsun and the KCIA can best be understood as products of the corrupt nexus of US-ROK government, military, intelligence and business relationships which has sustained US domination in a divided Korea for three decades.

The scandal reveals certain logical consequences of an economic strategy fostered by the Pak régime under US tutelage and rooted in the combination of export-oriented development and the leading role of international capital: that is the symbiotic relationship between the dictator and the multi-nationals at the direct expense of the Korean people, a relationship dramatically revealed in Gulf Oil's bankrolling of Pak's electoral victory in 1972.

From the early 1970s human rights issues provided a rallying point for critics of American policy. Donald Ranard, former

Director of the State Department Korea desk, a central figure
in pressing the Korea investigation, has explained the origins
of the search for a human rights component in US foreign
policy:

'The longest and probably most bitter foreign war in U.S.
history led many Americans to question the premises that
guided U.S. foreign policy, particularly as they related to
national security. To them it was fundamentally wrong, both
in terms of American traditions and values as well as
American security, for the U.S. to have as its allies in a so-
called "free world" some of the most repressive, brutal and
corrupt governments in the world. That such governments
were anti-communist no longer seemed reasonable enough
justification. The Kissinger era intensified this concern.'[60]

Few of the critics of US-Korea policy and of Koreagate, including many genuinely concerned about issues of morality
and foreign policy, have as yet confronted the structural relationship between economic strategies and the imperatives of
repression, nor for that matter the decisive American rôle in
creating the conditions for dictatorship in Korea. Democracy
can never flourish on the stony soil of a divided and occupied
nation. The central fact remains that developmental dictatorships relying on export-oriented development strategies and
currying the favour of international capital require heavy doses
of repression precisely because they violate basic interests of
the majority of people. Repression and corruption are integral,
structural features of ROK development, not merely the idle
whim of Pak Chung Hee. For this reason, Korea's high-speed
growth is at the centre of the present debate over the future
of the region.

III. The Korean Economy and US Policy
'South Korea today is one of just a few developing countries
with an income distribution more equal than Sweden's; rural
poverty has been drastically reduced; and because of this spec-
tacular economic progress, the continuing hostility of North
Korea and the unnerving effect of the South Vietnamese collapse, President Park Chung Hee has won grudging acceptance
of his authoritarian rule from a majority of South Korean

citizens. . . . What we want in Korea is a "German" solution —
stable co-existence of two governments in a divided nation.'
Donald Zagoria, 'Why We Can't Leave Korea.'

The Korean economic 'miracle' has been the focus of a carefully orchestrated campaign designed to sweeten the Pak
régime's image of unbridled repression and corruption in order
to justify continued US intervention in a divided Korea. By
the Fall of 1977, *Foreign Affairs, Business Week, Fortune, The
New York Times Magazine,* the Asian *Wall Street Journal* and
the World Bank had issued uniformly glowing reports on the
ROK's economic vitality and prospects, all within a six month
period. In Frank Gibney's words, South Korea is 'the world's
most striking case of an underdeveloped country working hard
and making good.'[61] In this view, South Korea is the new
Japan, embarked not only on a course of rapid economic
growth, but on the verge of entering the ranks of the advanced,
prosperous and democratic nations. The timing of the campaign suggests that it is directed precisely at blunting the edge
of Koreagate and martialing support for the Pak régime and
the US military presence in Korea.

Analysis of the ROK economy reveals the reasons for the
euphoria over the Korean performance among international
business interests: high speed export-oriented growth resting
on massive infusions of foreign capital has brought handsome
profits to international investors and to a small number of
Korean business and political associates.

South Korea is, to be sure, but one of many outposts for
American bank and corporate capital, but because it has
granted ideal conditions for exploitation by foreign capital, its
importance transcends the sum total of US loan and investment
capital. South Korea is being projected as a model to be
emulated by the nations of the Third World. In the years 1959–
75 the US provided $3·1 billion out of Korea's total capital
in-take of $9·1 billion, including $1·2 billion in public loans
and $1·8 billion in commercial loans.[62] The following partial
listing of US direct investors, a veritable who's who of
American industry, indicates the range of firms with direct
interests in Korea. Many of these firms have provided loans
several times larger than their actual investment. Both direct

investment and loans, moreover, date almost entirely from the last decade, with rapid growth continuing in the late 1970s.

Table 1
Leading American Firms with Direct Investment
in South Korea Exceeding $1 Million (1974)
Name of US Firm   Capital and Invest-
                                            ment Ratio
                                            ($ million)

Oil, petro-chemicals and fertiliser	Union Oil	$133	(50%)
	Gulf Oil	87	(50%)
	Caltex	2·75	(50%)
		49	(loan)
	Esmark & Skelly Oil	35·4	(25/25%)
	Dow Chemical	21	
	Skelly Oil	3·05	(50%)
		5	(loan)
		9·2	(aid)
	Associated Merchan-dising Corp.	16	
	Amoco International	5·25	(35%)
	Chemtex & Toray (Japan)	5·726	(50/50%)
	Continental Oil	·75	
		1·5	(loan)
Automobile and transport	General Motors	26·8	(50%)
	Dana Corporation	2·45	(50%)
	Eisenberg & Co.	1·67	(32·5%)
		14·75	(loans)
	Koreanic	1·25	(100%)
Electronics	Motorola	1	(100%)
		7	(loan)
	Doranco	·1	(100%)
		4	(loan)
	Semiconductor	2·8	(100%)
	(Fairchild subsidiary)	1·1	(loan)
	Control Data	3·2	(100%)
	Signetics	·62	(100%)
		1·55	(loan)
Computers	Sperry-Rand	3·5	(100%)
	Universal Management Systems	2	(95%)
	IBM World Trade	1·76	(100%)

Finance	International Finance	3·29	(39%)
	Back Bay Orient Enterprises	2·25	(70%)
Ship-building	Tacoma Shipbuilding	3·5	(70%)
Food and	Del Monte	2·4	(50%)
canning	Coco Cola Export	1·1	(100%)
		·03	(20%)
	Peavey Company	2·207	(loan)
Hotels	American Airlines	3·3	(50%)
		2·2	(loan)
Pharma-	Chas. Pfizer	1·4	(55%)
ceuticals		1·5	(loan)
Other	William Byrd & Chase International Investment	2·5	(100%)

Source: Kim Yong Bock and Pharis Harvey eds., *People Toiling Under Pharaoh* (Tokyo: Urban Industrial Mission and Christian Conference on Asia, 1976), pp. 192–97 from records of 45 firms with direct investment in Korea.
Note: The data should be taken as minimal figures, e.g., Gulf Oil's investment is much larger than indicated in this table, as is Japanese direct investment. As of 1974 at least 113 investments had been made by Japanese firms whose total investment of $475·3 million accounted for two-thirds of the total direct investment. Heading the list were such giants as Nippon Electric, Sumitomo Industries, Mitsui, Toray, Asahi Chemical, Mitsubishi, Kawasaki Heavy Industries, Marubeni, Chisso, Teijin and Nomura Securities.

Other major US firms with branches or subsidiaries in South Korea include Bank of America, Chase Manhattan, Citibank, Marine Midland, Esso Eastern, Westinghouse Electric, Bechtel International, Cargill Grain, Sears Roebuck, National Cash Register and Philco-Ford.[63]

These banks and corporations rank among the principal beneficiaries of an economic policy which serves foreign capital handsomely. It is the cruelest of illusions that with or without Pak Chung Hee the high growth export-oriented strategy of the ROK can provide the basis for a democratic Korean polity attendant to the over-riding needs of its people. The integral logic of repression and corruption in the ROK is part and parcel of an economic strategy which binds Korean working people in the service of state power and foreign profit.

Proponents of the Korean development model and of exposure of the corrupt US-Korean relationship symbolised by Koreagate are locked in a combat whose outcome will affect the future of the Korean peninsula and North-east Asia. This creates conditions for carrying public debate to the next stage of re-examining the record of three decades of US policy in Korea and the consequences for Koreans and Americans of US military, financial and political support for the division of the Korean nation.

The Korean people have paid a heavy price for three decades of American intervention: in a brutal war which produced little dissent in the US, in the division of land and people, in the perpetuation of a dictatorial structure reinforcing an economy harnessed to US, Japanese and European economic and financial interests, and in the permanent instability bred of the threat of war. The cancer of corruption which has characterised the relationship with the ROK has spread ineluctably back to the United States in the form of subversion of the American political process and the flight of jobs to Korea — principally, that is, to US and Japanese firms in Korea — in textile, electronic, shoe, toy and other industries. While Korea is unique in neither respect, the degree of corruption has reached proportions sufficient to generate sharp divisions within the American polity. President Carter's modest troop withdrawal proposals and hints of a diplomatic opening to the DPRK have set off shock waves in business, military, intelligence and political circles. These proposals deserve full support as first steps towards a solution. At the same time, three decades of American experience in Vietnam and Korea suggest that piece-meal measures will not cure the cancer. A just and lasting solution to the Korean problem requires the severing of US support for the Pak dictatorship and for permanent division of Korea, expanded relations with the DPRK, and the withdrawal of all American forces and weapons from the region, allowing the Korean people to solve in their own way the problems of peace, reunification and development.

NOTES

1. The force-modernisation programme was eventually extended to $1·8 billion in all forms of aid over seven years. Center for International Policy, *Human Rights and the U.S. Foreign Assistance Program Fiscal Year 1978. Part 2: East Asia* (1977), p.45 (hereafter CIP, *Human Rights*). Rinn S. Shinn, "The North-South Dialogue in Perspective," prepared for the Conference of Japanese and US Parliamentarians on Korean Problems, Washington, D.C., September 19–20, 1977, p.12 (hereafter Parliamentarians Conference).
2. *New York Times*, November 9, 1976.
3. General George Brown, Hearings Before the Committee on Armed Services US Senate 95th Congress, First Session, Fiscal Year 1978, *Authorization for Military Procurement, Research and Development* Part I, Authorization, p.413.
4. Henry Rowen, "Japan and the Future of Asia," *Orbis*, Vol.21, no.2, Summer, 1977, p.192. The author is former President of the Rand Corporation and a former deputy assistant Secretary of Defence. Rowen presents the case for a Japanese military build-up within the framework of US-Japan alliance while noting the capacity for rapid military build-up and an independent Japanese option.
5. For the origins of the integration concept see Herbert Bix, "Regional Integration: Japan and South Korea in America's Asian Policy," in Frank Baldwin, ed., *Without Parallel: The American-Korean Relationship Since 1945* (New York, Pantheon, 1974), pp.179–231.
6. "Statement of Secretary of Defense Harold Brown on the Amendments to the 1978 Budget and 1979 Authorization Request," *Department of Defense Appropriations for 1978*, February 22, 1977, p.15.
7. US Department of Defense, *Selected Statements*, September 1, 1977, p.23. From news conference in Seoul, July 26, 1977.
8. Creighton Burns, "Carter's Troop Plan Strikes Trouble," *The Age* (Melbourne), October 25, 1977.
9. Frank Gibney, "The Ripple Effect in Korea," *Foreign Affairs*, October, 1977; Donald Zagoria, "Why We Can't Leave Korea," *New York Times Magazine*, October 2, 1977.
10. US Congressional Budget Office, "Assessment of the Military Balance Between North and South Korea," reprinted in *Korean Review*, Vol.1, no.3, July, 1977, pp.15–40.
11. CIP, *Human Rights*, p.48.
12. Selig Harrison, "US Force Reductions and North Korean Policy," Parliamentarians Conference.
13. Sumiya Mikio, "Growth Economy and Unstable Society: Mechanism of the South Korean Economy," Parliamentarians Conference, pp.40–41.
14. Asian *Wall Street Journal*, March 24, 1977.
15. CIP, *Human Rights*, p.49.
16. 1976–78 arms sales and credits in US House of Representatives, *Foreign Assistance and Related Agencies Appropriations for 1978*, p.705; CIP, *Human Rights*, p.50.
17. Stefan Leader, "An Assessment of the Korean Military Situation," *Center for Defense Information*, May, 1977, reprinted in *The Korean Review*, Vol.I, no.3, July, 1977; CIP, *Human Rights*, pp.46–50.
18. Senator George McGovern, *The Congressional Record*, September 19, 1977; CIP, *Human Rights*, p.50.

19. Russell Spurr, "Seoul in Weapons Race," *Far Eastern Economic Review*, June 10, 1977, pp.110–11; CIP, *Human Rights*, p.51.
20. *Korea Week*, September 27, 1977.
21. *New Asia News*, November 18, 1977; *New York Times*, August 18, 1977; *Korea Week*, September 7, 1977; *Mainichi Daily News*, November 20, 1977.
22. Cf. the analysis in Bix, "Regional Integration," pp.179–80.
23. *Department of Defense Appropriations for 1978*, p.68. See also Takubo Tadae, "True Aim of US Forces Stationed in ROK," *Chuo Koron*, March, 1977, in *Summary of Selected Japanese Magazines*, March, 1977, p.31.
24. *Japan Times*, November 18, 1977.
25. Fujii Haruo, "Strategy and Moot Points of the Post-Fourth Defense Plan," *Shakaitō* January, 1977, in *Summary of Selected Japanese Magazines*, January, 1977, p.48.
26. "Japan Readies Major U.S. Aircraft Buy," *Aviation Week and Space Technology*, August 29, 1977.
27. Yamakawa Akio, "Turning Point in the Japanese Economy," *New Asia News*, November 18, 1977; Murray Sayle, "Japan's Miracle Turns Sour," *New Statesman*, November 11, 1977.
28. Senga Tetsuya, "SDF for Ensuring Safety of Territorial Waters Urged," *Economist*, March 1, 1977, in *Summaries of Selected Japanese Magazines*, July, 1977.
29. *Asahi Evening News* and *Japan Times*, October 20, 1977.
30. *Japan Christian Activity News*, October 21, 1977.
31. *New Asia News*, October 21, 1977.
32. Cf. Bix, "Regional Integration," pp.207ff.
33. Press Statement by Choi Duk Shin, Tokyo, November 18, 1977.
34. *Congressional Record*, September 19, 1977, p.1.
35. Bix, "Regional Integration," pp.200–08.
36. Gerhard Breidenstein, "Capitalism in South Korea," in Baldwin, ed., *Without Parallel*, p.240.
37. Kyong-dong Kim, "The Formation of the Entrepreneurial Elite in South Korea," *Asian Survey*, May, 1976, pp. 467–72.
38. Sumiya Mikio, "Growth Economy," p.38.
39. Pharis Harvey, "The Multinationals in Asia," *Christianity and Crisis*, March 15, 1976, p.45.
40. Baldwin ed., *Without Parallel*, "Introduction."
41. Baldwin, "America's Rented Troops: South Koreans in Vietnam," *Bulletin of Concerned Asian Scholars*, October-December, 1975, pp.33–40; Baldwin ed., *Without Parallel*, "Introduction," pp.29–30; Tad Szulc, "Too Much Rice, The Original Sin: Korea, Inc," *New Republic*, January 29, 1977, p.105.
42. Szulc, pp.103–04.
43. *Asahi Shimbun* (evening edition), December 17, 1977, and December 18, 1977; *Japan Times*, December 18, 1977.
44. Exhibit 60, "Results of TS Activities," Committee on Standards of Official Conduct, *Hearings Pursuant to House Resolution 252*, October 19, 1977 (hereafter *Hearings on HR 252*).
45. CIP, *Human Rights*, pp.46, 50, 54.
46. Committee on International Relations, Investigation of Korean-American Relations, "1976 Plan for Operations in the United States" (mimeograph; forthcoming publication), November, 1977. See also

"The Politics of Korean Studies in Europe," *Journal of Contemporary Asia*, Vol.7, no.3, 1977, pp.387–92; Sugwon Kang, "President Pak and His Learned Friends: Some Observations on Contemporary Korean Statecraft," *Bulletin of Concerned Asian Scholars*, October-December, 1975.

47. Exhibit 2, *Hearings on HR 252*. The most complete account of the Park Tongsun-KCIA connection is Maxine Cheshire's "Tongsun Park and the Korean CIA," *Washington Post*, August 28, 1977.

48. Exhibits 2, 8, 9, *Hearings on HR 252*.

49. *Stars and Stripes*, October 23, 1977.

50. *Washington Post*, October 15, 1977.

51. *Japan Times*, October 27, 1977.

52. Jeffrey Stein, "The CIA, the KCIA and Koreagate," Parliamentarians Conference.

53. *Washington Post*, August 28, 1977.

54. *Multinational Corporations and US Foreign Policy*, Hearings Before the Subcommittee on Multinational Corporations of the Senate Foreign Relations Committee, 1075, pp.4-12.

55. Szulc, "Too Much Rice," p.109; *New York Times*, November 8, 1976.

56. *Japan Times*, February 15, 1976.

57. *Asian Wall Street Journal*, March 10, 1977.

58. *Asahi Evening News*.

59. Harvey, "The Multinationals in Asia," pp.45–46.

60. CIP, *Human Rights*, p.1.

61. Gibney, "The Ripple Effect in Korea," p.161.

62. Yoshida Akiko, "Kankoku ni okeru kōdō seichō no mekanizumu" (The mechanism of high speed growth in Korea), *Keizai*, August, 1977, p.55.

63. *Korea Week*, October 26, 1977.

Section I

Division, Revolution and War

Chapter 1

The Political Background

Jon Halliday

Cold War fog still lies heavily over the question of Korea. It lies particularly thickly over the period between the Japanese surrender in August 1945 and the end of the Korean War in July 1953. This fog has to be dispelled and a fresh, unprejudiced look given to what was really happening in Korea in those years, especially at the political and social level.

First, *Korea was invaded by the US in September 1945 and the recently formed nationwide Korean administration based on the People's Committees was overthrown in the Southern half of the country which was occupied by the US.*[1]

On August 14, 1945 the US unilaterally promulgated a declaration known as General Order Number 1 which, *inter alia*, divided Korea into two at the 38th Parallel, ostensibly to facilitate the disarming of the Japanese forces: the Soviet army, which had already advanced deep into Korea, was to take the surrender North of the Parallel and the US South of the Parallel. The USSR accepted this arrangement, apparently without argument, even withdrawing from positions South of the Parallel. The Korean people, who had not engaged in aggression against anyone, were not consulted about this. The Koreans, however, disarmed the Japanese, freed political prisoners, and set up a functioning nationwide administration. This had all been done by the time the first US troops reached Korea, on September 8, 1945.

Second, *the vast majority of the Korean people demonstrably desired not only immediate independence for a united Korea, but also radical social and political policies.* North of the Parallel, the Soviet authorities recognised the local organisations, the People's Committees. Whatever influence they may have brought to bear on the selection of leaders, they allowed an essential continuity of popular institutions which

47

would be developed after the Soviet withdrawal in 1948. South of the Parallel, the US authorities refused to recognise them, reinstated the Japanese authorities, and embarked on a campaign to eliminate the radical left and, later, to disqualify even the centre and the moderate right-wing elements. It is important to grasp this aspect, since the US sabotage operation was not confined to dividing Korea, bad enough though that was; it also integrally involved trying to destroy the radical movement, which demonstrably had the support of the overwhelming majority of the population.

What were the results? On the one hand, the US Occupation was rapidly isolated, supported and assisted by only the far right and former collaborators with the Japanese. This is confirmed by official Western sources. General Ridgway, who, as Commander of the US/UN forces in Korea in 1951–53, was in a position to know, later wrote that the US, by confirming in office, 'the despised Japanese administrative officials . . . made a major blunder . . . that cost it the confidence and cooperation of the Korean people.'[2]

US-Korean Relations
'The Gooks don't need colleges. Let's close the place up and train them to be coolies.'
US officer, billeted in a university in South Korea, quoted in Alfred Crofts, "The Case of Korea; Our Falling Ramparts," *The Nation*, Vol.190, no.26 (June 25, 1960), p.554.

The 1946 'elections' in South Korea
'This is quite an election. . . . First, they let Syngman Rhee's boys decide the procedure. Second, to make sure nothing slips up, they hold the election in a series of four levels, so that the undesirables might be eliminated. Third, they let only family heads, or heads of ten families vote.

'They put all the possible opposition in jail, or drive it into the hills. . . . You can't beat the machine. It includes everybody in power, from the village cop and the landlord to the provincial governor.

'The machine is the same we found when we got here. For our purposes it's an ideal setup. It's organized military fashion. All you have to do is push the button, and some-where some cop begins skull cracking. They've been learn-ing the business under the Japs for thirty-five years. Why should anyone expect them to unlearn all they know now?' US Military Government officer, quoted by Mark Gayn in *Japan Diary*, p.398.

In October 1945, Syngman Rhee, an émigré conservative, returned from decades of exile in the United States. With US backing, he was promoted as the head of the régime in Seoul. John Gunther, hardly suspect as a radical, later wrote: 'It can be safely said that in the eyes of Hodge [the US commander] and Rhee . . . almost any Korean not an extreme rightist was a communist and potential traitor.'[3]

The other major result of the occupation was a tremendous upsurge in popular opposition to the US-Rhee régime — to its machinations for dividing Korea, and to its social and economic policies. Mark Gayn, then the correspondent for the *Chicago Sun*, describes the uprisings of autumn 1946 as 'a full-scale revolution, which must have involved hundreds of thousands, if not millions of people.' Gayn compares the events to 'some of history's great peasant revolutions.'[4] The leading US aca-demic authority of the time, George McCune, called the re-pression by the US and Korean rightists in the Taegu area then 'the Taegu slaughter.'

The UN and the Division of Korea

In 1947–48, the US, having failed utterly to get even utilis-able minority support within Korea, decided to shift the prob-lem to the United Nations, a formally international arena, but *de facto* with a built-in pro-US majority. Within the general strategy of *not* consulting the Korean people, this was, in effect, an attempt to internationalise the issue.

The main point about the UN operation is that, once again, the wishes of the overwhelming majority of the Korean people were ignored. The UN intervention and the project for hold-ing a separate election in the South alone were opposed not only by the Northern régime in Pyongyang, but also by the entire left and centre and even much of the right in the South

— indeed, by every political group except Syngman Rhee's minority régime. The opposition from the North is fairly well known. Less well known is that only the Rhee group in the South supported the US-UN project. In early 1948 the entire South Korean opposition, including some extremely conservative figures, joined with the Northern government in a series of initiatives designed to stave off the division of their country. In March 1948 the entire South Korean opposition issued a joint appeal against separate elections in the South. And in April the same leaders travelled to Pyongyang for a joint North-South Conference which endorsed the basic principles of: a) withdrawal of all foreign troops from Korea; b) no separate elections. Western sources rarely mention this crucial occasion. Yet, in the words of John Gunther: 'The South Korean delegation (to the Conference) included nearly every man of eminence in the country except Dr Rhee — even rightist leaders like Kim Koo, the heads of two of the chief political parties, and the chairman of the interim assembly.'[5] The establishment of an artificial UN interest was utilised to claim legitimacy for the division of Korea and for the régime installed in Seoul, and would serve the same purpose later when the US-led coalition invaded Korea in 1950. Yet, if one examines the record, the UN not only ignored the clear will of the Korean people; it claimed to have observed (i.e., effectively *checked*) an election which it did not; and further stated that this election was free and representative — neither of which was true.[6]

After the 1948 separate election in the South, the US set up a separate régime under Syngman Rhee based on Seoul — the Republic of Korea (ROK). The Democratic People's Republic of Korea (DPRK) was established later that same year, based on Pyongyang, and claiming to represent the whole country.

By this time most of the leaders of the southern Communist Party had moved to the North to avoid Rhee's police; conversely, many ex-collaborators and landlords had moved South. The establishment of the ROK was greeted by a new upsurge in popular opposition to the régime. The existing guerrilla movement expanded greatly, and in the autumn of 1948 there was a series of mass popular uprisings, accompanied by mutinies and defections to the guerrillas among the ROK armed forces. Between 1948 and June 1950 sizeable areas of the South were in a state of conflagration. Whereas in the North, the government had already (in 1946) carried out an extensive land reform and enacted laws for the formal equality of women, in the South there was no land reform, ex-collaborators commanded the army and the police, and women were being denied equality. The Seoul régime's campaign against the guerrillas, therefore, in the words of US General William Dean, Military Governor of Korea in 1947–48, 'consisted largely of burning the house of anyone the constabulary (army) or police even suspected of harbouring or co-operating with guerrillas.'[7] Large mountain areas were under guerrilla control, and many other parts of the country were under formal control by the Seoul forces by day, while the guerrillas exercised control at night.[8] Between 1948 and the middle of 1950 South Korea was seething from one end to the other. The army was not entirely reliable.[8a] The workers and farmers were outright hostile to the régime. Even in the capital, Seoul, Rhee was under attack, and retaliating with violence and torture. When the National Assembly launched an investigation into Rhee's financial affairs, Rhee had his police raid the Assembly: 22 people were arrested, of whom 16 were later found to have suffered either broken ribs, skull injuries or broken eardrums.[9]

From the start, the North had called for the withdrawal of all foreign troops. In 1948, the USSR withdrew its troops from the North, and in 1949 the US withdrew most — but not all — its armed forces. As well as keeping 500 troops in Korea, the US was training Korean military in Japan. The Rhee régime was visibly dependent on Washington for its very survival.

The Background and Politics of the 1950–53 War

The conventional Western picture of the Korean War is that the North launched an unprovoked attack on the South on June 25, 1950; occupied most of South Korea until September 1950; that, after the Inchon landing, the UN-US side re-liberated the South and then almost managed to free the North in late 1950; and that, although the West accepted a cease-fire roughly along the 38th Parallel, the UN-US side won a 'moral' victory, as shown by refugees, POWs and Communist atrocities.

The North's position is that the South launched an unprovoked attack on the North on June 25; that the North counter-attacked and liberated most of the South, with strong local support; that the UN-US-ROK side carried out many atrocities in both South and North, including the extermination of whole villages, napalming civilians, bombing irrigation dams, and using germ and chemical warfare. The North's overall assessment of the war is that it was a great victory.

In this welter of thesis and antithesis, what is the truth? And — also very important — what are the basic, fundamental questions? The first point is that the question 'Who fired the first shot on June 25?' is *not* the fundamental question. In fact, the conventional Western way of presenting — *or even questioning* — the 'origins' of the Korean War empties the struggle of its historical and political essence. The Korean War was the escalation of an ongoing civil war initially largely caused by and then overwhelmingly complicated by foreign intervention. Korea had been artificially divided against the wishes of its inhabitants. The Rhee régime represented virtually no one but itself and its US protectors. As well as the guerrilla war in the South, there had been literally thousands of armed clashes along and across the 38th Parallel prior to June 25.

Second, the evidence is extremely convincing that the desire for reunification and the disgust with Rhee and the US was incomparably stronger than any hesitations about the Northern régime, or about the kind of society which might emerge from unification via joint KPA-guerrilla liberation. As Alfred Crofts, a former member of USAMGIK (US Army Military Government in Korea), wrote in *The Nation*: 'Millions of South Koreans welcomed the prospect of unification, even on Communist terms. They had suffered police brutality, intellectual repression and political purge. Few felt much incentive to fight for profiteers or to die for Syngman Rhee.'[10] Among evidence that has often been quoted to support this argument one is: a) the very small number of people who left the capital, Seoul; the strongly anti-Communist book, *The Reds Take a City*, gives less than 7 per cent.[11] This is a pretty low figure, if one considers that the capital would have a high proportion of government officials, including police and army figures, who would reasonably be expected to want to make a get-away; it would also have a disproportionate number of the country's rich people; and probably also, given the fact it was the capital, and near the Parallel, a disproportionate percentage of the people who had left the North earlier (collaborators and landlords, according to Gayn).[12]

Other evidence cited includes the fact that a number of leading political figures in the South joined the North; the name most often cited is that of Kimm Kiu Sic, the leading surviving anti-Rhee conservative in the South.[13] But there were other striking defections, e.g., even Rhee's Minister of the Interior apparently went over to the DPRK in 1950.

But most material, whether of left or right, fails to go much beyond this and does not confront the really important issues of *political* struggle. While it is now generally acknowledged that Syngman Rhee was extremely isolated by June 1950, having secured the support of only 10–20 per cent[14] of those voting (on a highly restricted franchise and under conditions of terror) in the May 1950 elections, little is said about the other side of the coin — the desire of the vast majority of Koreans for radical social change within a united Korea. It is apparent from official DPRK statements that the decision implemented on and after June 25, 1950 was, in effect, an attempt to liberate the South, in conjunction with Southern political forces.[15]

Now, while there is little documented evidence on the state of the Southern political *organisations*, there is very strong evidence that the vast majority of the people in the South supported the overthrow of the Rhee régime and the reunification of the country. Not only did at least 93 per cent of the population of the capital stay put; but Rhee's army, in the words of the official US military history, 'disintegrated'.[16] The official US histories also record popular uprisings in places such as Taegu and Pusan, hundreds of miles from the 38th

Parallel — *on June 25, 1950.* There is no way to read the evidence except as indicating that the KPA (Korean People's Army) decision to cross the Parallel did indeed trigger the disintegration of the ROK state.

How did the Southern population react to the overthrow of Rhee and the concomitant political changes? A careful reading even of the Western evidence indicates that there was considerable support. General Dean, perhaps the strongest possible source on this, writes: 'the civilian attitude appeared to veer between enthusiasm and passive acceptance. I saw no sign of resistance or any will to resist.'[17] In fact, Dean records several examples of active Southern support for the liberation — including the persuasive fact that the KPA felt able to issue arms to some of the local inhabitants in the South — not something which could be done without secure political support. Even the material in *The Reds Take a City,* though lamenting the political activism involved, actually reveals that the new régime's basic platform was widely supported. The two key elements in it were land reform and equality for women, both of which carried enormous appeal. Moreover, it should be remembered that the new régime can not be characterised simply as a 'Northern occupation'; apart from the fact that Southerners filled many important posts in the DPRK prior to (and after) June 1950, many, perhaps most, of the leading political posts in the South up to September were filled by Southern Communists.

The extent of opposition to the Rhee régime is also confirmed by the fact that extensive guerrilla activity, of a kind only possible with a large popular base, continued for at least two years after the KPA was driven out of the South; and in some areas guerrilla activity continued up to as late as 1955.[18]

The conventional Western picture of the period late June–mid-September 1950 not only ignores the social and political realities of the South; it goes further and suggests, either explicitly or implicitly, that the liberation of the South was extremely unpopular. Why? Because, according to this version, the KPA committed numerous atrocities.

Since this is the conventional picture, it would seem necessary to scrutinise it. So long as this picture prevails in the

West, it will be that much easier for Washington, Tokyo, London and Seoul to oppose unification, on any terms at all, on the grounds that the population of the South rejected it in 1950 and would do so again.

The US Occupation and the South Korean Police
' "You must remember," said Maglin, "that when we took over last year, 12,000 out of the 20,000 men in the police force were Japanese. What we did, after sending the Japs home, was to push the Koreans up, and then build up the force by incorporating all the young men who had been helping the police. . . .

"Many people question the wisdom of keeping men trained by the Japanese. But many men are born policemen. We felt that if they did a good job for the Japanese, they would do a good job for us. It would be unfair to drive men trained by the Japanese out of the force." '
The (American) chief of the Police Division, Colonel William Maglin, cited in Mark Gayn, *Japan Diary*, p.391.

One most important aspect of the liberation of the South in June-July 1950 which has not been adequately considered is the question of the opening of the gaols and the release of the thousands of political prisoners. After June 25 the Rhee régime and the US military and civilian officials fled to Pusan, in the South-east corner of Korea, or to Japan. About 90 per cent of South Korea was freed, much of it before the KPA arrived. There is no credible evidence for atrocities by the KPA.[18a] However, when the gaols were opened — in itself a dramatic revolutionary gesture — those who had suffered under Rhee found the situation suddenly reversed, and their anger was not easily subject to political discipline — just as, for example in France at the time of the liberation in 1944. In considering this, it should be remembered that the Rhee police force was headed by former collaborators with the Japanese using, according to US official sources, the same methods as under the Japanese (see Box).[19] There is extensive and irrefut-

able evidence of the widespread use of torture and of indis-
criminate brutality inside and outside the prisons by the Rhee
police and right-wing goon squads. Under these circumstances,
it might be fair to set the question of 'atrocities' by either
the KPA or left-wing Southerners in the context of popular
justice.

What is sure is that there were atrocities in the South carried
out by the UN-ROK side. John K. C. Oh writes of the period
late 1948–1953: 'the civil liberties of countless persons were
often ignored. Frequently, hapless villagers, suspected of aiding the guerrillas, were summarily executed. . . . The most
notorious of these bloodbaths was the "Koch'ang Incident" in
which about six hundred men and women, young and old,
were herded into a narrow valley and mowed down with
machine guns by a South Korean army unit in February
1951. . . .'[20] This is a pro-Western writer, writing about *suspects*, and in the *South*. Moreover, this is only the most 'notorious' incident. This account not only serves to indicate the
level of political violence employed by the UN side, but also
confers inherent plausibility on DPRK and Southern opposition accusations of atrocities and mass executions by the UN
forces and Rhee officials during the occupation of the DPRK
in late 1950. After all, if civilians could be mowed down in
the South on *suspicion* of aiding (not even *being*) guerrillas—
what about the North, where millions could reasonably be
assumed to be Communists, or political militants?[21]

For a New Look at Everything Concerning Korea

This small book cannot hope by itself to reverse the decades
of misinformation, partial description and suppression of information practised by the West on the Korea issue. However,
we hope, especially in the light of the experience of US practice in and about Indo-China, that people will look again at
the evidence and think more deeply about the whole question
of Korea. We now know that the US lied consistently about
the Tonkin Gulf Incident (i.e., the 'origin' of the full-scale
US intervention in Vietnam); it lied about the whole social,
economic and political background to the struggles in Indo-
China; it invented 'atrocities' by the NLF, and suppressed infor-

mation about its own; it attempted to displace the discussion of popular support onto the false terrain of the 'refugee question'. Every one of these issues is present in equal measure as regards Korea. Moreover, one of the parties involved in both cases is the same — the USA. This in itself would seem more than adequate reason for renewed scrutiny of what really happened in Korea.

This is particularly urgent not only because of the danger of war caused by the presence of some 40,000 US troops and many hundred nuclear weapons in Korea, but also because of the terrible suffering being imposed on the people of South Korea by the US client régime headed by Pak Chung Hee The Pak régime exists today because the US invaded Korea in 1945; because Western nations supported the UN in dividing Korea and then went to war, first to maintain in power an unpopular dictatorship and then to try to destroy the DPRK; and because the US, Japan and other nations continue to support the dictatorship in South Korea as the basis for their own dominance in the region.

NOTES

1. Much about this period is still obscure, especially as regards reliable information on the strength and representativity of various political forces. The evidence provided by Dae-Sook Suh in *The Korean Communist Movement 1918–1948* (Princeton, 1967) indicates that the Communists were by far the largest and most popular political movement in Korea at the time the Japanese occupation ended. Most sources agree on the strength and representativity of the People's Committees (see, e.g., the detailed account in E. Grant Meade, *American Military Government in Korea* (London, OUP, 1951). Virtually all Western and pro-Western sources also agree that on September 6 a People's Republic, based on the People's Committees was established, or proclaimed (see, for example, Bruce Cumings, "American Policy and Korean Liberation," in Frank Baldwin, ed., *Without Parallel: The American-Korean Relationship Since 1945* (New York, Pantheon, 1974), pp.53ff; and Soon Sung Cho, *Korea in World Politics 1940–1950: An Evaluation of American Responsibility* (University of California Press, 1967), pp.65ff). DPRK accounts of the period do not, to my knowledge, confront the conflicting evidence and interpretations of the events; when they mention these (which is rarely), they deny any legitimacy to the People's Republic although other sources, e.g., Suh,

pp.298–9, indicate that there was Communist participation in the 'Republic'.

2. Matthew B. Ridgway, *The War in Korea* (London, 1967), p.7.
3. John Gunther, *The Riddle of MacArthur* (London, 1951), pp.166–7.
4. Mark Gayn, *Japan Diary* (New York, 1948), p.388.
5. Gunther, *op. cit.*, p.170.
6. The UN record shows that Commission members paid brief visits to only 2 per cent of the polling centres — i.e. did not *observe* the election in any meaningful sense of the word; (see my essay, "The United Nations and Korea," in Baldwin, ed., *Without Parallel*, esp. pp.119ff.).
7. William F. Dean, *General Dean's Story* (London, 1954), p.49; cf. p.54.
8. Cho, *Korea in World Politics*, p.232.
8a. In May, 1949, for example, two battalions of the Southern Army went over to the North with their officers. See Se-Jin Kim, *The Politics of Military Revolution in Korea* (Chapel Hill: University of North Carolina Press, 1972), p.55.
9. Andrew Roth, "Korea's Impending Explosion," *The Nation*, August 13, 1949, p.152.
10. Alfred Crofts, "The Case of Korea: Our Falling Ramparts," *The Nation*, June 25, 1960, p.547.
11. Introduction to John W. Riley, Jr and Wilbur Schramm, *The Reds Take a City: The Communist Occupation of Seoul* (New Brunswick, 1951), p.vi.
12. 'The refugees are the opponents and the non-conformists — collaborators, landlords, former policemen — and the Russian border patrols make no special effort to stop them.' (Gayn, *op. cit.*, p.491 — entry of May 3, 1947.)
13. Crofts, *op. cit.*
14. The figure depends on how one calculates direct and indirect support by different parties; for details, see John Kie-chang Oh, *Korea: Democracy on Trial* (Ithaca, Cornell University Press, 1968), pp.33–34.
15. I have discussed this at length in "The Korean Revolution," in *Three Articles on the Korean Revolution* (London, Association for Radical East Asian Studies, 1972) and *Socialist Revolution* (San Francisco), Vol.1, no.6 (1970).
16. Roy E. Appleman, *South to the Naktong, North to the Yalu* (Washington, D.C. 1962), esp. pp.129–131.
17. *General Dean's Story*, p.68.
18. Kim Chum-kon, *The Korean War* (Seoul, Kwang-myong Publishing Co., 1973), p.201.
18a. In fact, the former Chief of Staff of the South Korean Navy, Lee Yong Wun, has confirmed that the executions in the South immediately after June 25, 1950 which had been attributed to the KPA were the work of the Rhee régime (Speech by former Admiral Lee Yong Wun, New York City, April 2, 1977). Former South Korean Brigadier General Choi Suk Nam confirmed to the author that the accusations against the KPA on this score were untrue. "The North Korean Army . . . behaved very well." (Interview, New York City, April 3, 1977).
19. An adviser to the US Embassy in Seoul later wrote of the period prior to June 25, 1950: 'The jails in Seoul are overcrowded with political prisoners. Six weeks ago I inspected a police jail at Inch'on. The prisoners there were living under conditions I hesitate to describe in

this letter. It reminds you of a sense of the Divina Comedia (*sic*). Goya could have painted what we saw there. What is going to happen to the almost 10,000 political prisoners [in Seoul] . . .? It is hard to imagine the acts of vengeance and hatred which the people will commit if they survive the conquest of Seoul by their "liberators".' (Anonymous US official, letter cited in Frank Baldwin, ed., Harold Joyce Noble, *Embassy at War* (Seattle, 1975), p.255.)

20. Oh, *op. cit.*, pp.35, 206.
21. A Japanese source states that some 150,000 DPRK civilians were either executed or forcibly deported South during the occupation of the North in late 1950 (Tera-o Koro, *Sanju Hachidosen-no Kita* [North of the 38th Parallel] (Tokyo, Shin Nippon Shuppan-sha, 1959), p.24, cited in Koon Woo Nam, *The North Korean Communist Leadership, 1945–1965: A Study of Factionalism and Political Consolidation* (Alabama University Press, 1974), p.89); DPRK claims that the US-UN forces carried out large-scale massacres and conducted a scorched earth policy during the occupation of the North (the only time the US has ever occupied a Communist country) have never been disproved; Western sources are lamentably evasive on this crucial aspect.

Chapter 2

The War before Vietnam

John Gittings

'We fought in Korea, so that South Korea might remain free'
— President Johnson, May 4, 1965.

Korea was the war before Vietnam. It belonged to the age of cold-war innocence, when the Communists were indisputably the 'aggressors', evidently 'monolithic', and anyone who doubted their guilt was labelled a 'fellow-traveller'. It was also the age of cold-war trustfulness, when almost no one questioned the motives of the US Government, when civilians were bombed and dams were blasted with hardly a murmur in the West. As for germ warfare, or for that matter chemical warfare, the accusations were dismissed as a Communist libel upon the Free World.

The United States and 15 other Western and pro-Western nations sent troops to Korea.[1] At the end of the war the US admitted to 142,091 casualties, including 33,629 killed, and to a figure of 300,000 military casualties among the South Koreans. According to figures published by the North, the total of killed, wounded, and captured on the US-UN side was 1,567,000, of whom 405,000 were American. When the war ended in 1953, 2,500,000 refugees roamed the south, many of them having fled from Northern-controlled areas in fear the atomic bomb would be used against them.

About midday on June 25, 1950 the American journalist John Gunther was about to sit down to lunch in Japan with two important members of General MacArthur's staff attached to the US occupation headquarters. One was called unexpectedly to the telephone. He came back and whispered to Gunther: 'A big story has just broken. The South Koreans have attacked North Korea.'[2] Could it be, after all, as Gunther trustingly decided, a simple error in communication? For

60

South read North (and vice versa) and the cold war record is restored. Yet a new generation of Western scholars, younger and more radical than those who were moulded by the institutes and the foundations of the 1950s, see the origins of the Korean War in a very different perspective.

What Can You Believe?
On p.387 of *War in Peacetime: The History and Lessons of Korea* (Boston, Houghton Mifflin, 1969), J. Lawton Collins, Chief of Staff of the US Army throughout the Korean War, writes:
'There appears to be no doubt that on August 2, 1964, the Destroyer *Maddux (sic)* was intercepted and attacked by North Korean patrol boats.' Presumably Collins typed 'Korean' in error for 'Vietnamese' (itself an error!) and the editors and proof-readers at Houghton Mifflin missed the mistake altogether. The passage synthesises the particular combination of false information and blindness frequently found where Western discussion of Korea is concerned. If Collins can have the North Koreans triggering off the escalation of the Vietnam War, it should not be hard to make them responsible for the Korean War. . . .

Regardless of who 'started' the war, Korea was an artificially divided country in a state of incipient civil war. The division was not simply geographical, between North and South, but political, between progressive and more conservative forces. When the US divided up Korea in August 1945 and the USSR complied they did two things: they both intervened in *and* began to distort, an indigenous process of Korean revolution. The radical Korean administration based on the People's Committees, set up when Japan surrendered, was not recognised by the Americans, and Syngman Rhee was flown back in one of General MacArthur's private planes to set up a Rightist coalition. Local People's Committees were suppressed and more 'suitable leaders' — often with a record of collaboration with the Japanese — were found instead. In September and October 1946 a wave of strikes and demonstrations spread throughout South Korea. The present South Korean Government, in a handbook designed to show how beastly the Communists have always been, rather naïvely admits the widespread support that existed for the Left in 1946: 'In the general strikes that took place virtually all over the country, the workers shouted their opposition to the US military government as well as demands for Communist-style reforms of the political, economic and social systems'.

By 1949–50 the Left had been ousted from legal political life and driven into prison or underground in South Korea and Syngman Rhee was rapidly expanding his armed forces. He had received $440 millions in military aid since the end of the Pacific War. Defiantly, he threatened war. 'If we had our own way,' said his Defence Minister in October 1949, 'we would, I'm sure, have started up already. But we had to wait until they (the Americans) are ready.' Some Americans were backing away from over-committing their country to this unstable and unpopular régime. But John Foster Dulles (Acheson's chief Republican adviser) arrived in South Korea exactly one week before the war broke out in June, then departed for talks with the super-hawkish General MacArthur in Tokyo. He predicted 'positive action by the United States to preserve peace in the Far East.'[3]

Heavy fighting began early in the morning of June 25, 1950. Within hours, North Korean forces had advanced deep across the Thirty-eighth Parallel towards Kaesong and three days later had captured South Korea's capital of Seoul. On June 27 the United States put forward a resolution (which curiously had been drafted in the State Department before the war began) for a vote in the UN Security Council.[4] The resolution, calling on UN members to 'furnish . . . assistance to the Republic of South Korea,' was adopted in the absence of the Soviet delegate, who had been boycotting the Security Council for several months in protest against the absence of a delegate from the new Chinese Government.

But who began the war, and why? At one end of the spectrum there is the 'conspiracy' view of an international plot masterminded from Moscow. The argument goes that Stalin, thwarted in the West after the failure of his Berlin blockade, turned to the East, first inspiring revolution in Vietnam and China, then seeking to humiliate the United States in Korea. This theory ignores the clear evidence that Stalin, far from encouraging revolution in Asia, was distinctly unhappy about it, and that the Vietnamese, Chinese, and for that matter Korean peoples had every reason of their own to make revolution. Yet this myth of a co-ordinated international Communist plot was invoked by American leaders from Truman to Johnson, justifying intervention in Vietnam as it had previously in Korea. At the other end of the spectrum we find the original North Korean claim, almost completely ignored in the West, that the war was 'provoked' by South Korea. Karunakar Gupta in the academic journal *The China Quarterly*[6] recently claimed to have discovered *prima facie* evidence for a provocative attack, launched by the South against the Northern town of Haeju. The evidence has been disputed by other scholars, but many would argue that in a more general sense Syngman Rhee of South Korea provided ample 'provocation' in the preceding months, whether or not he was encouraged by Mr Dulles's visit to take more specific action. In 1975 'the former Chief of Staff of the South Korean Navy, Admiral Lee Yong Wun, stated that "ten months before the outbreak of war, at the beginning of August 1949, under secret orders from Syngman Rhee, I directly commanded a surprise assault on the North Korean military harbour of Monggump'o".'[6]

However, if Korea like Vietnam is regarded as a country artificially divided by the great powers the question of formal 'aggression' becomes legalistic, distracting attention from the origins and causes of what must be described as a *civil war*. The American writer Robert Simmons, author of a recent study of the Korean affair, concludes:

'There were constant and sizeable armed clashes and border incursions between the North and South for over a year before the final crisis. . . . Koreans were accustomed to the fighting and the possibility of war; each side believed that an early reunification was worth a war. While the Seoul régime enjoyed little popular support, it had announced its intention to invade the North and appeared to be preparing to do so. . . . The subsequent rapid North Korean victory was caused not by the size of its invading force, but rather a combination of superior firepower (tanks, artillery and planes), surprise, higher morale, and the support of a significant part of South Korea's population.'[7]

Whoever 'started' the Korean War, it was not in the interests of the Chinese, themselves still painfully picking up the pieces after 12 years of non-stop war against Japan and the Kuomintang. China was on the verge of demobilising part of its army; of starting to discuss its first Five Year Plan. Both had to wait for three more years. In late September, as the US forces counter-attacked and drove towards the 38th Parallel, China used diplomatic channels seeking to persuade the Americans not to send their own troops across the Parallel. When General MacArthur ignored instructions and went north, China sent a 'tripwire' force over the Yalu river, attacked the vanguard of the advancing Americans and then faded away. This second Chinese warning made a greater impression in Washington. A Chinese general was invited to talks at the United Nations, but on the day of his arrival, General MacArthur launched an all-out assault north towards the Manchurian border. Two days later, on November 26, a counter-attack was launched by the Korean People's Army with massive Chinese reinforcements which by January had forced MacArthur to fall back 60 miles south of the 38th Parallel.

It was an agonising decision for the Chinese leaders to take, partly because it was bound to intensify their dependence on the Soviet Union (Soviet 'aid' to the Chinese all had to be repaid, and the slate was not wiped clean till 1965). But Mao Tse-tung believed that a Korea unified under American rule, which is what the United Nations, dominated by Washington, now intended, would be the stepping-stone for an assault upon China. The Chinese Volunteers intervened not to liberate South Korea, but to force a return to the *status quo* ante and save the North from destruction. As the magazine *People's China* argued (December 16, 1950):

'If at the dawn of American democracy, Canada had been attacked by a ruthless invader who repeatedly bombed the State of Michigan and declared that the St Lawrence was not the real national boundary between Canada and the USA and had given repeated proofs of its hostility to the latter, would the democratic American people not have risen in defence of their neighbour and their own hearths and homes?'

Negotiations at Panmunjom. The name Panmunjom lingers on in the collective memory of Western historians and propagandists as the prime example of Communist 'intransigence' and it was invoked from 1965 onward to support accusations of 'stalling' or 'refusal to negotiate' against the North Vietnamese in the Indo-China war. Every college textbook echoes the same story: either China and North Korea were so 'bellicose' that they did not want peace, or Stalin prevented them from making it.

A contemporary judgement by US soldiers at the Korean front comes nearer to the mark. As reported by George Barrett in *The New York Times* (November 12, 1951):

'The unadorned way that an apparently increasing number of them [officers and enlisted men] see the situation right now is that the Communists have made important concessions, while the United Nations Command, as they view it, continues to make more and more demands. . . . The United Nations team has created the impression that it switches its stand whenever the Communists indicate they might go along with it.'

Three critical phases can be discerned in the first six months of the armistice negotiations, beginning in July 1951, at which the US-UN side upped its negotiating demands until it finally caused deadlock by refusing to return all Chinese and North Korean prisoners of war.

(A) The parallel issue: In July 1951 both sides had accepted a Soviet proposal — reflecting previous initiatives which included one by the UN Secretary-General — for an armistice along the 38th Parallel. But actual negotiations started with the United States refusing, 'as a matter of major principle,' to accept the parallel line. Secretary of State Dean Acheson much later conceded in his memoirs[8] that the Communists might have had cause to regard the American position as 'trickery' — though of course he denied that it was. Eventually the Communist side yielded the point, accepting that the eventual cease-fire would follow the line of actual control.

(B) The return of the POWs: the United States then raised the question of a prisoner-of-war exchange, saying it would be 'premature' to stop the fighting until this and other issues had been settled. Only days previous to this shift in November (when the Communists yielded on the parallel issue) the United States had called for a cease-fire without any other conditions — which the Chinese and North Koreans now accepted. By the end of December the Communists had conceded a second time, agreeing that a POW exchange should precede a cease-fire.

(C) The question of 'voluntary repatriation': Overnight the United States abandoned its emphasis upon a swift return of its own prisoners, now elevating the question of those Chinese and North Koreans who allegedly did not want to return to one of 'humanitarian' significance on which no compromise could be admitted. It was this issue which delayed the cease-fire and prolonged the casualty list for another year and a half — during which probably 500,000 were killed and wounded, the majority of them Korean civilians.

Thus by January 1952, the Communists had conceded the two main UN demands: An armistice line along the existing battlefront, not on the 38th Parallel, and a complete return of Allied prisoners before a cease-fire. Then, and only then, did the UN raise the question of 'voluntary repatriation'. More than 50,000 out of 150,000 North Korean and Chinese prisoners failed to go home, either voluntarily or under pressure, from their captors, at the end of the war.

The question of voluntary repatriation, far from being a purely 'humanitarian' issue as the United States claimed, was viewed largely as a means of scoring a propaganda victory over the Communists.[9] It was also the clear intention of some American officials to delay a cease-fire in the hopes of a more favourable outcome to the war. John Foster Dulles, by now Secretary of State under President Eisenhower, had this to say in April 1953: 'I don't think we can get much out of a Korea settlement until we have shown — before all Asia — our clear superiority by giving the Chinese one hell of a beating.'[10]

US bombing of Civilian targets (1952–53). A major factor in forcing the Communists to yield totally on the 'voluntary repatriation' issue — various compromise solutions were ruled out by the United States — was the intensive bombing of urban centres of population from the summer of 1952 onward and the blasting of vital irrigation dams in May 1953.[11] Little protest was aroused in the West by this type of warfare which, when attempted two decades later against North Vietnam, would lead to international condemnation. In particular, the attacks on the irrigation dams were reported routinely, if at all, by the Western press. Communist admissions that they caused widespread destruction of farmland and life were ignored.

The biggest raid of the war — against Pyongyang on August 29, 1952 — was reported by *The Times* of London with the deadpan observation that: 'Warning of the raid was given *fifteen minutes* [my italics] in advance by leaflet and Seoul radio to enable the civilian population to leave, but pilots reported that they saw no sign of movement.' Anyone who attempted to 'leave' would of course have been caught in the streets and subjected to low-level strafing by US Navy fliers who flew to rooftop level. 'The town was blowing up all over,' said one returning pilot. 'The smoke was the blackest I had ever seen.'

Six hundred and ninety-seven tons of bombs were dropped on the city; 10,000 litres of napalm were used 'with excellent results'; 62,000 rounds of ammunition were employed in 'strafing at low level,' according to the official communiqué. It was the fifth raid on the capital of North Korea within a month, and produced a death toll of some 6,000 civilians. Pyongyang's population, which had been 400,000 when the war started, had declined to one-fifth that number by its end, and the Australian journalist Wilfred Burchett reported that only two buildings remained intact by 1953. Over the period of the war the North Korean population as a whole is estimated to have declined from more than 9·5 million to less than 8·5 million.

Only the US/UN forces bombed from the air in the Korean War. Though there were hardly any protest marches in the West — certainly none on the scale that would be aroused later during the Vietnam War — the devastation of civilian

life and installations, including vital irrigation dams in the
final stage of the war, was staggering. As early as the end of
September 1950, the US Airforce had already dropped 97,000
tons of bombs and 7·8 million gallons of napalm.

Most of these atrocities aroused little attention in the West,
where US battle communiqués were regularly reported without comment. Here is a small part of the Far East Naval
Forces summary for the single day of May 19, 1953, published
routinely in the *New York Times* the following day:

> 'The North Korean cities of Pukchon and Songjin came
> under heavy bombardment from planes of Task Force 77 as
> the carriers USS *Boxer* and USS *Philippine Sea* unleashed
> their fury with nearly 200 sorties against the North Korean
> targets in excellent weather. A record number of 76 build-
> ings were demolished in one sector near Songjin as Sky-
> raiders, Corsairs and Panther jets co-ordinated strikes in
> the area. Smoke and flames billowed to 3,000 feet as numer-
> ous secondary explosions erupted.'

More concern was aroused, especially in Britain, by the use
of napalm, with protests from religious figures like the Bishop
of Birmingham and the Archbishop of York in the spring of
1952. René Cutforth has unforgettably recorded his first sight
of a napalm victim in Korea:

> 'In front of us a curious figure was standing, a little crouched,
> legs straggled, arms held out from his sides. He had no
> eyes, and his whole body, nearly all of which was visible
> through tatters of burnt rags, was covered with a hard
> black crust speckled with yellow pus. . . . He had to stand
> because he was no longer covered with a skin, but with a
> crust like crackling which broke easily.'[12]

In May 1953, US bombers began to attack the irrigation
dams supplying 75 per cent of the water for North Korea's
rice production. Five out of the 20 major dams were destroyed
before the armistice was signed. 'Floodwaters poured forth
and left a trail of havoc', the official history of the war records.
'Buildings, crops, and irrigation canals were all swept away in
the devastating torrent.'[13] US Commanders openly calculated
the effect of bombing the dams upon civilian morale in the

North. David Rees, author of *Korea: The Limited War*, explains why it was thought best to hit the dams one by one rather than launch a simultaneous attack:

'. . . gradual destruction of the dams would be best from psychological warfare considerations, so that the Korean farmers would tend to blame the Communists for prolonging the war, rather than the United Nations Command for initiating an all-out attack against food supplies.'[14]

Yet in the last result the savage bombing of North Korea was of very limited value in military terms, as would be the case a decade and a half later when Indo-China was saturated from the air. North Korea's combat effectiveness, wrote Hanson Baldwin (*New York Times*, July 2, 1953) 'actually . . . increased, rather than decreased, in the face of the Allied air attacks.'

Treatment of Prisoners of War. While in captivity, some US/UN prisoners received very rough treatment, especially during the first months of the war. Conditions were undoubtedly harsh, but the extremely bad living conditions which the US and other 'allied' prisoners had to endure were shared by their captors. American POWs were least able to adapt to Spartan living conditions. One army doctor reported that many would not eat Korean food and seemed to be waiting 'wistfully and unrealistically for the arrival of American chow.'[15] Official US statistics showed that 2,701 American prisoners died in captivity out of a total of 7,000, although the Turkish contingent of POWs (Turkey contributed troops to the UN Command) did not lose a single man. Low morale and uncertainty as to 'why we are fighting' led to American deaths and willingness to sign peace petitions — or, in the official view, to 'collaborate'.[16]

The 3,800 US Army prisoners who eventually returned from Korea were interrogated by special Joint Intelligence Processing Teams to establish what went wrong. As many as 30 per cent, the inquiry concluded, had committed 'technical' collaboration; more than 13 per cent were guilty of 'serious collaboration.' Yet the inquiry also concluded that 'the Army has not found a single verifiable case' where torture was used to win collaboration. Nor did prisoners who agreed to collaborate necessarily win better living conditions. Baffled, the Pentagon decided that a new code of conduct, backed up by 'a first-class training programme' would be necessary to prevent a repetition of the disturbing affair.

No account of the POWs' existence can be entirely black or white: what is clear is that American claims of maltreatment and 'brainwashing' were constantly exaggerated for propaganda purposes, as would again occur with the numbers games played by Presidents Johnson and Nixon over their POWs in North Vietnamese camps. For example, it was claimed in November 1951 that more than 5,500 US prisoners had been 'massacred' since the war began. Subsequent US casualty lists gave a similar picture by the device of treating the names of those 'missing' as POWs whose non-appearance must indicate that they had died in captivity, not (as was more likely) in action. Drowned in the hubbub of public outrage at this 'massacre', General Ridgway's headquarters announced calmly and *officially* that no less than 6,600 deaths 'resulted *primarily* [my italics] from the poor physical condition of the prisoners when they arrived at UN camps . . .'[17] Thus more POWs were admitted to have died in UN hands than were alleged to have done so in Communist hands. The hard conditions and lack of medical attention, regarded as evidence of 'atrocities' in relation to Northern treatment of their prisoners, were advanced as sufficient explanation for the deaths which occurred among prisoners in the South.

Later the riots on Koje Island where most of the North Korean and Chinese prisoners were concentrated could be less easily ignored by the Western press. On February 18, 1952, American-led soldiers killed 75 and wounded 139 prisoners. In May the American commander, General Dodd, was kidnapped by protesting prisoners. His deputy admitted — under duress, he pleaded later — that 'there have been instances of bloodshed where many prisoners of war have been killed and wounded by UN forces.'[18]

Germ Warfare. Any serious re-appraisal of the Korean War must end up by confronting the charge of 'germ warfare' levelled against the US and supported by the 'confessions' of 38 captured pilots, all of whom later maintained that they had yielded to torture. Here it is relevant to note that it has since come to light, by sheer chance, that US contingency plans did exist to use *chemical* warfare in Korea. In 1970 a storm of protest was aroused by US Defence Department plans to dump unwanted stocks of nerve gas (GB or Sarin) off the coast of Florida. The circumstances in which the gas was manufactured were then revealed. It had been stockpiled for use in Korea if the 1953 cease-fire broke down. As the *New York Times* reported (August 9, 1970):

'When American ground forces in Korea were overwhelmed by Chinese Communist human wave attacks near the Yalu river almost two decades ago, Pentagon policy-makers realised that the situation had forced a challenge upon them: Find a way to stop mass infantry attacks. . . . For a solution, the army dug into captured Nazi chemical warfare documents describing Sarin, a nerve gas so lethal that a few pounds could kill thousands of people in minutes if the deadly material were disbursed effectively.'

Can it be thinkable that the Pentagon should have contemplated using chemical warfare, outlawed by international agreement like germ warfare, but unthinkable that it should have contemplated the latter? What is at issue here is not a question of morality ('*Could* the United States have used germ warfare in Korea?') but a question of fact ('*Did* the United States . . .?') which is essentially a very simple one even if it may prove hard to answer conclusively at this distance of time. The evidence of research into germ warfare by the United States from the end of World War II onwards is well attested, including that of experiments with US personnel which resulted on occasion in death. Recent revelations make the North Korean charges inherently plausible: between 1950 and 1966 the US Army carried out germ warfare tests in at least 8 US cities, beginning with the release of 'harmless' bacteria in the drinking water system of the Pentagon in 1950 and culminating in the release of the bacterium *Serratia Marascens* in the New York subway system in 1966; we also know that the CIA secretly disseminated a strongly infectious virus of African swine cholera in Cuba in 1971, so that half a million pigs had to be slaughtered. If the US Army and CIA had no qualms about doing such things in Cuba and in the USA itself, the possibility of their having used germ warfare in Korea is certainly not to be dismissed out of hand.[19]

The circumstantial case is strengthened, too, by the revelation in late 1976 of the existence of a Japanese bacteriological warfare unit, the Ishii Unit or 'Unit 731', which had been working with and experimenting with the production and dissemination of cholera, plague and anthrax germs at a secret laboratory near Harbin in north-east China for 14 years till the end of the war in 1945. The principals of this unit escaped to Tokyo before the end of the war, taking important secrets and records with them. Subordinate members of the unit who fell into Soviet hands were prosecuted and punished for war crimes; the principals fell into American hands and the very existence of the unit was a closely kept secret for 30 years. Could their experience and expertise have been maintained by the Americans and used later in Korea?[20] Evidence from the Chinese and North Korean side was provided in a massive volume produced by the 'International Scientific Commission for the Investigation of the Facts concerning Bacterial Warfare in Korea and China', and in the various detailed confessions of US pilots in captivity. All these materials were of course dismissed by the US and apologists of the Western side as having been fabricated or exacted as a result of 'brain-washing'. Yet this was done in a remarkably perfunctory manner, with little attempt being made to demonstrate the various 'inconsistencies' and 'absurdities' which the documents were alleged to contain. Nor has this whole subject been regarded as a serious one for research in the two decades since the war ended. As with many other aspects of the Korean War, this has been a closed field where even to raise a critical question suggests to the great bulk of Western bourgeois scholarship that the questioner is not only partisan but perverse. Yet the whole edifice of cold war mythology, which provides the historical analogies to support current justifications for the maintenance of the American war machine at its menacing level, rests on the shaky basis of the official myth of the Korean War. It is high time that a critical spade was applied to its foundations.[21]

NOTES

1. As well as the 16 nations officially fighting, the Japanese Navy was also involved, *even in combat operations* — though this was only revealed very much later (see James E. Auer, *The Postwar Rearmament of Japanese Maritime Forces, 1945–71* (New York, Praeger, 1973), pp.63–67).
2. John Gunther, *The Riddle of MacArthur* (London, 1951), p.150.
3. Republic of Korea, *A Quarter Century of North Korean Provocations* (Seoul, 1974).
4. I. F. Stone, *The Hidden History of the Korean War* (New York, Monthly Review Press, 1969), pp.53–56.
5. "How Did the Korean War Begin?", *China Quarterly*, no.52 (1972); cf. discussion, *ibid.*, no.54 (1973).
6. Kyodo Tsushin report of June 25, 1975, cited in "Dokyumento," *Sekai*, September 1975, p.223.
7. Robert R. Simmons, "Korean Civil War," in Frank Baldwin, ed., *Without Parallel: The American-Korean Relationship Since 1945* (New York, Pantheon, 1974), pp.151–153.
8. Dean Acheson, *Present at the Creation* (London, 1969), p.633.
9. Admiral C. Turner Joy, the chief US/UN negotiator at Panmunjom, later wrote in his memoirs: 'It must be admitted . . . that besides humanitarian considerations, the major objective of the Washington decision to insist on voluntary repatriation was to inflict upon the Communists a propaganda defeat which might deter them from further aggression. It was thought that if any substantial portion of the ex-Communist soldiers refused to return to Communism, a huge setback to Communist subversive activities would ensue. I regret to say this does not seem to have been a valid point.' (*How Communists Negotiate* (New York, 1955), p.152.)
10. Quoted in Emmet Hughes, *The Ordeal of Power* (1963), pp.104–5.
11. The extent of US bombing in the first few months of the war is vividly portrayed by Major General Emmett ('Rosie') O'Donnell in testimony to the MacArthur hearings in 1951: 'I would say that the entire, almost the entire Korean peninsula is just a terrible mess. Everything is destroyed. There is nothing standing worthy of the name. . . . Just before the Chinese came in we were grounded. There were no more targets in Korea.' (Cited in Stone, *op. cit.*, p.312.)
12. René Cutforth, *Korean Reporter* (London, 1952), p.174; for more on British reactions, see chapter below on the UK and Korea.
13. Walter G. Hermes, *Truce Tent and Fighting Front* (Washington, D.C., 1966).
14. David Rees, *Korea: The Limited War* (London, 1964), p.381.
15. E. Kinkead, *In Every War But One* (New York, 1959), p.143.
16. Cutforth later recalled the effect on the US troops of the comparison between the behaviour of those they were fighting for and against: 'as the tales of mild and correct behaviour to prisoners and population by the Chinese began to filter through, and revelations of the [Southern] Republic's festering corruption piled up, these young men were left without ballast.' (*The Listener*, November 11, 1969, p.343.) Cf. Matthew B. Ridgway, *The War in Korea* (London, 1967), p.58, where he records

the Chinese returning wounded US troops during battle, and apparently
at some risk to themselves.

17. *Keesings Contemporary Archives*, p.11931.
18. Cited in Hal Vetter, *Mutiny on Koje Island* (Rutland, Vt., Tuttle, 1965),
    p.130. These revolts were in fact a joint operation by the POWs and
    the local population on Koje Island, which gave strong support to the
    POWs. The prison camp actions were a *political* move against the US-
    UN screening and 'voluntary repatriation.' Admiral Joy described the
    Koje uprising as the most successful initiative, which 'greatly jeopard-
    ised the major position of our delegation in the armistice conference —
    that relating to the exchange of prisoners' (Vetter, *ibid.*, p.137). Ridgway
    moved a battalion of tanks 200 miles to help put down the uprising,
    commenting: 'I wanted the killing machinery on hand to do a thorough
    job' (cited in Vetter, *ibid.*). In connection with 'screening', the Inter-
    national Committee of the Red Cross, according to the official US
    military history, 'protested vigorously against the tactics of the UNC
    [UN Command]. Violence, withholding food and water . . . and the
    use of force on hospital patients were heavily scored . . .' (cited in
    Hermes, *Truce Tent*, p.262).
19. The *Guardian* (London), December 23, 1976; the US daily, *Newsday*,
    reported in the (New York) *Guardian*, December 23, 1976; *Mainichi*
    and *Asahi* of the same date; *Asahi*, January 10, 1977 (on Cuba). See
    also "CIA Sought to Employ Truth Serum On Returning Korea War
    Prisoners," *Washington Post*, August 5, 1976. The CIA's programme
    of research into "truth serums" was conducted in part at Fort Detrick,
    Maryland, where, according to Chinese and North Korean claims, US
    pilots were trained in bacteriological warfare. The ramifications of
    this whole affair still await investigation.
20. *International Herald Tribune*, Nov. 20–21, 1976; Yoshinaga Haruko,
    'Ishii saikin butai no sengo sanjū nen' [The 30 postwar years of the Ishii
    bacteriological warfare unit], *Shokun*, September 1976.
21. See "Bacteriological Warfare," Jaap van Ginneken in *Journal of Con-
    temporary Asia*, Vol.7, no.2 (1977).

Section II

The South

Chapter 3

South Korean Society: The Deepening Nightmare

Walter Easey and Gavan McCormack

Many people in the West understand vaguely that political liberties in South Korea are severely curtailed under the military dictatorship of Pak Chung Hee. What is little known is the scope and depth of the comprehensive state apparatus of terror that maintains the régime in power — a régime which many nations, including all the NATO nations, recognise as the only 'legitimate' government on the Korean peninsula.

The Korean people have waged their struggle for independence, democracy and freedom for longer and at greater cost than any other people in modern times save perhaps the Vietnamese. From the beginning of the century they struggled heroically and despite the most savage repression against Japanese colonialism, and since 1945 they have had to contend with the intervention of the United States and other US-allied powers bent on frustrating the emergence of a unified, independent Korea, and with the depredations of semi-colonial régimes in the south supported or even appointed by the United States. From the nationwide anti-Japanese demonstrations of March 1, 1919, which resulted in thousands of deaths and what an American lawyer called 'an orgy of arrests, torture and village-burning'[1] up to the prayer meeting in the Catholic Myong Dong cathedral in Seoul in March, 1976, exactly 57 years later, which resulted in arrests and conspiracy sentences for a group of Christian clergymen and liberal political opposition leaders, to the labour struggles of 1977, there have been countless manifestations of the Korean determination to resist oppression and assert basic human rights and values.

The present régime in South Korea is maintained in power by a judicious combination of the stick of terror, torture, intimidation and harassment for the masses, with the carrot of wealth and privilege on a gargantuan scale for those bureaucrats and army officers who give Pak their co-operation. The extent of foreign control of the economy is such as to preclude even those token concessions to the middle and working classes found in fascist Italy and Germany. The secret police apparatus, records and personnel inherited from colonial days have been developed through the more modern refinements of the computer and the electrode into the sinews of a highly effective police state.[2]

South Korea has had only one brief spell of relatively liberal and open government in this century — the régime of John Chang (Chang Myon) which came to office through the instrumentality of the student-led movement which toppled the autocratic Syngman Rhee in April, 1960. Pak Chung Hee ended that brief spell by his military coup *d'état* in 1961. Through an Anti-Communist Law, a National Security Law, and the establishment of a Korean CIA (KCIA), the range of political expression was quickly limited, and sentiment in favour of unification of the country suppressed in the name of the twin goals of anti-communism and economic development. Within such strict limits, however, parliament (reopened in 1963), press, universities, and churches (there are over 4 million Christians in South Korea) continued to operate and to maintain some independence. These limited prerogatives have come under fierce attack since then. In 1971 Pak narrowly won the presidential elections in a straight contest with Kim Dae Jung (on whom see further below). It is now widely accepted that Pak resorted to massive ballot-tampering, bribery and intimidation in order to achieve this result. It is also known that he extorted a substantial and highly illegal contribution from at least one foreign investor — $3 million from Gulf Oil — to swell his campaign chest.[3]

In October, 1972, Pak announced that because 'disorder and inefficiency are still rampant around us' and because 'the political circles in our country are obsessed with factional strife and discord' a readjustment was necessary. It consisted in the suspension of the old constitution and its replacement by what Pak called a *Yushin* (literally 'renovation' but rendered into English by Pak propagandists as 'revitalisation') constitution, under which all limitations on his own tenure of the presidency were removed and he was empowered to appoint and dismiss at will Prime Minister, Cabinet Ministers, Supreme Court judges, to appoint one-third of National Assembly members by nomination, and to issue any emergency decree he thought necessary — in short, to govern as he saw fit.[4] 'Korea today is under the leadership of a government more undemocratic than any since Korea was liberated from the Japanese in 1945, and, I might add, with less justification', wrote Donald Ranard, Director (1970–74) of the Office of Korean Affairs at the US Department of State (*Far Eastern Economic Review*, May 23, 1975).

The power to issue emergency decrees and govern in accordance with them has been used to the full. Decree No.1 (January 1974) prohibited any 'denial, opposition or defamation' of the Yushin constitution; Decree No.2 ruled that offences against any Emergency Decree should be tried by Court-Martial; Decree No.4 (April 1974) banned the main student union, the National Democratic Youth and Student Federation, and specified penalties up to death for students absenting themselves from classes or examinations or engaging in any political activities; and the culminating Decree No.9, the principal one still in force, at the present time, ranged widest of all in banning 'Fabricating, disseminating false facts or making false presentation of facts.' Obviously only the régime is in a position to declare what is a 'false fact'. This last Decree also prohibits 'Denying, opposing, distorting or defaming the constitution, or asserting, petitioning, instigating, or propagating revision or appeal thereof by means of assembly, demonstration, or by using mass-communication media such as newspapers, broadcasts or news correspondence, or by making documents, pictures, records or other publications.'[5]

To reinforce this panoply of repression, however unnecessary such reinforcement might seem, there are numerous ways in which Pak has attempted to develop a positive, corporate-state ethic. All men between the ages of 17 and 50 are obliged to enrol in some form of military or para-military organisation, from the Militia, into which women as well as men are now drafted at 17, through regular conscription for three or four years from the age of 20, or membership in the National Student

Defence Corps in the case of students, to Militia or Reserve service which does not end till the age of 50. All citizens are being registered under a National Security Law which requires fingerprinting and under which detailed biographical records are kept in a central computer bank.[6] Anyone notified that he or she is under 'protective surveillance' under this law is obliged at once to report to the authorities details of his/her income, property, family, friends, religion and record of employment, and to establish to the satisfaction of the same authorities and through suitable guarantors that he or she is of a properly anti-communist spirit and faithful to the country and its laws. Failure to satisfy on any of these counts leads to prison.[7] The old Japanese fascist surveillance and mobilisation units, the *goningumi*, through which all citizens are organised into locality groups and to which the principle of collective responsibility and/or guilt in the case of any wrongdoing applies, have been reinstituted, and in the countryside the *Saemaul*, or 'New Village' movement serves a similar purpose in extending government control into each of the country's 35,000 villages.[8] The principal institution on which Pak depends in co-ordinating and executing the various measures described here is the Korean CIA, recently described by an American professor who was formerly US Cultural Attaché in Seoul as 'a vast, shadowy world of an estimated 100,000 to 300,000 bureaucrats, intellectuals, agents and thugs.'[9]

The universities have been a thorn in the side of South Korean régimes from the time of Syngman Rhee. The Emergency Laws, arrests, detention and torture, compulsory enrolment in military groups and the prohibition of any non-academic organisation (the so-called 'circles') have served at least temporarily to put a brake on activism among the country's 220,000 university students. To complement these steps professors who are suspected of wavering in their loyalty to Pak and the Yushin system are also now being systematically weeded out. Under a law passed through the National Assembly in June, 1975, all university teachers have to have their appointments confirmed by a screening committee after which they are given contracts for periods ranging between one and ten years. Between 400 and 500 of the country's 9,019 college instructors were dismissed in the first six months of the law's operation, most of them for obviously political reasons.[10] As for the press, the last flicker of its independence was snuffed out in 1975 after massive sackings from the *Dong-A Ilbo* (the country's leading daily) and after a crisis brought on by government pressure on business which resulted in a sudden cessation of advertising revenue to the paper. There is also a pathetic irony in the fact that, in the land which so many western liberal democratic nations joined under a United Nations resolution to fight to keep out of the clutches of international communism, members of the National Assembly should have to complain that Korean news is regularly excised from their copies of western and Japanese papers, while *Pravda* and even Pyongyang's *Rodong Sinmun* are ignored by the censors.[11]

There are several main grounds upon which this institutionalised repression is sometimes defended. One is that it is an unpleasant necessity in the present stage of capital accumulation and development which will soon be obviated by rapid economic growth and greater prosperity. When this happens, present controls can be relaxed and the society can afford the luxury of liberal democracy. But it should be clear from our analysis of the South Korean economy[12] that this is highly unlikely. The direction of economic growth is such as to lead not to eventual independence, wealth and equality, but to increasing subjection to foreign control, mass impoverishment and heightened inequality.

The second, and principal, rationale offered by defenders of the régime is that of external danger so great and so imminent as to leave no alternative to the garrison state. This too, however, is patently untrue. There is now very persuasive evidence to show that many of the crucial incidents used by the Pak régime to foster this sense of crisis and insecurity and to justify its own continuance have been either fabrications or deliberate provocations. Such measures have been adopted in particular at times when the régime has been under greatest pressure from popular discontent.

Thus, in 1964, when the terms on which Pak proposed to 'normalise' relations with Japan sparked widespread protest

throughout the country, martial law was declared, the opposition silenced, and the proposed changes carried out in an
atmosphere of crisis and fear created by the exposure of a
northern 'plot'. Thirteen people were arrested and charged
with membership of a 'People's Revolutionary Party', which
was supposed to have been manipulating the student and popular demonstrations in the interests of a northern-sponsored plot.
The prosecutors and courts, however, still at that time retained
a degree of judicial independence and found the charges so ill-
founded that they first acquitted all but two of the defendants
and then when the government insisted on a retrial, found all
guilty under the Anti-Communist Law, but of such trivial
matters that half were given suspended sentences and the others
sentences of from one to three years. No evidence was presented
of the existence of any 'People's Revolutionary Party', or of
any northern connections.[13]

In 1971, when once again popular unrest was rising, Pak
threatened martial law unless given immediately extraordinary
powers to deal with what he described as 'North Korean preparations for an invasion' and a step-up in infiltration of agents
and communist terrorism. The *New York Times*, in an editorial on December 28, 1971, noted that 'Outside observers,
including the State Department and the American Embassy in
Seoul' could detect no sign of these 'threats', and that 'The
external threat Mr Park evidently fears is not military attack
but just the opposite — detente.'[14]

1974 was evidently a critical year for the régime, and there
are striking examples of both fabrications and provocations
engineered by it. Early in the year domestic opposition to Pak
was running high and massive demonstrations were anticipated
in Seoul on March 1, the anniversary of the 1919 demonstrations against Japan. Just at this time, however, an 'unprovoked northern naval attack' occurred on some southern ships
in the Yellow Sea. A frenzied campaign of vilification and war
readiness followed, including a massive anti-communist rally
in which one million people were mobilised in Seoul on
February 21. Domestic protest against Pak was swamped.[15] In
April a second 'People's Revolutionary Party' case broke.
Several of the 1964 defendants were among those arrested,

tried, and, on the basis of confessions extracted from them under torture, convicted. A second naval clash occurred on June 28, while the trials were in progress of another batch of opponents of the régime. Eleven days later, while the mood of crisis and hysteria was still high, the poet Kim Chi Ha and six others involved in the so-called case of the National Federation Youth and Students were sentenced to death, and on July 16 an ex-President, Yun Po Sun, together with a number of pastors and professors, was arraigned for trial. Both of the naval incidents seemed at the time to involve some suspicious circumstances, and early in 1975 the former Chief of Staff of the South Korean Navy himself reported that, according to his former naval subordinates, both had been deliberately provoked by the south.[16] In April, 1975, the eight 'People's Revolutionary Party' defendants were executed, one day after their appeals had been rejected, and an Amnesty International observer, who was in Seoul at the time, wrote after a careful review of the evidence and the circumstances surrounding the affair:

'It is the considered opinion of this mission that the above facts point to the case having been fabricated by the Korean authorities. . . . The PRP case of 1964 had been fabricated in an attempt to rouse the Korean people's feelings on the North-South issue. This we find to have been the aim in 1974; it was further an attempt to arouse prejudice against academic, church and other demands for liberalisation.'[17]

Again in 1975, in the wake of the American collapse and withdrawal from Indo-China, a badly rattled Pak spoke repeatedly of the imminent danger of northern attack, sponsored mass anti-communist rallies, and announced the most stringent of his Emergency Decrees, the 9th, ostensibly to cope with the increased danger of attack.[18] Yet his claim was denied by the highest levels of American military and diplomatic officialdom. Thus Kissinger on May 13: 'I don't think that North Korea is planning any military move'; the US Embassy and the 8th Army command in Seoul in the same month stressed that the military situation was quiet, with no change having occurred for months and there being absolutely no signs of mobilisation in the north; Assistant Secretary of State Habib in June: 'It is inconceivable that North Korea should be planning any attack'; and Defence Secretary Schlesinger on July 6: 'There is basically little likelihood of a DPRK attack on the south, and particularly over the past few weeks such a possibility has been remote'.[19] This, of course, should not be taken to imply that the North is indifferent to repression in the South. Its position is rather that, while the North will not export revolution,[20] it cannot be expected to stand idly by if revolution breaks out. As Kim Il Sung put it in his speech in Peking on April 18, 1975: 'If revolution takes place in South Korea, we, as one and the same nation, will not just look at it with folded arms but will strongly support the south Korean people.'[21]

Those who suffer the brunt of repression in the South are neither communists, nor advocates of armed struggle, nor clandestine agents of Kim Il Sung. Those arrested and imprisoned have included many of the leading intellectuals, lawyers, artists, church leaders and writers, people who are plainly not communist, and of whom a good many are anti-communist. Kim Chi Ha has given an explanation of this phenomenon: 'In South Korea, Lao Tzu, Confucius, Jesus, the Buddha, anybody and everybody concerned with fundamental truth or essential reality would be a communist.'[22] There are even those in South Korea who believe that the real northern agent, the real secret operative for Kim Il Sung is President Pak himself, since by crushing and eliminating the liberal opposition, like Ky and Thieu in Vietnam before him, he ensures that in the long run unification will be more likely to occur on northern terms, after the collapse of the south through its own corruption and the total alienation of a despotic régime from its people.[23]

Harassment of the opposition extends well beyond the frontiers of South Korea. The case of the students, artists and intellectuals abducted from various European cities in 1967 and 1969 to be imprisoned, tortured and almost murdered, is dealt with below.[24] In 1973, the leading political opponent of the régime, Kim Dae Jung, who had been enjoying considerable success in organising the Korean community in Japan and the United States, was kidnapped from his hotel in Tokyo and whisked back to Seoul, again by CIA agents. In June, 1975, 500 South Korean coal miners in West Germany joined in demonstrating against constant surveillance and harassment by Korean CIA agents there.[25] Since 1975 there has been a stream of revelations from various Congressional hearings in Washington about the activities of the Korean CIA in the United States: threats and intimidation against publishers of anti-Pak newspapers, attempted bribes to Congressmen, and manipulation of academic 'front-groups'. Dr Lee Jai Hyon, former Director of the South Korean Information Office in New York, summed up by saying that these operations were based on 'the three basic techniques of seduction, pay-off and intimidation.'[26] Since late 1975 the Korean community in Japan has been the object of another concerted campaign as numerous of its members, students, businessmen and so on, are arrested during visits to Seoul and arraigned under the Emergency or Anti-Communist laws. By late May, 1976, four had been sentenced to death, the supposed ringleader of the group being Pak Ok Kwang, the 27-year-old public relations officer of the Korea Junior Chamber of Commerce from Osaka, Japan. These young Japan-born Koreans were charged with visiting the north secretly and then penetrating campus groups to stir up anti-government feelings, contacting army officers and preparing to take action in the event of a coup. Like others before them, they were convicted on the basis of confessions extorted by torture and despite evidence to show that they had been in Japan at the time of their supposed visits to the north.[27]

The cases of the politician Kim Dae Jung and the poet Kim Chi Ha illustrate best the character of the régime. The former is particularly bizarre. All outside observers from the chief of the US State Department's Korean department[28] to the Tokyo Metropolitan Police Department[29] agree that Korean Embassy/CIA staff were responsible for Kim's kidnapping in Tokyo in August, 1973. The two governments concerned were acutely embarrassed by the affair and eventually, in 1975, agreed to bury it, Kim being promised eventual release and the Korean consular official whose fingerprints were found at the scene of the crime quietly resigning. By this time, however, Kim had been indicted for 'irregularities' in the 1971 election campaign in which he almost unseated the President. *Inter alia*, he was charged with imputing that Pak, if elected, intended to emasculate the constitution and govern for life — which is, of course, precisely what Pak proceeded to do. While his trial was in progress it was revealed, in the course of Senate Multinationals Sub-Committee hearings in Washington, that at least one major American company, Gulf Oil, had been forced to pay a levy of $3 million to Pak's campaign funds in that same year.[30] This episode, prominently reported in the US and Japanese media, was completely censored from the Korean media, but it appears to be the case that, were it ever to come before the Korean courts, it would render Pak himself liable to a possible death penalty on several counts — accepting foreign funds for his campaign, exceeding the legal limit on campaign funds and so on. Instead, Kim Dae Jung was given a 12 month sentence for *his* transgression — outspokenness — and, while excused from actual incarceration because of his poor health, he then took part in the prayer meeting in Seoul Catholic cathedral on March 1, 1976, at which a call was issued for the restoration of democracy.[31] As a result he was again arrested and tried on much more serious charges under the 'Emergency' decrees. With him in the dock stood a representative group of the country's leading intellectual and religious figures: Yun Po Sun, 80 years old, former President, a devout Presbyterian; Chung Yil Hyung, former Foreign Minister; I Tae Young, winner of the 1975 Magsaysay award; five Catholic priests, and some well known Protestant ministers, including the venerable Quaker Ham Sok Hon, who is also known as Korea's Gandhi.[32] Prison sentences were announced on August 28, 1976, ranging from two to eight years, with eight years for both Kim Dae Jung and Yun Po Sun. Yun was not jailed, a concession to his age. For Kim, whose health has been ruined by his experience of the 1973 kidnapping, by various KCIA attacks and jail privations, the sentence may be tantamount to a death penalty.

The poet Kim Chi Ha, a Catholic, has spent a good deal of the last ten years in prison. To read his poetry is to understand why, for no totalitarian régime could tolerate writing as

evocative, as scathingly critical of the régime, and as steeped
in the popular culture of his people as this. Only wide scale
international protest prevented Pak from having him executed
in 1974, after a conviction for having given money, some of it
provided him by the renowned Catholic bishop Chi Hak Soun
(Daniel Chi), to help the student opposition. In February,
1975, Kim Chi Ha was released from prison in a partial
amnesty prompted by fears that the régime was getting such
a bad name that its vital aid funds from Washington might
be cut. In an act of astonishing courage, within weeks of his
release, Kim published detailed accounts of the torture of
prisoners such as he had come to know during his own in-
carceration, and in particular of the reasons for believing the
case of the 'People's Revolutionary Party', in which eight men
were hanged in April, to have been a frame-up. At this
he was again arrested, charged under the Anti-Communist
law (since his writing is alleged to benefit the north), and
on December 30, 1976, was sentenced to another seven years.[33]

Kim Chi Ha's two best known poems are 'Five Bandits',
published in 1970, and 'Groundless Rumours', published in
1972. The former is a scathing satire on the politicians, generals, bureaucrats, plutocrats and high officials who wax fat
on the sufferings of the people while cravenly selling the
country out to foreign interests:

'Now the last bandit and his cronies step out: Ministers and
vice-ministers, who waddle from obesity, sediment seeping
from every pore. With shifty, mucous-lined eyes, they command the national defence with their golf clubs in their left
hands, while fondling the breasts of their mistresses with
their right.

And when they softly write "Increased Production, Increased Export and Construction" on a mistress's breasts,
the woman murmurs, "Hee-hee-hee, don't tickle me!".'[34]

'Groundless Rumour' begins with the story of a poor man
who, because he curses the authorities for depriving the people
of their freedom, is sentenced:

'And it is hereby solemnly declared in accordance with
the law

that from the body of the accused shall be cut off im-
                                                    mediately,
after the closing of this court,
one head, so that he may not be able to think up or spread
groundless rumours anymore;
two legs, so he may not insolently stand on his own two
                                              feet anymore;
one penis and two testicles, so that he may not produce
                            another seditious like himself.'[35]

However, even after the execution of this terrible penalty, the
man's trunk continues to beat against the prison walls, disturbing the complacency of the rich and powerful. To continue
the résumé of the poem as given in the magazine *Ronin*:

'Later a king, not unlike South Korean President Pak
Chung Hee, appears. The king is pregnant with a giant
serpent's egg. The regal advisers with one accord state that
the only remedy against the embarrassing egg is to eat the
raw livers of all communists — which the king dutifully
proceeds to do. Having devoured all the communist livers,
the king seeks a more general remedy and determines to
digest the livers of all Christians as well; at which point
general rebellion breaks out.'[36]

The voice of the poet has for the moment been stilled; general rebellion seems unlikely although new waves of protest in
the Fall of 1977 linking University and Christian activists
with the workers' movement suggest the beginning of a new
stage. But there is no easy solution to the repression in South
Korea — by change to a more 'liberal' régime, for example —
since repression is integral to the very structure of the economy and constitutes part of the attractiveness of South Korea
to its foreign backers. The problem of repression has to be
understood in its full economic and international context, as
is made clear in the chapters that follow.

NOTES

1. Amnesty International, *Political Repression in South Korea* (Report by William J. Butler), New York, 1974, p.2.
2. The 1974 and 1975 Amnesty reports cited in notes 1 and 5 record an array of torture techniques that is sickeningly familiar from our knowledge of fascist states elsewhere — the use of water, fire, heat, cold, electricity, sleep deprivation and so on.
3. *Newsweek*, May 26, 1975, p.39.
4. Committee on Foreign Relations, US Senate Staff Report, *Korea and the Philippines, November, 1972*, Washington, 1973, p.5; for brief résumé of main portions of the Yushin system, Amnesty International, *Political Repression, op. cit.*
5. *Ibid.*; for complete text of Decrees 1 to 9, see *Korean Studies* Vol.1, No.10 (October, 1976). An Amnesty International mission in the spring of 1975 was told that under South Korean law the following were forbidden:
   i. The publishing of an essay that argues that the death sentence is morally indefensible;
   ii. an allegation that the present Government of Korea neglects the rights of the poor and under-privileged;
   iii. a public statement that torture is used to extract false confessions from individuals under interrogation by the KCIA. (*Report of The Mission to the Republic of Korea, 27 March-9 April, 1975*, p.8–9).
6. *Korea Newsletter*, no.36, January 16, 1976.
7. T.K., *Sekai*, September, 1975, p.188.
8. John Saar, the *Washington Post*, February 15, 1976.
9. Gregory Henderson, Samuel B. Knight professor at Case Western Reserve University, Cleveland, in testimony before Subcommittee on International Organisations, Committee on International Relations, US House of Representatives, March 17, 1976, "Proceedings of the US House Hearings on the Activities of the KCIA," *Korean Studies Supplement* March, 1976, p.11.
10. *New York Times*, March 14, 1976.
11. T.K., *Sekai*, June, 1976, p.235.
12. See following Chapter.
13. On the 'People's Revolutionary Party' generally, see *Korea Newsletter*, nos.6 and 17, August 1, 1974, and January 15, 1975, and Amnesty International, *1975 Report, op. cit.*, pp.22ff.
14. Cited in *Korea Newsletter*, August 1, 1974.
15. On these naval incidents, see the two issues of *Korea Newsletter* cited in n.13 above.
16. *Ibid.*
17. Amnesty International, *1975 Report, op. cit.*, p.34.
18. In a 40-minute radio broadcast on April 29, 1975, for example, Pak stated that 'The time has passed for discussions on whether the North will attack the South' and stressed that the attack would certainly come before the year was out. 'Every citizen is a soldier,' he said, 'I too am resolved to fight to the death together with the six and a half million citizens for the defence of Seoul.' On May 10 approximately 1·4 million

to 2 million people were mobilised in an anti-communist rally in Seoul. Emergency Decree no.9 was proclaimed on May 13, and the Prime Minister, Kim Jong Pil, repeated on June 11 that the North had completed its war preparations and was looking for a pretext to invade the South. (See "Dokyumento," *Sekai*, July, 1975, pp.173, 175; September, 1975, p.214.)

19. "Dokyumento," *Sekai*, July, 1975, p.186; Brian Woodward, " 'Jinkakuto' shokei to sono ato" (The executions in the 'People's Revolutionary Party' case and the aftermath), *ibid.*, p.141; "Dokyumento", *Sekai*, September, 1975, pp.221–4. These quotations are translated back from the Japanese and therefore the wording may differ slightly from the original.

20. Kim Il Sung in Mauritania on June 2, 1975: 'We have no intention of imposing communism on South Korea. The revolution of the northern half cannot be exported.' "Dokyumento," *Sekai*, September, 1975, p.203.

21. *Peking Review*, no.17 (April 25), 1975, p.17.

22. T.K., *Letters from South Korea* (Tokyo, Iwanami Shoten, 1976), p.403.

23. T.K., *Sekai*, June, 1975, pp.124–5.

24. See Chapter 9.

25. "Dokyumento," *Sekai*, September, 1975, p.208.

26. Andrew Rees, *Guardian*, July 13, 1976. For the full text of Dr Lee's June 10, 1975 testimony to the Subcommittee on International Organisations of the Committee on International Relations of the House of Representatives, see "Human Rights and Democracy in South Korea," *Korean Studies*, 1976, pp.37–45.

27. For a detailed treatment of this phenomenon: "Dokyumento," *Sekai*, March, 1976, pp.142–4; and *The November 22nd Spy Case*, a pamphlet published by the November 22nd Rescue Committee, c/o Tsutonda Church, 3-7-25 Tondo-cho, Takatsuki-shi, Osaka, Japan.

28. Donald Ranard, Chief of the US State Department Korea section between 1970 and 1974, in testimony on March 17 to House of Representatives Subcommittee, *Korean Studies Supplement*, March, 1976; also in interview, *Yomiuri Shinbun*, March 26, 1976.

29. *Japan Times*, November 5, 1973.

30. *Newsweek*, May 26, 1975, p.39.

31. Full text in English of "Declaration for National Democratic Salvation" is given in *Ampo*, vol.8, no.1, 1976, pp.40–41.

32. *Far Eastern Economic Review*, May 21 and June 11, 1976.

33. For a small selection of recent writing on the plight of Kim Chi Ha: Frank Baldwin and Bruce Cumings, *New York Review of Books*, August 7, 1975, pp.3–4; Robert Whymant, *Sunday Times*, May 16, 1976; *Far Eastern Economic Review*, June 4, 1976.

34. Kim Chi Ha, *Cry of the People and other poems* (Hayama, The Autumn Press, 1974), p.45.

35. Text, *ibid.*, pp.60–89.

36. *Ronin*, Vol.1, no.4 and 5, August, 1972, p.6.

Chapter 4

The South Korean Economy: GNP Versus the People

Gavan McCormack

'The ordinary citizen here is quite free. We have a free economic system. Anyone is free to set up a firm or a factory.' South Korean Premier Choi Kyu Hah, March, 1976.[1]

South Korea and two other dictatorships, Taiwan and Brazil, are the three most frequently cited examples of capitalist Third World economic 'development'. By conventional standards the statistical indices of growth are indeed remarkable. At the same time observers have, in muted fashion, registered concern over evidence that the 'miracle' is springing up on the stony soil of a highly inequitable and repressive social order. Where a connection has been drawn between the two, however, it has commonly been to argue that political repression is a temporary, regrettable but necessary phenomenon associated with the stage of generating economic take-off, and that equitable distribution of wealth and the apparatus of political liberalism can, and perhaps must, be postponed. This is also the position adopted by official spokesmen for the South Korean government, although the Premier, in the passage cited above, takes his stand firmly in the nineteenth century by proclaiming that 'freedom' means the 'freedom to set up a firm or a factory'.

Our view is that growth and industrialisation have undoubtedly occurred but that expansion of the economy is no end in itself. The *particular kind* of industrialisation policies the Pak régime has pursued have achieved the paradoxical feat of combining increased production with greater poverty. The economic distortions and dislocations have been enor-

This essay draws heavily on the pioneering research of Kim Chang Soo, particularly his article "Marginalization, Development and the Korean Workers' Movement," *Ampo*, Vol.9, no.3, and his criticism of an earlier draft of this paper.

mous, while the fruits have been either appropriated by a tiny élite or remitted abroad. Continuation of the South Korean economy along its present trajectory is likely to lead to greater inequality and immiseration for the vast majority of the people, as well as expanded economic control by foreign capital.

The evidence for the South Korean economic 'miracle' can be resumed by several sets of statistics.[2] From 1962, the year in which the Pak Chung Hee régime introduced its first Five-Year Plan, to 1976, the Gross National Product (GNP) grew at an average annual rate of approximately 10 per cent, reaching 15.9 per cent in 1969, 16.5 per cent in 1973 and 15.2 per cent in 1976. Exports, a mere $54.8 million in 1962, grew steadily, exceeding $5 billion in 1975 and, despite the continuing world recession, $7.7 billion in 1976. They reached $10 billion in 1977. *Per capita* GNP rose in the same period from negligible amounts to $380 at the end of 1974 and approximately $700 in 1976. During three successive five-year plans the importance of manufacturing industry to the economy has steadily increased and that of agriculture has shrunk. Known in world markets not long ago almost exclusively for its light consumer goods, in the past five to ten years South Korea has developed a substantial heavy and chemical industry sector; it boasts an impressive ship-building capacity; and it has already begun to compete effectively for overseas contracts in construction, ship-building and other areas. Is it, in short, developing into a second Japan?

The figures establish beyond doubt that growth has occurred, and the record is particularly impressive in the light of the economic troubles experienced globally since 1973. The figures have no mystic significance, however, and must be interpreted.

The first main characteristic of the South Korean economy stems from the nature of its inception as an American protectorate on the East Asian continent. The US has already paid out a total of $4.5 billion in straight grants to Seoul; and on post-1945 Korean-related expenses (i.e., costs which include those of the Korean War itself), it has spent a staggering $189 billion, more than on any other country except Vietnam.[3]

Washington has always been, and remains, the ultimate under-writer of the régime.

The second main characteristic is the fact that economic growth over the past ten years, the period of dynamic expansion, has been based overwhelmingly on exports. This policy rested in turn on foreign capital induction in the 1960s, in the form of capital goods imports from Japan and Vietnam War earnings paid by the United States.

Giving priority to the export sector is a common feature of economic policies in recent years in the capitalist Third World.[4] It is a policy which was adopted after the failure of attempts in the 1960s to promote industrialisation by giving priority to import substitution, in other words, to industrialise by first producing domestically some of the goods that were being supplied by manufacturers in the advanced countries. The reason for the failure of this policy is disputed, but at least it is clear that it bred inefficient industries, generated corrupt government bureaucracies and ran counter to the interests of the multi-nationals which it sought to limit or displace. It also conflicted with a separate, and, even more important, multi-national interest that also became clear about the late 1960s — that is, to integrate to their own advantage the favourable conditions of cheap and skilled labour, cheap land, and absence of labour organisation and pollution control, by establishing branches of their own manufacturing industries in North and South-east Asia and producing goods there for the world market. Import-substitution policies ran directly counter to the interests of international capital on both these counts and it is therefore hardly surprising that such policies were gradually abandoned.

The countries of the region, South Korea most prominent among them, have given increasing priority to the production of goods for export over production of goods for the home market. Concentration on an export strategy aimed at world markets has had as a corollary the infusion of massive amounts of Western investment and loan capital and technology, resulting in deepening dependency. The manufacturing sector of the 'national' economy thus becomes denationalised and turned over to multi-national business as a setting for the growth of its competitive processing, manufacturing or marketing activities.

The degree of foreign capital infusion into the economy between 1959 and 1975 is set out on the accompanying table. The fact that the United States and Japan between them account for 57·9 per cent of the $8·9 billion total (US: 34·2 per cent; Japan: 23·7 per cent) is immediately striking. Where the United States was responsible for 38·5 per cent of all commercial loans in this period, Japan was responsible for 65·5 per cent of all direct investment.[5] Because Japanese involvement is concentrated in the manufacturing sector, through this direct investment, it tends to be more conspicuous. But it is important to note that the most important source of capital is not investment, which actually amounts to less than 10 per cent of the total, but loans, in which the United States share is crucial, and in which the EC countries are also heavily involved.

The most important components of the export sector in 1976 were textiles and clothing (35 per cent of all exports) and electrical appliances (10 per cent).[6] Conditions in these industries are discussed in greater detail below, but in the context of attractiveness to foreign investers it should be noted here that the decisive factor in these labour-intensive industries is low wages. Wages in manufacturing industry in general in South Korea are about one-eighth of the equivalent in Japan (according to a September, 1975, study);[7] they are even lower in textiles and electrical appliances, which rank among the lowest paid of all.[8] These are the areas in which the amounts of foreign capital involved is often small, and in which small- and medium-scale Japanese enterprises, facing extinction because of their inability to compete with the monopolies at home, are prominent. To avoid the squeeze at home they become exploiters abroad. The average Japanese investment in the 694 Japanese joint ventures in South Korea is only $830,000 (as of 1975), as against an average in US joint ventures of $1·4 million.[9] This concentration of Japanese investment in the low-wage, labour-intensive manufacturing export sector makes the Japanese rôle in the economy peculiarly conspicuous. Forced to expand in order to survive, these small-

and medium-scale foreign capitalists expect to recover their capital in five years at most,[10] and they do it by securing

Table 1
Foreign Capital Intake
(in million $)

	1959–73	1974	1975	Total 1959–75
America	2,314·2	481·1	334·4	3,129·7
Public loans	1,009·6	45·0	105·6	1,160·2
Commercial loans	1,138·3	403·9	220·3	1,762·5
Direct investment	166·3	32·2	8·5	207·0
Japan	1,470·6	460·2	161·2	2,092·0
Public loans	416·2	222·5	40·0	678·7
Commercial loans	674·5	142·9	18·4	835·8
Direct investment	379·9	94·8	102·8	577·5
EC	1,084·8	333·6	244·1	1,662·5
Public loans	111·1		98·3	209·4
Commercial loans	955·3	331·6	94·0	1,380·9
Direct investment				
IBRD/IDA/IFC	525·8	85·0	409·4	1,020·2
Public loans	525·8	85·0	382·5	993·3
Commercial loans			26·9	26·9
Direct investment				
ADB	244·2	89·0	101·5	434·7
Public loans	244·2	89·0	101·5	434·7
Commercial loans				
Direct investment				
Other	323·4	223·5	102·3	649·2
Public loans	0·9	15·0		15·9
Commercial loans	311·2	208·5	63·9	583·6
Direct investment	11·3	0·7	38·4	49·6
Total	5,963·0	1,672·4	1,352·9	8,988·3

Source: Yoshida Akiko, " 'Kankoku' ni okeru kōdō seichō no mekanizumu," Keizai, August, 1977, p.55. From South Korean official statistics.

cheaper labour and longer hours in Korea than they can get anywhere else. Japanese companies in Korea, moreover, handle 52·7 per cent of total exports and 64·2 per cent of total imports.[11]

While Japanese capital is particularly strong in the light industry sector, American capital, by contrast, is concentrated in strategically important capital-intensive and high-profit areas. Thus petroleum is 100 per cent controlled by subsidiaries of US corporations such as Gulf, Caltex and Union,[12] in joint ventures with the ROK government, while the petro-chemical sector is also dominated by foreign (largely, but not exclusively, American) capital in 50:50 joint ventures with the South Korean government. In the petro-chemical industry, Kim Chang Soo discusses the astonishing case of a group of US companies, including Gulf, International Mineral, Skelly Oil and Swift Agricultural Chemicals, which extracted $92 million in profits from joint petro-chemical ventures with the Korean government, to which neither they nor the Korean government had actually committed a cent.[13] All the investment funds were provided by low interest US AID loans, i.e., by the American taxpayer. The Korean government enforces the sale of the fertiliser to farmers at grossly inflated prices and thus could guarantee high returns in advance to the foreign corporations involved. The mechanism employed by these corporations, often US in origin, is much more sophisticated and 'discreet' than that of the manufacturing sector investers, but the level of exploitation is greater. The Korean people are the object of a joint 'rip-off' by the multi-nationals and their own government.

Loan funds, which are channelled primarily into the large-scale and heavy industries, serve important political as well as economic purposes. A substantial proportion of all 'aid' funds to South Korea is creamed off in bribes and kick-backs and finds its way into the hands of the ruling political and technocratic *élite*; thereafter, some of it goes into the hands of allies and supporters of that *élite* in Washington and Tokyo. Estimates as to the amounts consumed vary, but the figure of 20 per cent is frequently suggested and, according to Kim Hyung Wook, former KCIA Chief, testifying in Washington in June,

1977, Pak Chung Hee's own *personal* share amounts to a staggering 5 per cent.[14]

The remainder serves a no less important political purpose: that of ensuring the dependence on the régime of the Korean business *élite*. Funds are disbursed according to government discretion. In South Korea, where normal interest rates, on which small businessmen and farmers depend, are extraordinarily high (16–18 per cent annually), privileged access to foreign loan funds at 9 per cent interest is an incalculable boon to the big business supporters of the régime. The importance of good official connections for financing large enterprises (those with more than 200 employees) is evident from the following table, which reveals the near monopoly of large firms concerning access to foreign loans:[15]

Table 2
Composition of Enterprise Capital in 1975
(in per cent)

	Own capital	Bank loan	Foreign loan	Other debts
All enterprises	24.0	30.3	15.0	30.7
Large enterprises	23.7	30.3	15.3	30.7
Small enterprises	41.5	23.8	0.6	34.1

But this only begins to suggest the enormous financial burden under which Korean firms operate. Critical is the category 'other debts', which reportedly are comprised principally of loans by company executives to their own firms, where interest rates typically range between 3 and 3.5 per cent *per month*. It is above all the larger export-oriented firms which operate under the constant pressure of enormous loan payments which can be met only by the rapid expansion of sales. The process is one which simultaneously drives the economy forward while concentrating wealth in the hands of financiers, both domestic and foreign.

During the period of high growth of the economy between 1966 and 1974, large enterprises made use of their privileged positions to increase from 1.6 to 5.2 per cent of all enterprises;

their number of employees grew from 39·7 to 62·7 per cent of all employees; and the value-added accruing from their enterprises increased from 57·5 to 74·6 per cent of the total. The South Korean economy is embarked in short on a programme of rapid concentration.

As both investment and loan totals grow, the accumulated repayment obligation to foreign bankers and investers has become a serious burden. Outstanding foreign debt increased from $3·3 billion in 1973 to at least $8·1 billion by the end of 1976, with $4·6 billion of the total provided by commercial loans.[16]

The debt problem has been compounded by the fact that every increase in the flow of exports has been achieved only at the cost of a proportionate increase in imports, as a result of which there has been a consistent deficit in the international trading account for every year between 1962 and 1976. This deficit has been most substantial in the years of highest growth, around a billion dollars a year between 1968 and 1973, rising in 1974 to nearly $2·5 billion.[17] It required a massive bail-out by the United States, the World Bank and other multilateral agencies in 1975 when South Korea's current account deficit reached $3·3 billion and when rising US Congressional criticism of the Pak régime's repression prevented expansion of bilateral aid.[18]

As South Korean trade approaches balance for the first time in 1977, the economy remains extremely vulnerable. Its level of dependence on foreign trade is extraordinarily high, having soared from 2·9 per cent in 1960, just before the present régime came to power, to 62 per cent ($18·8 billion) in 1975. It is expected to reach $28 billion in 1981, 83·5 per cent of a $33·5 billion GNP.[19]

With the exception of Hong Kong and Singapore, trading nations with no significant agricultural population, no other nation approaches this level. The Japanese figure, by contrast, is below 20 per cent.[20] Of course, Japan is a major trading nation. But the economy's growth is firmly rooted in the domestic sector.

South Korea's domestic economy is depressed precisely as a consequence of policies designed to provide the cheap and plentiful labour force required by the export sector. The result is an extreme form of economic dualism, with the dynamic of the export and foreign sectors achieved at the direct expense of domestic agriculture and industry. Not only is South Korea's debt level already very high, but its economic planning is postulated on the ability to sustain into the indefinite future a comparable rate of foreign capital inflow. Fulfilment of the fourth five-Year Plan (1977–81) is tied to the intake of an additional $10 billion in foreign capital, an amount roughly equal to the total intake under all preceding plans. South Korea's planners themselves acknowledge, however, that close to an equal sum ($9·4 billion) will have to be remitted abroad in order to service the accumulated foreign debts during this period. By 1981 the government projects a $15 billion foreign debt, 25·6 per cent of anticipated GNP. And in that year $2·6 billion will be paid out in debt servicing, as against only $1·9 billion coming in.[21]

The question of South Korea's debts should be seen in a broad international context. Since 1973–74 the role of credit in the financing of world trade has increased enormously. Third World debt (non-OPEC Third World debt to the West) was estimated at $171 billion at the end of 1976.[22] This enormous increase in credit has been a key mechanism used by contemporary capitalism to keep world trade — historically crucial to uneven development — moving and growing. The great bulk of loans to Third World nations has gone to approximately a dozen countries whose dictatorships have provided optimum conditions for foreign capital at the expense of their people. The rôle of South Korea, which is a subordinate, not an autonomous, economy, within imperialist strategy as a whole, is such that it cannot be characterised by the figure for debt in isolation. Foreign capital is paying for something, and is getting a return on its investment. From a technical point of view, it is not inconceivable that imperialism can go on recycling the debts more or less indefinitely, while making handsome profits on trade.

There is a further and most important observation to be made about South Korea in the global context. Between them, three politically ultra-dependent Third World territories, Hong

Kong, Taiwan and South Korea, account for a strikingly high percentage of Third World exports of manufactured goods to the advanced industrial economies; in 1968 the figure already surpassed one-third.[23] The United States has made no secret of the fact that it sees this group of special political cases (in effect, all three are territories artificially amputated from socialist countries) as the spearhead of a 'black-leg' campaign against the demands of the Third World for global economic change.[24] Under the Pak régime, South Korea represents a politically protected reservoir of labour both against the Third World and against the working classes in the advanced capitalist countries. The ability of the Pak régime to sustain its export drive and the continued flow of foreign loans and investment rests on its ability to keep wages depressed.

The 1977–81 plan calls for maintaining the primary dependent orientation of the economy towards the United States and the secondary one towards Japan: $2·2 billion to come from the former and $1·8 billion from the latter.[25] It can be assumed that the economic benefits derived by the joint sponsors of the system will be in a similar ratio. There are, however, very special aspects about the relationship with Japan (on which see also Chapter 8 below). Japanese expansion into South Korea has accelerated greatly since the late 1960s, when the limits to the high growth of that decade became apparent as people became aware of the appalling level of destruction of the Japanese environment through uncontrolled pollution, and as wage increases and an explosive inflation in land values increased business costs and threatened competitiveness in world markets. Since 1969, Japanese business has devised a series of plans for solving some of these problems through the industrialisation and gradual incorporation of the South Korean economy into the reproductive capacity of Japan.[26] Viewed in this light, Korea's grandiose economic projections continue to unfold in step with the designs of Japanese capital. Korea's emphasis on heavy and chemical industries perfectly complements Japanese plans to restructure domestic industry by restricting high polluting heavy industry and emphasising computer-related and other knowledge-intensive advanced technologies.

Since the real foreign capital inflow between 1977 and 1981 will be minimal, allowing for debt servicing, the question arises as to how the goals of the plan — an increase in GNP by 1·7 times to $31 billion and an increase in exports by 2·6 times from $7·7 billion to $20·2 billion — are to be met.[27] The answer is by greatly stepped-up exploitation of the Korean people and further lashing of the economy to foreign capital. One important source of additional investment capital is taxation. With foreign capital to account for only 12 per cent of South Korean investment between 1977 and 1981, a substantial portion of new investment is to derive from increased taxes on the Korean people.[28] Taxation levels, which have risen sharply over the past 15 years, are expected to continue their ascent.[29]

Table 3

	Taxes as percentage of revenue	As a percentage of GNP
1963	40·9	8·9
1975	80·5	16·4

There is obviously a limit, however, to the extent to which tax levels can be raised without provoking social tensions beyond the point of containment. In October, 1977, for example, a wave of shopowner boycotts in Seoul protested the latest value-added tax imposed by the régime.[30] The quest for funds has therefore led the South Korean régime to adopt some unusual, and even bizarre, expedients, which when considered in sum are perhaps best described as taking the path of a mercenary state.

The export of labour has become South Korea's most successful growth industry. The origins of this business lie in the juicy construction contracts awarded South Korean companies in Vietnam as part of the 'offset' arrangements under which the US paid for the services of Korean troops in the war. Overseas work contracts in 1975 reached a total of $850 million, and this was only the beginning. While the government has been reticent in publishing data for fear that other countries will rush to compete, authoritative sources have indicated that overseas construction contracts exceeded $4 billion in 1977 and are projected to reach $10 billion in 1978.[31] This work is over-whelmingly concentrated in the Middle East, although the export of skilled labour, nurses and miners to countries like Canada and West Germany, and seamen to crew foreign, especially Japanese, ships is a much older phenomenon.[32] (On this, see Chapter 10 on Korea and the Middle East.)

The export of young men and women, commonly in KCIA-policed contingents, is complemented by the promotion of prostitution as a foreign-exchange earner. In 1973, for example, 93 per cent of the 411,000 Japanese tourists who visited South Korea were unaccompanied males, and the availability of prostitutes is an important part of the tourist promotion campaign, particularly in Japan.[33] Estimates of the number of prostitutes range as high as 200,000.[34] South Korea's income from tourism virtually doubled, from $141 million in 1975 to $275 million in 1976, and is expected to reach $800 million by 1981.[35] Many women, including illegal immigrants, are despatched to work in Japan. There can be no more revealing indication of the depths of degradation to which the Pak régime has sunk than the speech by the then Minister of Education, Min Kwan Sik, on the occasion of his visit to a South Korean high school in Tokyo in April, 1973, in which he referred to 'the laudable patriotic sentiments of the large number of South Korean *kisaeng* and nightclub hostesses who have come to Japan selling their . . . for the nation.'[36]

Apart from the shameless trafficking in the bodies of the country's women, the South Korean government also co-operates with foreign adoption agencies in 'exporting' Korean babies to the West, at the rate of about 5,000 per year. The government does not appear to be directly involved in profiting from this racket, but it tolerates it because it simultaneously brings in foreign currency and reduces the child welfare budget.[37]

The reconstruction of the domestic Korean economy in order to accomplish foreign-capital-fired, export-oriented growth has had the most marked effect on Korean agriculture which has stagnated throughout the boom years. By keeping a deliberately low ceiling on rice prices through the dumping of cheap American grain surpluses, the government has enforced a rapid decline in rural incomes, from 83 per cent (as compared to urban incomes) in 1966 to 53 per cent in 1968 and to 59 per cent in 1970.[38] A mere 6·8 per cent of all foreign capital introduced into the economy between 1959 and 1974 went to the agricultural sector, though it employed the largest number of people.[39]

Ironically, the necessary precondition of the chosen pattern of growth, the mobilisation to the cities of a cheap, depressed labour pool, has had a doubly debilitating effect: the domestic economy has been depressed because of the low purchasing power of the masses, and grain imports have been a large drain on foreign currency reserves, costing $450 million in 1974, $689 million in 1975 and $459 million in 1976.[40] Some aspects of the way in which American 'aid' rice sent to Korea has been used to strengthen the Pak régime, even while bringing ruin to Korean farmers, have only recently come to light. Rice imports from the United States to South Korea between 1970 and 1973 totalled 1·5 million tons, 40 per cent in excess of actual food needs.[41] One result was that Korea's self-sufficiency in grain fell steadily, from 94 per cent in 1965 to 80 per cent by 1970; in 1976 it stood at 75 per cent.[42]

There is no doubt, however, that the Pak régime's agricultural policy accomplished what it set out to accomplish. A rural population of 16·1 million in 1967 fell to 12·8 million in 1976, from 54·4 to 35·7 per cent of the total population. According to Kim Chang Soo's study, this means that, if natural increase is taken into account, 6·7 million farmers left the land. Many who remain, as many as 43 per cent according to a recent government estimate, are in full or in part tenant farmers. These families, among the poorest in Korea, pay an average rent of 40–60 per cent of the crop.[43] Many destitute farmers and their families, forced to leave the land, went to Seoul, whose population, less than 2·5 million in the early 1960s, increased to 4·7 million in 1969 and to 7·5 million in 1977. Seoul now has the largest proportion of its population concentrated in the capital of any country in the world, and approximately 2·5 million of Seoul's citizens are squatters, living in slum conditions and under constant government harassment.[44] Obviously, not all of this massive influx can be employed. In the past decade, employment in all non-agricultural sectors increased by only 2 million (1 million in the manufacturing sector).[45] The large surplus pool of unemployed or semi-employed serves the function of keeping wages down and making labour organisation more difficult. Kim Chang Soo summarises the process as follows:

'In short, in the last decade millions of peasants, forced off the land, have moved to the "periphery" of cities. They are in the "periphery" both in the sense that they live as squatters in the outskirts of the city and also in the sense that they serve as marginal labour in the urban economy. Large numbers are left unemployed or work at starvation wages. Among the 6,365,000 non-agricultural workers, the low-income class earning below the official "minimum" standard amounts to more than 5,400,000. The origins of this marginal population lie in the export-oriented industrialisation policy and its guided decline of the agricultural economy.'[46]

Only 17.8 per cent of jobs (in 1974) were in mining and manufacturing; 49.8 per cent were still in agriculture and fisheries; and 34.5 per cent were in the 'service' sector, most of them, nearly 3.5 million, simply classified as 'other'. This enormous category comprises the ' "service workers" such as maids, porters, carriers, bus girls, tour guides, peddlars, shopkeepers, day labourers and prostitutes . . . those whose livelihood is least stable and whose work caters predominantly to the foibles of the rich and of foreigners and can not be considered productive.' The economic rationale for the destruction of the agricultural sector is not to be found, therefore, in the need to shift the population from agriculture into industry, but in the desire to provide a pool of sufficiently depressed, unorganised and cheap labour to attract multi-national investors.

The actual unemployment rate is impossible to determine accurately, since the government figure of 4.5 per cent is based on the exclusion from the 'unemployed' category of anyone working as little as one hour a week. A more realistic estimate, based on 40 hours a week, gives a figure of about 30 per cent for the country as a whole (a good deal higher in Seoul).[47]

Employers prefer women, especially unmarried young women, since they cost less than half their male equivalents, and in many of the large export enterprises they constitute 70 to 90 per cent of the work force.[48] In 1976 the average woman worker earned 44 per cent of the wage of the average male worker.[49] In the Masan Free Export Zone 76 per cent of the 24,500-strong work force is made up of women.[50]

The heavy reliance on female labour in the key export sectors of textiles and clothing (one-third of all exports) helps hold costs to the barest minimum. The average monthly wage in 1975 was 30,393 won (approximately $62) in textiles, around 25,152 won (approximately $52) in clothing, as against an average in the manufacturing sector of 38,378 won (approximately $79).[51] In the Seoul garment industry in 1970 one-half of the 27,000 person labour force was below 15 years of age, working up to 16 hours a day, in conditions so bad that many suffered from eye infections, tuberculosis or pneumonia.[52] A 1976 report made it clear that conditions remained very bad: in the Pyonghwa market, where 150 clothing factories are located, it is often impossible for workers to stand upright, due to additional floors being installed in the buildings to maximise space.[53] Women are grossly exploited in other sectors too: bus conductresses in Seoul work an 18-hour day, and it is apparently not uncommon for them to fall asleep on their buses, at least one young woman having died in a fall from her bus as a result.[54]

In March, 1976, the Office of Labour Affairs of the South Korean government reported that the average male worker received a salary of $93 per month. The same government's Economic Planning Board held, however, that the minimum requirement for the average family was $142.[55] This is a standard that is met by only a small fraction of the work force; in fact, in 1974 it was met by only 13 per cent of workers (the figure then standing at $113) and there is no evidence that there has been any improvement since.[56] The South Korean wage pattern reveals a sharply polarised income distribution, with the vast majority living on the margins of subsistence, as indicated in the following table.[57]

Table 4
Wage Structure of Non-agricultural Sectors
(in thousands)

Monthly wage	Number of employees	Percentage	Cumulative total of workers	Cumulative percentage of workers
Less than 20,000	248	3·9	248	3·9
20– 30,000	3,608	56·7	3,856	60·6
30– 45,000	1,158	18·2	5,014	78·8
45– 70,000	281	4·4	5,295	83·2
70– 90,000	320	5·1	5,615	88·3
90–120,000	355	5·6	5,970	93·9
120–200,000	291	4·6	6,261	98·5
200–500,000	98	1·4	6,359	99·9
Over 500,000	6	0·09	6,365	100·0
Total	6,365	100·0	6,365	

Source: Material submitted to the House Finance Committee, reported in *Dong-A Ilbo*, June 19, 1977. See also the editorial in *Dong-A Ilbo*, July 14, 1977.

The statistic of *per capita* GNP, often flaunted by the régime as if to suggest it represents an average actual annual income, is meaningless in a country where the inequalities in the distribution of wealth are as pronounced as they are in South Korea and where inflation has eaten into hard-won wage increases. Sumiya Mikio, a leading Japanese economist, has demonstrated that the statistical effect of a nominal rise in *per capita* GNP between 1968 and 1973 from $100 to $373 was achieved only at the cost of a substantial real deterioration in living conditions.[58] At the same time, Kim Chang Soo has documented the fact that the rate of exploitation — that is, the ratio of the respective share of the total product appropriated by capital to that of labour — has continued to rise as the growth of labour productivity has outstripped real wages between 1970 and 1974.[59] South Korea's Engel's co-efficient (the ratio of food to total consumption expenditure) is considered by experienced labour experts to be 55–60 per cent (government figures place it at 40 per cent). Sumiya observes that over 55 per cent 'indicates a semi-starvation situation.'[60]

Neglect of safety standards on the part of management and government is another way in which profits are maximised. Officially reported industrial disabilities increased 2·7 times between 1970 and 1976, when they reached 95,289. Between 800 and 900 workers are being *killed* each year in industrial 'accidents', a level which appears to be 3 to 5 times the ILO average.[61] It is a measure of the kind of society that South Korea has become that employment, even in such conditions, should seem desirable to the displaced masses who throng the slums and shanty towns of Seoul.

Under these circumstances, labour organisation is weak, and designedly so. A mere 14 per cent (712,000) of the labour force is unionised, and they in unions which have been carefully cultivated by management and government as instruments of social and economic control.[62] They have consistently been denied the right to affiliate with the ILO. Far from being autonomous organisations, they are directly controlled by the government's Office of Labour Affairs through the medium of the Federation of Korean Trade Unions. As Kim Chang Soo comments: [63]

'Any attempt to form a new (alternative to the officially licensed) labour union is illegal. In small shops with less than 16 workers, the right to organise, not to mention the right to strike and to collective bargaining, is not permitted. It is necessary to get government permission to organise a labour union in the bonded areas or in foreign capital-affiliated companies. Thus, the three basic rights of labour, the right to organise, to collective bargaining and to strike, are in effect prohibited. Therefore, genuine labour movements in Korea take the form of "guerrilla struggle". Anyone attempting to create a true labour movement committed to defending the interests of the workers must be prepared to face dismissal, arrest, imprisonment and torture.'

Export-led industrialisation, it should be clear, has little to offer the working or unemployed masses. This is not to say that it is without support; quite the contrary. The success of the present régime in pursuing the distorted form of industrialis-ation that has been described has won it considerable support which it would be foolish to deny. The benefits drawn from the system by big business have already been mentioned; a rural capitalist *élite* is thriving; and the attractions to university students of the kind of salaries that high growth makes poss-ible for them — monthly 120,000 to 150,000 *won* or approxi-mately $240 to $300 — may make it easier for some to overlook the injustices of the régime.[64] Even here, however, the pressures are intense. The 50,000 spring, 1978, college graduates will enter a job market in which big businesses em-ploying 200 or more workers reportedly plan to hire only 8,000 high school *and* college graduates.

In short, the 'success' of the economy is based on the formula

Growth = Dependence + Repression.

A weakening of the repression or a challenge to the dependence would certainly disrupt the growth, but it is also the pre-con-dition for a policy of true development. As Kim Chang Soo's important paper makes clear, it is the Korean workers upon whose labour the industrialisation of South Korea has been built but who have been exploited, impoverished and 'mar-ginalised' in the process, who have seen the fruits of their labour transferred either to the repressive and unproductive *élite* at home or to foreign capitalists. In 1977, the growing number of strikes in the face of severe repression provides the clearest sign that they are deepening their understanding of the mechanism of their oppression. Once they fully grasp it, the Pak dictatorship and the political economy it supports cannot last.

However, true economic development in South Korea will not be accomplished easily. An end to the Pak régime may be a precondition, but it is no more than that, for South Korea, like North Korea, is the unnaturally truncated half of one country, Korea. Only with its re-unification, however long-term a prospect that may be, can the energies, resources and talents of a single people be shifted from false policies of confront-ation and militarisation — implicit in the division — and con-centrated on the pursuit of development in the interests of all the people.

NOTES

1. Quoted in *Far Eastern Economic Review* (hereafter *FEER*), March 16, 1976, p.16.
2. Statistics from Yoshida Akiko, " 'Kankoko' ni okeru kōdō seichō no mekanizumu" (The mechanism of high growth in South Korea), *Keizai,* August, 1977, p.64; Kim Chang Soo, "Marginalisation, Development and the Korean Workers' Movement," *Ampo,* Vol.9, no.3, (July–November 1977); Gerhard Breidenstein, "Capitalism in South Korea," in Frank Baldwin, ed., *Without Parallel: The American-Korean Relationship Since 1945* (New York, Pantheon, 1974), p.235. All figures cited are from official South Korean government sources.
3. Breidenstein, p.240; Center for International Policy, *International Policy Report,* Vol.1, no.1 (December 1975), p.2
4. The best general treatment of the whole phenomenon of export-oriented industrialisation is the book-length special number of *Ampo,* "Free Trade Zones and the Industrialisation of Asia," Vol.9, no.2, (1977).
5. Additional data for 1976 is given in Economic Planning Board, *Kyungje Baeksuh, 1977* (hereafter *Economic White Paper, 1977*), pp.286, 293. Data from Korean language sources provided courtesy of Kim Chang Soo. Direct investment at the end of 1976 totalled $953·7 million and loans for the years 1959–76 reached $11·3 billion on an approval basis.
6. *Economic White Paper, 1977,* Yoshida, p.59.
7. *Akahata,* March 2, 1976, cited in Yoshida, p.64.
8. For tables of salary by sector, see: Don Long, "Repression and Development in the Periphery: South Korea," *Bulletin of Concerned Asian Scholars,* Vol.9, no.2 (April-June, 1977) for 1975 figures, and Yoshida, p.66, for 1976 figures.
9. Kido Jun, "Nihon dokusai shihon no tai 'Kan' shinshutsu" (Japanese monopoly capital's thrust into South Korea), *Keizai,* August, 1976, p.71. The figure of 694 joint ventures is from "Bei, Nichi, 'Kan', kankei no gen kyokumen" (The present juncture in American, Japanese, South Korean relations), *Zadankai* (Round-table discussion), in *ibid,* p.37.
10. *FEER,* August 12, 1977, p.28.
11. Nakagawa Nobuo, "Kankoku no 'oiage' setsu ni igiari" (There is another opinion on Korea's catching up with Japan), *Asahi Journal,* January 13, 1978, p.101.
12. Yoshida, p.58.
13. Kim Chang Soo, p.26.
14. *The Washington Post,* June 6, 1977.
15. Yoshida, p.60.
16. *Economic White Paper, 1977,* p.447. Compare Long, pp.29, 32.
17. For a table of imports and exports for 1962–1975, see Yoshida, p.64.
18. Center for International Policy, *Human Rights and the Foreign Assistance Program,* Fiscal Year 1978, Part 2, East Asia (Washington, 1977), p.53.
19. *Economic White Paper, 1977,* pp.76, 79.
20. Sumiya Mikio, *Kankoku no keizai* (The South Korean Economy) (Tokyo, 1976), p.39.

21. Yoshida, pp.61–62; Long, p.29.
22. *IMF Survey*, September 5, 1977, p.282. At the end of 1973 the figure was $93 billion.
23. UNCTAD, *Trade in Manufactures of Developing Countries: 1969 Review*, p.41.
24. *FEER*, January 16, 1976, p.19.
25. Kido Jun, pp.68–69.
26. For various versions of Japanese plans since 1973, see *Zadankai*, pp.35–37; also see the Chapter on Japan below.
27. Kido Jun, p.70.
28. Yoshida, p.61.
29. *Ibid.*, p.65.
30. *New Asia News*, October 21, 1977.
31. "Hashiru Kankoku" (Running Korea), *Asahi Shimbun*, December 1, 1977; *Asia Research Bulletin*, January 31 and June 30, 1976; *Financial Times*, April 27, 1976; *Time*, August 9, 1976, p.30; *Middle East Economic Digest*, July 16, 1976.
32. *FEER*, January 9, 1976, p.129; *Spare Rib*, Vol.47 (1976); Matsui Yayori, "Women's Predicament: Why I Oppose Kisaeng Tours — Unearthing a Structure of Economic and Sexual Aggression," in White Paper on Sexism — Japan Task Force, *Japanese Women Speak Out* (Tokyo, 1975).
33. *Shūkan Gendai*, October 25, 1975. See also Hasegawa Kazuto, "South Korea's Blue House: The KCIA in the Bedroom and Ford in the Garage," *Ampo*, Vol.7, no.1 (Winter, 1975), pp.35–39.
34. *Time*, June 4, 1973.
35. *Economic White Paper, 1977*, p.473.
36. The word omitted here from the minister of Education's address was an explicit and obscene Korean gangster expression. Chung Kyung Mo, "The Second Liberation of South Korea and Democratization of Japan," *Japan Interpreter*, Vol.9, no.2 (Summer-Autumn, 1974), p.179.
37. "Panorama," BBC television programme on the international baby adoption business, March 15, 1976; text in *The Listener*, March 18, 1976.
38. Kim Young Hee, "A Report on the Saemaul Movement," *Sekai*, November, 1976; cited in Kim Chang Soo, p.28.
39. Kim Fa Hyo, "Minami Chōsen ni okeru 'keizai kindaika ron' hihan" (Critique of 'economic modernization theory' in South Korea), *Chōsen Shiryō* (Materials on Korea), August, 1977, p.35.
40. *Economic White Paper, 1977*, p.269; Sumiya, p.202.
41. *FEER*, April 18, 1975; Tad Szulc, "Too Much Rice: The Original Sin," *The New Republic*, January 29, 1977; Long, p.35.
42. Ministry of Agriculture and Fishery, Republic of Korea, *Nong chong Suchup, 1977* (Agricultural memos, 1977).
43. Kim Chang Soo, p.22. Sumiya Mikio, "Growth Economy and Unstable Society: Mechanism of the South Korean Economy." Paper prepared for the Conference on Japanese and U.S. Parliamentarians on Korean Problems, Washington D.C., September 19–20, 1977, pp.23–24.
44. Kim Chang Soo, p.28; Long, p.35.
45. Kim Chang Soo, p.29.
46. *Ibid.*, p.30.
47. "Kankoku rōdō undō ni kansuru hōkoku" (Report on the labour movement in South Korea), *Sekai*, June, 1976, p.250; Long, p.35, suggests

a figure of 22·5 per cent of the "economically active population of the country as a whole." See also Kim Chang Soo, pp.29–30.

48. "Kankoku rōdō undō," pp.250–54.
49. Kim Yoo Hwan, "Kyungje kaepal kwa imkeum" (Economic development and wage policy, *Shin Dong A* (New East Asia), December, 1977, p.127.
50. "Masan yūshutsu jiyū chiiki no jittai chōsa" (Investigation into the actual conditions of the Masan Free Export Zone), *Sekai*, May, 1975, p.46.
51. For average wages by sector, see Yoshida, p.66.
52. Breidenstein, p.254.
53. "Kankoku rōdō undō," p.252.
54. Kim Chang Soo, p.34.
55. Richard Halloran, *New York Times*, March 20, 1976.
56. A study based on 1975 statistics concluded that they had deteriorated: Chung Kyung Mo, *Korea Newsletter*, Vol.35, December 15, 1975–January 1, 1976, pp.3–4. Kim Chang Soo, p.30, calculates that in 1976 85 per cent of workers in the non-agrarian sector earned less than the minimum living salary fixed by the government.
57. Kim Chang Soo, p.30.
58. Sumiya Mikio, "Oitsumerareta Kankoku keizai" (South Korean economy in a corner), *Sekai*, September, 1975, p.37.
59. Kim Chang Soo, p.30.
60. Sumiya, "Growth economy," p.28.
61. *Korea Herald*, July 10, 1977.
62. "Kankoku rōdō undō," p.247.
63. Kim Chang Soo, pp.32–33.
64. *Zadankai*, p.40.

Section III

The North

Chapter 5

North Korea. Development and Self-Reliance: A Critical Appraisal

Aidan Foster-Carter

Introduction

North Korea (or, to give it its proper name, the Democratic People's Republic of Korea — hereafter DPRK) has been perhaps the least known country in the world as far as the West is concerned. Two sorts of reasons for this may be adduced. First, and most important, there is the 'curtain of ignorance' (as Felix Greene has called it) with which in the era of the Cold War the West tried — and, until Vietnam, largely succeeded — to blot out all appreciation of the development of communist states, especially in Asia. China was obviously the main example here, but the DPRK suffered still more: not only was Korea in any case a relatively small and little known country in the West, but above all the unique distinction of being made war on by the 'United Nations' — and the way in which that war has consistently been misrepresented[1] — served to reinforce the DPRK's image in the West as the ultimate international pariah. Also, while in the case of China the West has finally opened its eyes in the last five years, we continue obdurately not to 'recognise' the DPRK;[2] and 'non-recognition' in this formal, diplomatic sense bespeaks a deeper refusal to examine the experience and lessons of a country whose development over the last thirty years is actually very significant.

The second obstacle to a proper understanding originates with the DPRK itself. There are two aspects to this. First, hard data on the country are few and far between: for instance, official statistical information on the economy has become scarcer since the mid-60s and almost non-existent in the 70s (apart from relative indices, which are hard to interpret). 'Social science' in the DPRK also seems remarkably opaque;[3] and, despite somewhat increased opportunity in recent years for Westerners to visit the DPRK, such trips are so standardised as to be informative only within prescribed limits.

Secondly, the DPRK has of course been conducting its own publicity campaign over the last five years or so, largely through the medium of large and expensive newspaper advertisements.[4] These have probably made the name of Kim Il Sung better known, but it must be seriously doubted whether they have won the DPRK any new friends. The attribution of every detail of the DPRK's undoubted successes to 'the respected and beloved leader' is something not easy for a Westerner, and especially a Western socialist, to understand. Almost certainly the whole campaign has been counterproductive for the DPRK. We hope that the following account will, *inter alia*, at least help to throw some light on why the DPRK insists on presenting itself in this way and thereby creates a unique problem for would-be sympathisers, who are quite prepared to offer solidarity but draw the line at what they see as sycophancy.

Background and Brief History

Both sets of problems arise as soon as we begin to examine the origins of the DPRK. The conventional Western view denies all autonomy to Korean political processes, and attributes the rise of a communist state in North Korea simply to the entry in 1945 of the Soviet Army and their few Korean protégés, including Kim Il Sung.[5] Conversely, DPRK accounts are more or less silent on the Soviet contribution (as they are also on the Chinese role in the Korean War), and see 1945 as the climax of an independent guerrilla anti-Japanese campaign waged — mainly in Manchuria — by Kim Il Sung since the 1930s.[6] The former view is patently false, while the latter (to say the least) contains considerable lacunae. What *both* versions consistently down-play is the predominance of leftist and Communist currents within Korea itself by 1945. One point on which (for once) they tend to agree is the fragmentation and factionalism of Korean Communism from the 1920s. The Party had to re-form on four occasions in the

1920s after being infiltrated and broken up by the Japanese secret police; and in Comintern circles in the 1930s. Korea was apparently a byword for factionalism. But it is also true, as acknowledged in the major Western-language account of Korean Communism, that the communists 'succeeded in wresting control of the Korean revolution from the Nationalists; they planted a deep core of Communist influence among the Korean people . . .'[7] That influence is nowhere better illustrated than by the network of People's Committees which — despite three decades of oppression and clandestinity — sprang up within two weeks of the end of the war in 1945; they disarmed the Japanese, convened a congress, promulgated various reforms and established a nationwide administration before the American Commander, General Hodge, arrived on September 8.[8]

In some ways it is hardly possible to tell a separate story of North as opposed to South Korea until at least 1948 (when the 'DPRK' was proclaimed, after and in response to the declaration of the 'Republic of Korea' in the South), or even 1950. And this in turn is because it is scarcely possible to separate the strands of nationalism and communism in this period. United front politics were predominant; conversely, Syngman Rhee's attraction for the Americans was that 'he was the *only* Nationalist leader who opposed an alliance with the Communists.'[9] In the South, the US refused to recognise the People's Committees, but set up its own military government and reinstated Japanese officials and collaborators: the consequent oppression provoked furious resistance, including full-scale uprisings, which in a sense led naturally into the events of June 1950. In the North, inasmuch as '[the Peoples' Committees] owed little if anything, to the initiatives either of the Soviet forces . . . or [those] of Kim Il Sung', both of those groups worked with and through them, which must have helped ensure Kim's legitimacy.[10]

Early Developments in the North, and the Japanese 'heritage'
Those in the West who now grudgingly admit that the DPRK is no puppet tend to portray this as a fairly recent development, and persist in seeing it as a Soviet or Chinese satellite at least until after the Korean War. And yet, while

the presence of the Soviet Army doubtless helped to resolve the initial question of state power, and the Chinese People's Volunteers later were crucial in ensuring the state's very survival, it would be wrong to underplay not only (as we have seen) the radical mood of the Korean people in 1945 but also the determined independence of mind of Kim Il Sung himself. It should be remembered that 'for almost a decade . . . North Korea's was the only ruling Communist régime in a post-colonial third-world nation.'[11] As such, the DPRK faced problems that were unprecedented. Nonetheless, within twelve months North Korea carried out what has been called 'the most comprehensive reform program yet seen in the entire Third World.'[12] In order to understand the significance of this, we should look briefly at the type of economy and society that the Korean communists inherited in 1945. This was, primarily, a colonial economy, of a particularly exploited and distorted type. In McCune's words, 'the old economy was pushed back . . . but not supplanted':[13] typically, the pre-capitalist mode of production (usually labelled 'feudal') coexisted in subordination and articulation to the newly dominant capitalist one.[14] There thus persisted a fairly strong rural gentry,[15] in *de facto* alliance with Japanese colonialism. The latter meanwhile proceeded in two stages.[16] At first, Korea was seen primarily as an agricultural and settler colony: in 1925 there were 525,000 Japanese in Korea, and by 1942 80 per cent of forests and 25 per cent of cultivable land were Japanese-owned (often by finance companies rather than individual landlords). The combined pressure of feudal and colonial extortion led to agricultural pauperisation. 56 per cent of farm households had only 5.6 per cent of the land, rice consumption per head declined by almost half between 1912 and 1936, and by 1945 more than two million Koreans had been driven off the land into Japan itself where they took the harshest and worst-paid jobs.

Later, after the crisis of 1929–31, Korea came to be seen as a source of raw materials for Japanese industry, eventually providing all Japan's magnesite, graphite and cobalt, 85 per cent of molybdenum, 22 per cent of bauxite, 14 per cent of coke, 11 per cent of steel, and 16 per cent of fertilisers. There was a certain industrialisation, in Korea, but not *of* and *for*

Korea (in Suret-Canale's words, 'pas auto-centré'): in particular there was no machine-tool industry, and Koreans were later to complain that the railway networks led only from the mines and factories to the sea. The Korean share of the capital involved was only 11 per cent in 1938, and even this had declined to 3 per cent by 1943; on the other side, in the same year the working class numbered nearly $\frac{3}{4}$ million. Very few Koreans were given technical or managerial posts: this was in keeping with Japanese cultural policy, characterised by one scholar as '*de facto* apartheid',[17] which went so far as to forbid the use of the Korean language.

Such was Korea in 1945. (It should be added that most of the mining and industry were in the North, while the South was the agricultural centre: as in Vietnam, the monstrosity of partition was economically irrational too.) In North Korea swift measures were taken, of which the most significant was the agrarian reform of March 1946,[18] which created an economy of private small farming that was to last through the war till 1954. There was also labour legislation, and most industry was nationalised: since the latter had overwhelmingly been Japanese-owned, even such hostile critics as Scalapino and Lee admit that nationalisation was 'not only natural but also relatively simple . . . an act of nationalism as much as of socialism.'[19] Thus far, the reforms were more democratic than socialist; Kim Il Sung acknowledged that 'economic construction in our country at the present time is not socialist.' (He added: 'Nor, of course, is it going in the direction of capitalism.')[20] But already there could be heard the note of self-reliance which would later become such a dominant theme of the DPRK's ideology and practice: in 1948 Kim stated that 'it is quite possible for us to develop the national economy independently. . . . We should not send out [raw materials] to foreign countries, but should proceed in the direction of processing all of them at home to produce finished goods.'[21]

Much of the DPRK's story over the next quarter of a century consists of a single-minded and largely successful journey along that path. (Already by 1949 *per capita* national income had more than doubled since 1945.)[22] But first there was to be a devastating intermission along the way.

War and Reconstruction

It is difficult to exaggerate the scale of the disaster which the war of 1950–3 inflicted upon North Korea — indeed, upon Korea as a whole. Perhaps the most graphic comment is that of General O'Donnell, head of Bomber Command in the Far East: 'Everything is destroyed. There is nothing standing worthy of the name. Just before the Chinese came in we were grounded. *There were no more targets in Korea.*'[23] It is said that in Pyongyang only two buildings remained intact: its population was reduced from 400,000 to 80,000. The DPRK's military casualties numbered about half a million with a million civilians missing; North Korea's population fell by over one million from 9·62 million in 1949 to 8·49 million in 1953. Every major industrial enterprise was destroyed: power production in 1953 was only 26 per cent of what it had been in 1949, fuel 11 per cent, chemicals 22 per cent, and metallurgy 10 per cent.[24] Agriculture was dealt with, as in Vietnam, by the deliberate bombing of the dikes which provided water for 75 per cent of the DPRK's rice production. In the first three months of the war alone the US air force dropped 97,000 tons of bombs and 7·8 million gallons of napalm. The results, according to one American writer, 'rivaled Dante's *Inferno.*'[25] The DPRK's unremitting hatred of the USA, which outsiders sometimes find puzzlingly extreme and indecently virulent, makes sense in response to this horrific experience without parallel in modern times; it may be necessary to go back to Genghis Khan to find a precedent for such total material destruction.[26]

Even so — though it seems an obscenity to make such judgements — the war might be said in retrospect to have given the DPRK certain perverse 'advantages' in its subsequent development. Joan Robinson has spoken of the North Koreans' 'patriotic rage and devotion expressing itself in enthusiasm for hard work';[27] and it seems plausible enough that the experience of the war helped to promote a sense of national purpose and unity. Also in view of the massive destruction (both urban and rural) as well as population movements, we can assume that by 1953 such few bourgeois as remained, and any incipient *Kulaks*, had little stomach for a fight and indeed very little left to fight for. At all events,

private industry's share of gross industrial product, which
from 27·6 per cent in 1946 had already declined to 9·3 per
cent in 1949, fell again during the war to 3·9 per cent and by
1958 (0·1 per cent) was virtually extinct. Similarly on the land
private ownership which in 1953 still produced 92 per cent of
agricultural output and occupied 95 per cent of land, had
totally disappeared five years later by 1958;[28] moreover there
is general agreement that this was accomplished without large
scale violence.[29] This was seen as a necessary step towards a
modernised and productive agricultural sector, and production
did increase accordingly. More than this, in the aftermath of
war there may in any case have been no alternative: 'A destitute people lacking animals, implements, seed, and labour
power could not easily survive alone.'[30] Similarly, massive
state investment was needed to get industry going again; and
— perversely again — both wartime destruction and aid from
socialist countries can be said to have made possible (as did
Marshall Aid in post-war Germany) the development of a
modern industrial society.

Yet it is crucial to stress that this possibility, which became
a reality, was in no way an inevitability. On the contrary,
DPRK accounts admit that there were policy disagreements
over the proposed direction and character of post-war reconstruction. The leadership were determined to invest as much
as possible in heavy industry, even at the cost of present consumption (The official formula of the 1954–56 plan was 'priority development of heavy industry with simultaneous development in agriculture and light industry,'[31] but this should
perhaps be understood in a long-term sense (as in the Korean
economists' comment below, as there is no doubt that people
in the DPRK at this time had, as they put it, to 'tighten their
belts').[32] Such a policy may well have seemed harsh at home.
Yet the reasoning behind it was clearly spelled out by two
DPRK economists to Ellen Brun and Jacques Hersh:

'The[y] wanted us to "eat" all resources and foreign aid,
living well for a short period and then having nothing. Our
party rejects this line. Because without giving priority to heavy
industry we would have been unable to stabilise the people's
livelihood, our defence power would have suffered, and we
would have been unable to lay the foundation of an indepen-

dent national economy. As a matter of fact, heavy industry is the foundation for agricultural and light industrial development. When we make more farming machines, we produce more rice, when we make building equipment, we produce many more houses, and with vessels we can catch more fish.'[33]

Interestingly, it seems that Korea's allies joined in such criticisms. It has been alleged that 'socialist industrial countries argued that the DPRK instead of importing most machines should acquire consumer goods from them.'[34] At the third Korean Workers' Party Congress in April 1956, when the Five Year Plan, in whose framing the Russians apparently had not been consulted, was announced, the Soviet delegate reportedly foresaw 'difficulties' and 'argued indirectly for a greater degree of attention to consumer needs and the agricultural section';[35] while, according to Brun and Hersh, he also reminded Koreans that their country *leans upon* the co-operation and fraternal, mutual assistance of the socialist states.[36] (The Soviet delegate was none other than Leonid Brezhnev.) Similar disagreements were to arise later in the early 1960s, when the DPRK — which had never joined Comecon, but kept observer status since 1957 — strongly criticised the theory of an 'integrated economy' of the socialist countries, saying that it would 'reduce in the long run the economy of each country to an appendage of the economy of one or two countries.'[37]

Kim Il Sung got his way, despite attempts in 1956 (inspired by 'de-Stalinisation' in the USSR) to unseat him,[38] and his authority has not been overtly challenged since. Whatever one's view of the official hagiography which now surrounds him, and attributes virtually every decision ever made on every topic to his guidance, there can be no doubt that at this crucial juncture at least he was responsible for a difficult decision to chart a course not previously mapped out by any other country. In that sense his far-sightedness can be said to be a major cause of the DPRK's subsequent remarkable development.

'Juche' and 'Chollima': Economic and Social Development in the DPRK

The twin watchwords of the DPRK provide a good indicator of its values and achievements. 'Juche' is often inter-preted as 'self-reliance'. Such a notion had been implicit in the political practice of the preceding guerrilla movement. It is no coincidence, however, that it was elevated into the central plank of the DPRK's political ideology in December 1955, at a time when the leadership faced the difficulties described in the foregoing section.[39] In this connection, *'Juche'* expressed a theme which Kim Il Sung also spelled out more explicitly: 'Some advocate the Soviet way and others the Chinese, but is it not high time to work out our own?' But, as Gordon White points out, *Juche* is more than just an opportunist political response to overweening allies and their 'flunkeys' at home: for it also strikes directly at the earlier cultural traditions of *sadae* ('rely on the great') and *mohwa* ('emulate China') which had paralysed previous generations of Korean intellectuals. It must, too, be seen as a riposte to the specifically *cultural* assault (described above) of Japanese colonialism on Korea — and also, nowadays, to the 'Cocacolonisation' of South Korea by the US. (The term is also in use in South Korea, in a simi-lar sense.) White sums it up as 'a form of psychological de-colonisation'; indeed, any reader of Fanon should have little difficulty in understanding what is involved.

But there is a second strand to the *Juche* idea, which has been less understood although it is philosophically more pro-found than the 'sitting on our own chair'[40] aspect (its con-ceptual roots in classical Marxism are certainly stronger), and which is of no less relevance for understanding the develop-ment of the DPRK. This is brought out in a very interesting recent speech by Kim Il Sung: 'The Juche idea is based on a philosophical theory that man is master of everything and decides everything . . . [it provides] a powerful weapon to cognise [sic] and transform the world.'[41] Elsewhere in the same speech Kim several times insists that people must act 'with the attitude of a master'[42] and speaks of the need to 'transform nature and society.'[43] This is surely the quintessen-tially Marxist theme of *homo faber*, Promethean man, whose nature it is perpetually to be transforming Nature, and whose history is made of that dialectic of transformation. Kim him-self has stated, 'We are not the author of this idea. Every Marxist-Leninist has this idea. I have just laid a special emphasis on this idea.'[44] *Juche* involves being 'independent *and* creative':[45] the former is well known, the latter is what we are stressing here. It would be hard to imagine a more powerful modernising ideology than this combination in a country that has had to combat the cultural legacy of both colonialism and rural traditionalism.

These themes illustrate much that is specific to Korean communism: the pronounced emphasis on *material* well-being (which should not however be equated with material incentives); the goals of 'working classising' the peasantry (rather than, as sometimes in China, learning from them)[46] and later of 'intellectualising' the whole society; or the fact that Kim can point proudly to 'the black smoke rising'[47] over what was once a land sunk in stagnation.

'Chollima' is simpler: a mythological winged horse, it symbolises very rapid growth. Let us now turn to this. It is the key claim of the DPRK that 'our once underdeveloped colonial agrarian country was converted in a historically very brief period into a socialist industrial state.'[48] Western studies, while querying individual data here and there, do not dissent in essence from this judgement. Thus even an article bearing the title "Overstatement of North Korean Industrial Growth 1946–63"[49] concludes that the accomplishments are 'very impressive' (at least as compared with other Communist countries), including an 'unprecedented' growth of industrial output by 36 per cent per annum between 1956 and 1959.

This particular article relates only to the industrial sector, and stops at 1963. Joseph Sang-Hoon Chung considers the entire compass of the DPRK economy up to 1969 in his seminal (and far from uncritical) work, and reaches similar conclusions: 'North Korea has made a giant stride since 1945 in her drive toward industrialisation and economic viability . . . calling the North Korean feat a miracle perhaps overstates the case but nevertheless dramatises her achievements.'[50] This alludes to Joan Robinson's article "Korean miracle" whose verdict was that 'All the economic miracles of the postwar world are put in the shade by these achievements.'[51] And René Dumont, who is not normally noted as an enthusiast for collectivisation, goes so far as to say that: 'In agriculture and probably industry too, North Korea leads the socialist bloc.'[52]

There are two ways of illustrating the DPRK's performance. One is to use statistics, like those for industrial production quoted above. Agricultural production (which Chung
incidentally reckons to be the DPRK's weakest link)[53] also
recorded high annual rates of growth: 10 per cent for 1954–60,
and 6·3 per cent for 1961–70, which, as Breidenstein notes,
are 'very high rates for the rural economy which had much
less growth potential than the manufacturing industries.'[54]
'Moreover, grain output has continued to increase since 1970,
reaching a reported total of 8 million tons in 1976, an unprecedented figure both in absolute terms and in terms of output
per area.' But statistics only make sense within a framework
that emphasises qualitative and structural factors. It is not
just that the DPRK economy has grown fantastically fast:
what matters is its structural transformation, and the manner
of its growth. Thus in less than twenty years between 1946
and 1965 the share of industry and agriculture as components
of national income was almost exactly reversed: from 16·8 per
cent and 63·5 per cent to 64·2 per cent and 18·3 per cent. Similarly, technical and industrial workers comprised 65 per cent
of the labour force by 1963, while in the same year agricultural
workers (74 per cent in 1946) were 42·8 per cent.[55] There can
be no doubt, then, that the DPRK has, as it claims, made the
qualitative leap to being an industrial state, and (as a *Le
Monde* writer put it) 'one of the greatest economic powers in
Asia.'[56]

Besides statistics, a brief description may illustrate these
themes. The 'Juche' urge to do as much as possible at home
and with one's own resources is seen above all in the emphasis
on the machine-building industry; the DPRK is now reported
to be 98 per cent self-reliant in machine tools, and their general quality has been assessed as comparable to Soviet and
better than Chinese.[57] ('Self-reliance' in this context is not inconsistent with 'pirating' of — say — a Soviet original, and
then producing a copied design in Korea — as in the story of
the Russian tractor which was taken apart, duplicated, re-
assembled, and would only go backwards.)[58] Needless to say
they got it right eventually, and today the DPRK produces all
its own tractors; the point being that, unlike most small under-
industrialised Third World countries, the DPRK is thus not

at the mercy of late deliveries from abroad, expensively priced technology, or exploitation through control of patent rights. In other instances, however, there has been complete originality. The artificial fibre vynalon was developed by a Korean scientist in Japan in 1939, using a coal base. In the DPRK in the 1950s, since coal was scarce and needed in Industry, the inventor managed to change the raw material base to limestone (which was abundant). Today vynalon provides the great bulk of the DPRK's clothing. By the mid- to late 1960s it was estimated that overall the economy was self-sufficient in 70 per cent of its raw materials.[59]

Current preoccupations of DPRK industry well illustrate the level and type of development that has been reached. Automation and remote control by television of productive processes at the Hwanghae iron and steel complex is said to have 'doubled or trebled' production, while cutting the labour force by a quarter. A 4,600 metre earth-moving conveyor belt completed in 1975 was said to replace 'a large labour force and 80–90 heavy duty lorries.' In the same year was opened what was claimed to be the longest transport pipeline in the world, 98Km long, across a mountainous route carrying iron ore from the Musan mine to the Kim Chaek iron and steel works in Chong'in. Also in 1975, a 20,000 ton freighter was launched. Electrification of railways 'has nearly doubled their transport capacity, reduced the consumption of fuel to one fifth, saved much labour force, and markedly enhanced culture in the operation of railways.'[60]

What comes across in reports like these, apart from an obviously advanced level of industrialisation, is an emphasis on saving resources, especially fuel and labour — which are indeed two things that the DPRK is short of. Lacking oil and coking coal, it obviously makes sense to electrify railways (the electricity is produced by hydropower, which is abundant in the DPRK). Shortage of labour[61] is an unusual attribute for a Third World country (only Mongolia comes to mind). Apart from secular factors like population loss in the war this mainly seems to be self-induced, and as such is a tribute to Korean industrialisation — and incidentally one in the eye for contemporary neo-Malthusians, as W. Rosenberg emphasises, who ascribe underdevelopment to overpopulation.[62]

The labour shortage has also affected agricultural development, ensuring that consistent efforts have been made to modernise agriculture and thus free as many workers as possible for industry. Four areas were singled out: irrigation, electrification, mechanisation, and 'chemicalisation'.[63] The irrigation network is now nationwide, and extends to 37,000Km. Rural electrification is also claimed to be 100 per cent. As for mechanisation, there are now some 80,000 tractors (a high figure in relation to population and cultivated area). Rice transplanting machines were introduced in 1974, and the total mechanisation of autumn harvesting was anticipated within 2–3 years.[64] A significant pointer to this is the repartitioning of fields into standardised shapes and sizes, doubtless to facilitate mechanisation.[65] As for chemicals, Kim Il Sung has produced a variant of Lenin's 'Communism equals soviets plus electrification' with his dictum 'Fertiliser Is, So To Speak, Rice, And Rice Is, So To Speak, Socialism!'[66] Chemical fertiliser production reportedly reached 3 million tons in 1975.[67]

All this has paid off: a Japanese economist recently claimed that DPRK output at 5·9 tons of rice per *chongbo* (= c. 1 hectare) had surpassed even the Japanese figure of 5·8.[68] Considering that the South was traditionally the 'rice-bowl', and that only 20 per cent of the mountainous North is cultivable, performance has been impressive. The DPRK has consistently been a net importer of cereals, but this is because by taking advantage of world relative prices it can sell rice and import wheat — which is both a financial and a nutritional gain.[69] Given that it is still necessary to draft large numbers of the urban work force seasonally into the countryside,[70] the technical revolution in agriculture will no doubt continue.

Needless to say, development on this scale would not be possible without a considerable investment in human capital. In this context, the educational system of the DPRK is one of its most striking achievements. From 80 per cent illiteracy under the Japanese, near-universal literacy was early achieved. In 1975 there was introduced an eleven-year universal compulsory education one year ahead of schedule. In the same year there were said to be 150 universities, 600 higher specialised schools, 4,100 senior middle schools, 4,700 primary schools, and no less than 60,000 nurseries and kindergartens.[71] (This last figure reflects what one Danish visitor has reckoned to be the most comprehensive nursery facilities in the world;[72] which in turn is not unconnected with the fact that — again perhaps uniquely — women form virtually 50 per cent of the labour force.) There are a million technicians and specialists, 200,000 teachers (one for every 25 students), a million higher students, and a grand total of 8·59 million people, half the population involved in one or other phase of the education process — 3·5 million at nursery and kindergarten and 5·09 million between primary school and university.[73] It was intended that all working people would attain middle school level or above in 1975: adult education is strongly emphasised, and the goal of 'intellectualising the whole society' is now proclaimed. All students would henceforth learn more than one technical skill, sport, and musical instrument. There is an emphasis on 'all-round' education, with a strongly technical bias.[74] Certainly the DPRK's strategy of self-reliant industrial development would have been hard to conceive without this emphasis on science and technology.

North and South Korea Compared

It is easy to talk about the DPRK as a country in its own right, which of course it is. But one must never forget — as certainly Koreans never forget — that in fact it is only half of a country cut in two, and that reunification as a goal and the existence of a separate State in South Korea are constant pre-occupations of the DPRK. In addition, it is of course of general interest to compare the development of capitalist and socialist systems. Breidenstein[75] recently carried out the exercise, and his conclusions are striking. Looking first at growth rates, until the early 1960s it was an extremely one-sided race: from 1954 to 1962 the average annual growth in national income was 22·1 per cent in the North, and 4·7 per cent in the South. (Per capita, the respective figures were 17·2 per cent and 0·8 per cent.)[76] During the 1960s the South did better, with an average of 9·3 per cent between 1961 and 1970 (including higher rates in the later years), as compared with a slower rate 8·9 per cent in the North. Gross Industrial Output between 1954 and 1970 grew at an average annual rate of 23·5 per cent in the North, 15·3 per cent in the South. Agricultural output in the South, however, grew at only 2·7 per cent in the 1950s and 4·4 per cent in the 1960s, compared with the North's 10·0 per cent and 6·3 per cent.

Breidenstein also compares some absolute output figures, and finds that *per capita* in 1970 'North Korean energy production in 1970 was at least 2·8 times higher than the South Korean, steel production 4 times, pig iron more than 100 times, cement 1·5 times, chemical fertilisers 2·5 times, rice production about 1·2 times, and textile fabrics 2·5 times.' South Korea, however, would almost certainly have the edge when it comes to consumer goods like appliances, cars, watches, radios and TV sets.

The ultimate 'statistic' is, of course, national income per head. Here different definitions make comparisons almost meaningless, and variations abound. One source for 1973 gave $373 for South Korea, $330 for North Korea.[77] The DPRK in 1974 claimed $1,000 for themselves,[78] and $50 ('the lowest in the world') for South Korea.[79] The former seems exaggerated, the latter blatantly ridiculous. Conversely, a Southern source in 1976 gives the ratio of Southern to Northern GNP as 3·6:1[80] (*per capita* this would be 1·66:1, given population figures of 15·5 million for the North and 33·6 million for the South, in 1974).[81] Breidenstein, less polemically committed and working with the more detailed figures which are available for 1970, gives $375 for the North and $252 for the South; but after allowing for an over-valued Southern exchange rate and high inflation, as well as lopping off an estimated 35 per cent for 'services' in order to establish comparability with the North (which does not include these in its own national income accounts), the Southern figure reduces to $110 — less than one-third of the North's.[82]

Meaningful comparisons, as we have stressed, must go beyond abstract statistics to look at structural and qualitative considerations.[83] And it is here, perhaps, that the DPRK scores most. South Korea (as discussed elsewhere in this volume), for all its belated 'miracle growth', is a house built on sand, utterly vulnerable to the storms of the world economy, a classic illustration of extreme dependency. The crucial point is that, contrary to the advocates of so-called 'export-led growth', there is no evidence of any Third World country having attained self-sustaining growth on the basis of an open export economy. As Samir Amin puts it, there are *two* types of capitalist development, *'autocentré'* and *'extraverti'*. The core capitalist countries who exemplify the former did not start off as the latter, but on the contrary owe their development to a Keynesian (or one might call it *Juche*) development of the home market and its demand potential. Conversely, the *extravertis* began their capitalist life as export economies: their dynamic is thus qualitatively different from the *autocentrés*; and will never lead into it but only to growing 'marginalisation' of the masses, ruin and revolution.[84]

On the other side of the coin, the Guyanese economist Clive Thomas in a recent path-breaking study has expounded a feasible development strategy for Third World countries, based on what he calls two 'iron laws of transformation': converging resource use with demand, and converging needs with demand. Space forbids a detailed treatment here; but it is remarkable how time and again Thomas' profound theoretical model (derived by opposition, as it were, from the neo-colonial experience in Africa and the Caribbean) of an economy growing and industrialising on the basis of inputs from its own resources and outputs sold to its own people corresponds to the actual pattern of development in the DPRK.[85]

The 'Quality of Life'

It remains to consider certain aspects of the social and political structure of the DPRK, which raise issues that should not be ducked. Up to now we have discussed the DPRK's development mostly in terms of total economic indices. But how do these translate in terms of people's everyday lives? And what price has been paid?

On the level of material well-being, we can accept the sober judgement of a recent New Zealand writer: 'In the North of Korea, poverty, though not frugality, has been abolished.'[86] The policy of priority to heavy industry, necessary in the long run to create the basis of light industry too, has in the short term inevitably meant that light industry, (and agriculture) have received relatively less investment; and this has led to admitted difficulties in the supply, quality, and variety of consumer goods.[87] Nonetheless, the almost free supply of housing and utilities,[88] the provision of comprehensive free health and educational services, and the abolition of all taxes (another claimed 'first in the world'),[89] plus an adequate supply of the basic necessities, altogether seem to endorse Rosenberg's judgement. In addition, the worst period of 'primitive accumulation' is certainly over: the seven year plan (actually 1961–70, extended, it seems, because of difficulties due to increased defence expenditure) began to restore the balance towards light industry and consumer goods, and this trend has continued. The DPRK now produces *inter alia* its own TV sets, radios and watches, and increasing emphasis is laid on washing machines and refrigerators ('to free women from the burden of household work').[90] What is certain is that improvements in living standards will only come about in a gradual and egalitarian manner, unlike in South Korea where extremes of wealth and poverty coexist.

But is there a deeper, spiritual 'price'? Even a sympathetic account admits that 'it is difficult to imagine a society more tightly organised than contemporary North Korea.'[91] Membership of the Korean Workers' Party (KWP) is proportionally higher than in probably any other Communist country;[92] and no citizen of the DPRK can be uninvolved in one or more of the various youth, trade union, women's, students' militia or other organisations.[93] Kim Il Sung recently called for an intensification of the 'ideological revolution' in order that people 'will think and act the way the Party wants them to, anytime and anywhere' (yet in the same sentence they are also admonished to '[give] full scope to their revolutionary spirit of *self-reliance* in the attitude of *masters of the revolution*').[94]

Needless to say, the standard Western literature on the DPRK abounds with terms like 'Stalinism' and 'totalitarianism'. Both of these rather miss the point. Cumings argues that the emphasis on organisation, rather than 'a mere commitment by the KWP leadership to power for power's sake,' should be understood as a reaction to the earlier 'debilitating factionalism', as well as to an historical tendency of local-level bureaucrats to be high-handed and a law unto themselves if not held in check. (Hence also the DPRK's emphasis on the 'mass line'

—understood, however, as being strictly from the top down.)[95] Equally, 'Stalinist' seems inapt, inasmuch as the DPRK leadership appears not only to have achieved its goals without widespread bloodshed or the physical liquidation of any social group, but also (as even its critics admit) to 'command the allegiance of the great majority of the North Korean people at this time',[96] rather than ruling by terror.

More to the point, perhaps, is Scalapino's earlier — and somewhat quaint — charge against the DPRK of 'abolishing privatism'[97] (sic). By means of deliberate planned techniques of socialisation, starting quite literally at birth,[98] the DPRK leadership pursues its avowed aim of a 'monolithic ideological system'[99] using preventive measures rather than drastic surgery: as Joan Robinson succinctly puts it, 'no deviant thought has a chance to sprout.'[100] This no doubt maximises national unity and the spirit of self-sacrifice, but one may doubt whether it could ever eliminate totally all dissent or even difference of opinion.

This question cannot, of course, be separated from the content of the DPRK's ideology, and especially the relentless emphasis on the role of Kim Il Sung. No service is done either to socialism or to the people of Korea by those who simply reproduce the DPRK's own self-presentation, which indeed we believe to be harmful to its own cause. In two crucial areas, namely the DPRK's relations with the Third World and above all its image in the South, the way the North presents itself has been and continues to be directly counter-productive. In both cases, admiration of the DPRK's economic achievements and of its egalitarianism is tempered by the way the Korean revolution is presented as though it were the work, largely or wholly, of one man — its leader. True, the DPRK now has relations with nearly 100 countries,[101] and is generally accepted in the Third World as the legitimate state of Korea (e.g., its admission in 1975 to membership of the non-aligned movement). On the other hand, as the editor of *North Korea Quarterly* perceptively remarked, this should be taken more as 'the reflection of a general international trend' rather than a substantive compliment, considering that 'the primitivism of their diplomacy and public relations work have won the North Koreans a special place among the ranks of the world's most

insular peoples.'[102] As for the South Korean revolution —
what happened to it? It is to be hoped that sooner or later
the DPRK leadership will recognise that while Westernised
Third World audiences (and that includes South Korea) are
increasingly ready to 'buy' their economic development, which
certainly speaks to their condition, and to respond to the
message of independence and creativity implicit in Juche, they
may be much less inclined to do so if the Koreans insist on
presenting their politics in simplistic terms of inspired and
charismatic leadership.[103]

Conclusion

There is much that the Third World in particular can learn
from the development of the DPRK, if only they are prepared
to penetrate the public mask. There is no intrinsic reason why
the Korean model should not be followed by a great number
of ex-colonial countries, whose problem is much less (as is
sometimes alleged) a lack of resources — let alone 'over-popu-
lation' — than the lack of a political will, movement, and
strategy to construct a 'self-centred' economy. Doubtless the
growing crisis of the Third World will open some eyes to the
DPRK's achievements.[104] At all events it is interesting to note
that in recent years the DPRK's own self-identification has
shifted more and more to a 'Third Worldist' position. In a
major speech late in 1973, Kim Il Sung's main foreign policy
slogan was 'Let us unite with the peoples of the world who
advocate independence'.[105] He argued that 'Today the third
world forms the battle front where the anti-imperialist struggle
is raging most fiercely', and stressed the need for economic
co-operation between third world countries which would bring
about 'rapid progress even without relying on big Powers.'[106]
This is in striking contrast to the DPRK's previously mentioned refusal to join Comecon, and general suspicion of so-
called socialist international integration; significantly, the
references in this speech to the 'international communist movement' are few and perfunctory.[107] (The DPRK's recent ac-
cession to the non-aligned movement is thus less incongruous
than has sometimes been suggested.)

In assessing the DPRK it is important to take the longer
view. Future historians will have to admit that in the 1950s

and 1960s this was the first ex-colony to carry out 'primitive accumulation', largely on the basis of its own resources, and lay the foundations for a modern industrial state. Due credit for this achievement will be given to Kim Il Sung and the 'Juche' line. It will also be noted that the process of 'primitive accumulation', which elsewhere in the world has involved hideous cruelties — slavery in the Americas, child labour in England, the massacre of a class in the USSR — was *relatively* painless in the DPRK, and that this, too, is unprecedented: one generation certainly sacrificed its comfort, but not its whole life. Moreover, as elsewhere, this laid the basis for sustained expansion of a 'self-centred' economy. The stress given not only to Kim Il Sung, but to his father, grandfather and son, too, as members of a 'revolutionary family,' and the fact that numerous relatives are reported to hold high offices in the party and the state raise serious questions about the political institutions of the DPRK;[108] but however these are eventually understood, the achievements of the Korean Workers' Party are clearly remarkable and will be remembered long after the tottering neo-colony in South Korea has finally collapsed, and Korea has regained its rightful and age-old unity.

Postscript, November 1977

During 1977 the clamour in the Western press about the DPRK's debts subsided considerably. One reason for this may have been the Western banks' decision to roll over the loans to the DPRK, and thus their desire no longer to have the DPRK portrayed as an unreliable client, but rather the exact opposite.

Early in 1977 a group of four European banks which had been involved with lending to Pyongyang renegotiated what appeared to be the bulk of the DPRK's borrowings from Western Europe by, in effect, postponing some payments immediately due and lengthening the terms of maturity on other, medium-term borrowings (the total of which came to about £85m).[109] Japanese banks had earlier come to similar arrangements with the DPRK. The upshot was that 'unorthodox' DPRK behaviour vis-à-vis the world capitalist banking system had not deterred the latter from continuing to advance credits to Pyongyang.

NOTES

1. The Korean war is discussed elsewhere in this volume.
2. A petty illustration: in 1966 the DPRK soccer team came to the UK for the finals of the World Cup. A proposed design for a commemorative postage stamp, featuring the flags of the sixteen nations competing, was vetoed by the Foreign Office on the grounds that the British Government did not 'recognise' the DPRK.
3. See, for instance, the volume of proceedings of the 'Social Science Conference' held in Pyongyang in 1972, whose 400 pages contain little except paeans of praise to the leadership of Kim Il Sung (*National Conference of Social Scientists* (Pyongyang: Social Science Publishing House, 1972)).

   Doubtless a more academic social science — at least in economics — must exist in the DPRK; but it is not publicised. The contrast in this respect between Korean materials and those of other socialist states (e.g. *Vietnamese Studies*, and other scholarly work produced from Hanoi) is striking.
4. Some examples from *The Times*: two quite informative 8-page supplements, 11–12 April, 1973; a full page speech welcoming the Syrian President (October 25, 1974); the DPRK constitution (1½ pages of very small print), (December 27, 1974); the Supreme People's Assembly resolves to implement agricultural policy (over half a page), (January 22, 1975); Kim's New Year Address (a full page), (January 24, 1975). The 1976 New Year Address took a full page in the *Sun* on two days (Jan. 30–31st, 1976).

   The campaign was discussed by David Blundy in the *Sunday Times* (May 11, 1975), whose sardonic tone is typical of Western response to the DPRK ads. Blundy mentions a full page advertisement in the *Sunday Mirror* of May 4, 1975, which will have cost some £6,000.
5. See most of the standard and all the official Western accounts, e.g., the US State Department's *North Korea: A Case Study in the Techniques of Communist Takeover* (US Government Printing Office, 1961).
6. See, e.g., *Brief History of the Revolutionary Activities of Comrade Kim Il Sung* (Pyongyang, FLPH, 1969); or at greater length, Baik Bong *Kim Il Sung Biography* (3 vols; Tokyo: Miraisha, 1970, and other editions). It should be noted, however, that Kim Il Sung himself in 1945 referred to the Soviet Army as having played the 'decisive role' (in a speech of August 20, 1945, cited in Kim Il Sung, *On Juche In Our Revolution* (Pyongyang, FLPH, 1975), Vol.1, p.104), and in 1975 both the 30th anniversary of liberation (August 15th) and the 25th anniversary of the entry of Chinese People's Volunteers into the Korean War (October 25th) were celebrated in Pyongyang with respectively Soviet and Chinese delegations, both of whom were warmly thanked for their countries' assistance. See the account in *North Korea Quarterly*, Vol.2, No.3–4 (Jul-Dec. 1975), pp.10–11 and 42–46.
7. Dae-Sook Suh, *The Korean Communist Movement 1918–1948* (Princeton, 1967), p.132; see also Suh's companion volume *Documents of Korean Communism 1918–48* (*ibid.*, 1970). Little is added to Suh's account by Robert Scalapino and Chong Sik-Lee's massive *Communism in Korea*, London, 1972. See Gerhard Breidenstein's review of the latter in *JCA*, Vol.3, no.3 (1973), pp.350–55.
8. Jon Halliday, "The Korean Revolution," *Socialist Revolution*, Vol.1, no.6, Nov.-Dec. 1970, pp.95–135. This section owes much to Halliday's pioneering resurrection of the issues in the five crucial but largely

forgotten (or misrepresented) years between 1945 and 1950. Source material for this period includes: George McCune, *Korea Today* (London, 1950); Mark Gayn, *Japan Diary* (New York, 1948); Gregory Henderson, *Korea: The Politics of the Vortex* (Cambridge, Mass., 1968). On the broader international context of postwar Korea, which is not discussed here, see: Soon Sung Cho, *Korea in World Politics: An Evaluation of American Responsibility* (Berkeley, 1967), and Joyce and Gabriel Kolko, *The Limits of Power: The World and United States Foreign Policy, 1945–52* (New York, 1972).

9. Halliday, *op. cit.*, p.107 (emphasis in original).

10. Bruce G. Cumings, "Kim's Korean Communism," *Problems of Communism*, Vol.23, no.2, Mar.-Apr. 1974, p.34. According to Cumings, however, Baik Bong's 'hagiographic' biography of Kim ignores the People's Committees 'because Kim Il Sung played no role in initiating them' (*ibid.*, n.41). On the People's Committees and on the 1945–50 period generally see the same author's "American Policy and Korean Liberation," in Frank Baldwin ed., *Without Parallel: The American-Korean Relationship Since 1945* (New York, 1974), pp.39–108.

11. Cumings, *op. cit.*, p.38.

12. Ellen Brun and Jacques Hersh, "Aspects of Korean Socialism," *JCA*, Vol.5, no.2, (1975), p.141. (See also their book on the DPRK, *Socialist Korea* (Monthly Review Press, 1977).)

13. McCune, *op. cit.*, cited by Brun & Hersh, *loc. cit.*

14. The concept of 'articulation' of modes of production has been developed in recent years by French marxist economic anthropologists endeavouring to conceptualise the precise character of the impact of colonial capitalism on pre-capitalist modes of production. See P.-P. Rey, "Sur l'articulation des modes de production," in his *Les Alliances de Classes* (Paris, Maspero, 1973). There is a summary and discussion in English in Barbara Bradby, "The Destruction of Natural Economy," *Economy and Society*, 1974.

15. Cumings (*op. cit.*), following J. B. Palais, argues that the balance of power between the rural aristocracy and the centralised bureaucracy of the Yi dynasty was much more to the former than is often thought, and that the seeming autocracy of the latter was, in Palais' words, 'merely a façade' (p.29).

16. The following account of Japanese colonialism is mainly based on J. Suret-Canale, *La Corée populaire: vers les matins calmes* (Paris, Editions Sociales, 1973), pp.27–32, who in turn uses *inter alia* such important Russian-language sources as G. V. Griaznov, *Socialist Industrialization in the DPRK* (Moscow, 1966).

17. Henderson, *op. cit.*, p.76.

18. Brun & Hersh provide a thoughtful account of the political reasoning behind this and other early economic and social reforms. Crucial data and useful economic analysis will be found in the key work on the DPRK economy, Joseph Chung's *The North Korean Economy: Structure and Development* (Stanford, Hoover Institution Press, 1974).

19. Scalapino and Lee, *op. cit.*, Vol.2, p.1196; cited by Brun & Hersh, p.144.

20. Quoted in Brun & Hersh, *loc. cit.* (Kim Il Sung, *Selected Works*, Vol.1, p.36).

21. Quoted in Cumings, *op. cit.*, p.36 (Kim Il Sung, *op. cit.*, pp.188–9).

22. W. Rosenberg, "Economic Comparison of North and South Korea," *JCA*, Vol.5, no.2 (1975), p.90; cf. J. Chung, *op. cit.*, p.146 (table 41).
23. Quoted in I. F. Stone, *op. cit.*, p.312.
24. Rinn-sup Shinn *et. al.*, *Area Handbook for North Korea* (Washington, US Government Printing Office, 1969), p.297. Quoted by Gerhard Breidenstein, "Economic Comparison of North and South Korea," *JCA*, Vol.5, no.2 (1975), p.176 (fn. 6).
25. Robert R. Simmons, "The Korean Civil War," in F. Baldwin, ed., *op. cit.*, pp.168–170. See also Halliday, *op. cit.*, and John Gittings, and "Talks, Bombs and Germs: Another Look at the Korean War," *JCA*, Vol.5, no.2 (1975), pp.205–17. (Part of the North's population loss will consist of refugees, a fact which has traditionally been invoked as *prima facie* evidence of people 'voting with their feet' against Communism. However, as Halliday observes: 'Bombing, when it is conducted by only one side, means that there is only one place to which a civilian can escape — behind the lines of the side that is doing the bombing' (*op. cit.*, p.127). Among support he cites is a magazine article of the period, entitled "How Refugees are Made" (*Christian Century*, Jan. 23, 1952). More recently, the same propaganda trick backfired in both Laos and Cambodia, whose erstwhile governments made much play about their swelling refugee populations — even as the area they controlled inexorably diminished.)
26. Wilfred Burchett, *Again Korea* (New York, 1968), p.65.
27. "Korean Miracle," *Monthly Review*, Jan. 1965, p.43 (also in her *Collected Economic Papers*, Vol.3, pp.207–215). Professor Robinson visited the DPRK in 1964.
28. J. Chung, *op. cit.*, p.61 (table 18) and p.11 (table 3).
29. Chung, *op. cit.*, p.12; Scalapino & Lee, *op. cit.*, p.1067.
30. Scalapino & Lee, *op. cit.*, p.1067.
31. Quoted in Chung, *op. cit.*, Appendix A, p.164. (The word 'light' is omitted, doubtless in error.)
32. A phrase frequently used by DPRK officials.
33. *Op. cit.*, p.146.
34. Brun & Hersh, *loc. cit.*
35. Gordon White, "North Korean Chuch'e: The Political Economy of Independence," *Bulletin of Concerned Asian Scholars*, Vol.7, no.2 (Apr.-Jun. 1975), p.47.
36. *Op. cit.*, p.149, citing "Third congress documents." (It is not made clear whose is the emphasis.)
37. Cited in White, *op. cit.*, p.48, along with a number of other fascinating quotations from DPRK sources taking to task 'some people' (*sc.*, the USSR) who, from their emphasis on 'traditional production' and 'natural economic advantage', sound for all the world like fully-fledged Ricardian equilibrium theorists!
38. The factional struggles within the Korean Workers' Party, which at their zenith in 1956 prompted the personal intervention of Mikoyan and P'eng Teh-Huai (the Chinese Minister of Defence) to restrain Kim Il Sung, are discussed by Scalapino and Lee, *op. cit.*, especially pp.510ff.
39. Kim Il Sung, "On Socialist Construction," *On Juche*, cit., p.486. White, *ibid.*, p.45. The discussion and quotations in this paragraph are derived from his pp.44–46.

40. Benjamin Page. "North Korea: Sitting on Its Own Chair," *Monthly Review*, January 1969. (The metaphor is attributed to Kim Il Sung.)
41. "On the Thirtieth Anniversary of the Korean Workers' Party" (9 October, 1975). Reproduced in full in *NKQ*, Vol.2, no.3–4 (Jul.-Dec. 1975), pp.76–107; the quotation appears on p.80. Also Pyongyang, FLPH, 1975.
42. E.g. pp.83, 93; cf. pp.79 ('masters of their own destiny') and 88 ('attitude of masters of the revolution').
43. P.77 and p.80; cf. p.89 ('. . . even from the fetters of nature . . .').
44. Answers to journalists of the *Mainichi Shimbun*, September 17, 1972, in Kim Il Sung, *Answers to the Questions raised by Foreign Journalists* (Pyongyang, 1974), p.286.
45. "On the Thirtieth Anniversary . . .," *op. cit.*, p.80.
46. B. Cumings, *op. cit.*, compares Korean and Chinese attitudes on these points (pp.29–33).
47. I have been unable to trace this reference, which occurs in one of Kim Il Sung's speeches. (It is no idle boast: Harrison Salisbury confirms that the major chemical complex of Hamhung produces worse smog than even Los Angeles (*To Peking and Beyond* (London, Arrow, 1973), p.200.) To be fair, the DPRK government does claim that industrial plants are sited well away from residential areas in order to minimise pollution.)
48. "On the 30th Anniversary . . ." *op. cit.*, p.85.
49. By Pong S. Lee, in *Journal of Korean Affairs (JKA)*, Vol.1, no.2 (July 1971), pp.3–14. Scrutiny reveals that the alleged overstatement is not enormous: Lee recalculates an average annual industrial growth rate of 15·6 per cent for the period 1949–63, as against the DPRK's figure of 17·4 per cent.
50. *Op. cit.*, p.151.
51. *Op. cit.*, p.208.
52. *The Hungry Future* (London: Deutsch, 1969, p.137).
53. E.g. *op. cit.*, pp.55–56.
54. *Op. cit.*, p.171.
55. J. Chung, *op. cit.*, pp.146–7 (Table 41).
56. Philippe Pons, *Le Monde*, July 1, 1974.
57. Harrison Salisbury, *op. cit.*, p.200.
58. Retold among others by Mark Gayn, in a report from the DPRK which is broader in scope and deeper than the (sub-editor's?) title might suggest: "The Cult of Kim," *New York Times Magazine* October 1, 1972. (I am grateful to Dr Ivar Oxaal for this reference.)
59. Burchett, *op. cit.*, pp.138ff.
60. See reports reproduced in *NKQ*, Vol.3, no.1, p.31; Vol.2, no.2, p.46; Vol.2, no.3–4, pp.66–7; *ibid.*, pp.63–4; and Vol.2, no.1, p.43.
61. See Chung, *op. cit.*, pp.92, 94, 160.
62. *Korea North and South: A Tale of Two Systems* (forthcoming), especially Ch.2. (I am grateful for the opportunity to see this manuscript.)
63. The classic source is Kim Il Sung's *Theses on the Socialist Rural Question In Our Country* (Pyongyang, FLPH, 1968, but originally adopted in the DPRK in 1964).
64. Figures from Fujishima Udai, article reproduced in *NKQ*, Vol.2, no.3–4 (1975), pp.136–7. Figure for tractors from *Korean Review* (Pyongyang, FLPH, 1974), p.94.

65. *NKQ*, Vol.2, no.1, pp.32–3.
66. *NKQ*, Vol.3, no.1, p.14.
67. Jun Nishikawa, "DPRK's Economy Developing Under Banner of Juche Idea," reproduced in *NKQ*, Vol.3, no.1, pp.57–61.
68. Fujishima Udai, *loc. cit.*
69. See Chung, *op. cit.*, p.143, also pp.151–2. Chung cites Chong-Sik Lee, "Notes on North Korean Import and Export of Cereals," *JKA*, Vol.1, no.4 (June, 1972), pp.54–6.
70. See, e.g., Russell Spurr's generally interesting reportage from the DPRK in *FEER*, 8th and 15th July 1974; he 'met a senior official who had just spent four days transplanting rice along with the rest of the population of Pyongyang.' (July 8, 1974, pp.29–30.)
71. Figures as given in the Supreme People's Assembly in April, 1975; reported in *NKQ*, Vol.2, no.2, pp.50–52.
72. Ellen Brun, "North Korea: A Case of Real Development," *Monthly Review*, Vol.22, no.2 (June 1970), pp.25–37.
73. *NKQ*, Vol.2, no.1, p.71.
74. See n.70 for source of figures. On the slogan of 'intellectualising the whole society,' see, e.g., *NKQ*, Vol.3, no.1, p.78, reporting a three-part *Rodong Sinmun* article of February 24, 1971, on this theme.
75. *Op. cit.* The ensuing figures all come from Breidenstein unless otherwise indicated.
76. Yoon T. Kuark, chapter in J. S. Chung ed., *Patterns of Economic Development* (Kalamazoo, Michigan, Korean Research and Publication Inc., 1966).
77. *FEER Asia Yearbook*, 1975, pp.239 and 285.
78. As reported in April 1975: *NKQ*, Vol.2, no.2, p.49 (The Editor of *NKQ* comments: 'This may be a little exaggerated, but not necessarily so unfounded as South Korean and/or pro-South Korean commentators maintain').
79. *Korean Review, op. cit.*, p.149.
80. *Korea Herald*, January 13, 1976: reproduced in *NKQ*, Vol.3, no.1, p.56.
81. Population figures given in *FEER Asia Yearbook*, 1976, pp.237, 281.
82. *Loc. cit.*, p.190.
83. W. Rosenberg's article and forthcoming book extend the comparison over a wide range of social as well as economic indicators.
84. Samir Amin, "The Theoretical Model of Capitalist Accumulation," *Review of African Political Economy*, no.1 (1974).
85. *Dependence and Transformation* (London, Monthly Review Press, 1974); see a summary of some themes in his "Industrialization and the Transformation of Africa," pp.325–360, in Carl Widstrand, ed. *Multinational Firms in Africa* (Uppsala; Scandinavian Institute of African Studies, 1975). For example, Thomas insists that smallness, and hence limited economies of scale, are not a crucial constraint; that socialist agriculture must be large scale, capital intensive, and modernised, thus freeing a labour force for other sectors; that choice of technique is less important than choice of raw-material input; that substitutability of raw materials is possible and desirable (cf. vynalon in the DPRK); and speaks of industrialisation as 'man . . . mastering the material environment' (in Widstrand, ed., p.346), in the very language of *Juche!*
86. W. Rosenberg, *op. cit.* (book), p.171.
87. Chung, *op. cit.*, pp.73 and 150.

88. A recent American visitor gives a figure of rents in Pyongyang as only 2 per cent of family income. Fred J. Carrier, *North Korean Journey* (New York, International Publishers, 1975), p.87.

89. *Korean Review, op. cit.*, pp.135–6.

90. *ibid.*, pp.92–3.

91. B. Cumings, *op. cit.*, p.28.

92. Scalapino and Lee, *op. cit.*, p.714.

93. "On the Thirtieth anniversary," *op. cit.*, p.82: 'Today all our people are affiliated with some units of working peoples' organizations.'

94. *ibid.*, p.88.

95. Cumings, *op. cit., passim.*

96. Scalapino and Lee, *op. cit.*, p.843.

97. "Patterns of Asian Communism," *Problems of Communism*, Vol.20, no.1–2 (Jan.-Apr. 1971), pp.2–13.

98. See a fascinating article by Hyung-Chan Kim, "Play as Methods [sic] for Political Education in North Korean Preschools," *JKA*, Vol.3, no.2 (July 1973), pp.33–41.

99. See, e.g., Kim Il Sung, *op. cit.*, ("30th Anniversary . . ."), p.82.

100. *Op. cit.*, p.214.

101. *FEER*, October 24, 1975.

102. *NKQ*, Vol.2, no.3–4, pp.3–4.

103. The writer can confirm this from observing responses to DPRK publicity in Africa, where it tends to be seen as (at best) eccentric and amusing. The DPRK seems to operate a full embassy in every country with which it has relations, a luxury long since abandoned by the UK. In Tanzania, for instance, a very large new embassy *and* a 'Cultural Centre' have been recently erected. The large sums thus expended on publicity by the DPRK might be expected eventually to prompt some reflections in Pyongyang on whether they are being deployed to the best effect.

104. On the other hand, President Nyerere of Tanzania managed to side-step the issue neatly when, having admired the DPRK's industrial growth, he concluded that the moral for Tanzania was that *agriculture* 'is the industry we have'! (J. K. Nyerere, *Freedom and Development;* Dar es Salaam; Oxford UP, 1973, p.40). To the contrary, the lesson of the DPRK is precisely that it *was* a typical colonial agricultural economy which transformed itself into an industrial one.

105. This is the title of Section IV of Kim Il Sung, "On the 30th Anniversary of the KWP," *op. cit.*, p.99.

106. *ibid.*, pp.100, 104.

107. In five pages there are 24 references to the Third World, compared with only six to the international communist movement.

108. Robert Whymant, "The war of fact and fiction," *FEER*, April 9, 1976; *NKQ*, Vol.3, no.1, 1976, p.73.

109. The *Times* (London), March 11, 1977.

APPENDIX A

The DPRK's Debts

It is all too typical of the pattern of Western 'non-recognition' — and hence non-cognition — of the DPRK that, while its economic achievements have for years gone virtually unreported, allegations of recent balance of payments difficulties have been given wide publicity.[1] These should be put in perspective. First, there are inconsistent (and sometimes self-contradictory) reports of the exact figure involved: thus the *Korea Herald* (Seoul) in September 1975 quoted a sum of $1,715m, yet five months later the same source suggested it was $1,150.[2] (Presumably the DPRK had not in the meantime at a stroke repaid $600m.) Other estimates of the position at the end of 1975 ranged from $2,144m ($1,242m to non-communist countries and $902m to 'the Soviet Union' — which presumably includes other Communist countries), according to (unnamed) 'South Korean sources',[3] to 'a recent US estimate compiled in Tokyo' of $430m to the West and $700m to Communist states.[4] The most widely quoted figure as at the end of 1975 appears to be about $1,000m to the West and $700m to the Soviet Union.[5]

Second, whatever its amount, this figure represents borrowings agreed by both parties, and as such is a perfectly normal feature of commercial life, whether of individuals (e.g., a mortgage, or hire purchase) or nations. It should not be, as one suspects it has been, confused with *overdue* debt *repayments*, which even the Seoul government estimates to be no more than $114·5m.[6] Of this more in a moment.

Third, there can be no doubt that the aim of those 'South Korean sources' who have so energetically publicised this mote of the DPRK is primarily to distract attention from the massive beam in their own eye. As the (by no means pro-Pyongyang) editor of the *North Korea Quarterly* observed in 1975, the DPRK's then total estimated debt of $1,700m was very much less than the equivalent South Korean figure of some $5,800m.[7] And, while none of the latter was then actually overdue, a very detailed recent study estimates that South Korea needs to pay $1 billion annually just to service its existing debts, and concludes — or rather opens — with the words: 'The Republic of Korea is headed for default on her debts abroad and economic chaos at home . . .'[8]

Nonetheless, despite exaggeration and partisan motivations, the smoke is not wholly without fire. Yet the smoke signals may mean something quite different — even opposite — to what has been suggested: far from signifying an economy in deep trouble, they may paradoxically testify to its long-run advance and strength despite short-term problems of cash flow. As Chung notes, the value of the DPRK's trade has risen steadily throughout its history.[9] Typically the balance has been unfavourable (though not very), although this improved in the late 1960s. The small deficits were covered by aid and long term credits, which between 1949 and 1962 totalled some $1·37 billion.[10] The decline of such assistance since the early 1960s supports Chung's comment on the DPRK's 'unique' achievement of having 'effectively utilised foreign aid in its program for industrialisation'[11] — in contrast to the common situation in the Third World (and not least in South Korea), where 'aid is necessary to maintain the system that makes aid necessary.'[12]

Examination of the changing composition of the DPRK's trade reveals what Chung calls a 'phenomenal shift'[13] in its commodity structure. Minerals, which in 1953 constituted 82 per cent of exports, had shrunk to 7·2 per cent by 1969; while in the same period metals increased from 9 per cent to 39·6 per cent. As for imports, machinery and equipment have consistently comprised 20–30 per cent (30 per cent in 1969), while fuels increased from 9·8 per cent in 1953 to 19·3 per cent. All this attests, as Chung allows, to the successful pursuit of a policy of import-substituting industrialisation, often aspired to but rarely achieved elsewhere: 'North Korea was transformed from a raw-materials-exporting-and-capital-importing nation to a semifinished-products-exporting-and-capital-and-semifinished-products-importing-nation.'[14]

Import substitution seems to have gone furthest in semifinished manufacturing (metals etc.), and in light industry (consumer goods). Typically, it had not by 1970 reduced the import of capital equipment: the latter, after all, is what is required first in order to produce the import-substituting goods. Besides, the increased share of fuels in the import bill illustrates not only the DPRK's most serious resource weakness but also its industrial growth (which has made more fuels necessary).

It is these two factors, coupled with an apparent change in the direction of foreign trade, which may help to explain the evolution of the DPRK's trade in the 1970s (although it must be stressed that hard data for the last few years are extremely scarce, confused, or unreliable).[15] Certainly the DPRK must have been hard hit, like everybody else, by the massive jump in world oil prices from 1973. As for capital goods, it has been plausibly suggested that the DPRK's current need for the most advanced technology in computers, automation and electronics has forced it to look elsewhere than the USSR (traditionally its major supplier of industrial plant) to the West;[16] such a diversification of trading partners might in any case have seemed politically judicious. Trade with the non-Communist world as a percentage of total trade had increased steadily from almost nil in the mid-50s to 27 per cent by 1969.[17] Current estimates (unsourced) put the proportion as high as almost half (although other figures contradict this).[18] Whatever the precise figure, it is clear that in the early 1970s the DPRK went on a major buying spree for Western technology: some 90 projects were reported.[19] This was to be paid for partly by short-term credits (2–3 years)[20] given by the other nations concerned, and partly no doubt by increased exports.

What then happened? The more hostile commentators have blamed an allegedly 'poor industrial base' and 'outdated port facilities'[21] for the DPRK's failure to deliver. DPRK sources themselves have privately admitted the latter, and added such factors as shortage of foreign currency, worldwide food and energy problems and the recession in capitalist countries[22] (which last has prompted a sharp fall in the price obtainable for tungsten, tin, and zinc, which are the DPRK's main hard currency earners).[23] Similarly, both Swedish and Japanese creditors have noted opportunities as yet unexploited for the DPRK to sell its manufactured consumer goods abroad, which would earn foreign exchange;[24] although it is possible that in the Third World sales of these (and also of machine tools) may be increasing. There is evidence, too, that the DPRK is relatively inexperienced in the ways of international trade — and, for that matter, not particularly concerned about its commercial reputation: a fall in raw material prices prompted the DPRK to renege on certain contracts for the supply of metals, leading it to be blackballed on the Baltic Exchange.[25] Finally, one point which recent discussions have overlooked is a persistent cyclical pattern in the DPRK's foreign trade, whose previous worst imbalances have always been towards the end of a particular Plan period (Chung suggests a scramble for imports to ensure that targets are met in time).[26] With the 1970–76 6 year plan reportedly fulfilled last year, this could again be a factor as it was in 1959 and 1969.

When one considers that virtually all nations (including communist ones) do much of their trading on credit and are thus normally in the position of owing very large sums to each other, the DPRK's problem scarcely appears serious. At worst, it temporarily bit off more than it could chew. Even now, the DPRK's dependence on trade (exports plus imports as a proportion of national income) is no more than 30 per cent; whereas for South Korea, with ten times the DPRK's volume of trade, the figure for 1974 increased to an astonishing 77 per cent.[27] There is little doubt that the purchase of advanced technology (soon no doubt to be reproduced at home), a continuing expansion of domestic energy sources (especially hydroelectricity), plus growing exports of consumer goods and machine tools as well as metals, will ensure the continued expansion of the fundamentally self-reliant DPRK economy. For this is a house built on stone; whereas for the house built on sand which is South Korea's ultra-dependent economy, the prospects are shaky indeed. In any case, time will tell.

NOTES

1. See, e.g., *New York Times*, February 26, 1976, "North Korean Lag on Debt Reported" (pp.43 and 47), as well as sources cited below.
2. *Korea Herald*, September 28, 1976 and February 26, 1976, reproduced in *North Korea Quarterly*, Vol.2, no.3–4, pp.110–113, and Vol.3, no.1, p.71, respectively.
3. Susumu Awanohara, "Pyongyang's Time Runs Out," *FEER*, April 9, 1976.
4. Edith Lenart, "A Vicious Circle for Pyongyang," *FEER*, December 19, 1975.
5. See the table in *NKQ*, Vol.2, no.3–4 (1975), p.11 (this also appears in no.1, p.59).
6. *Korea Herald, loc. cit*; cf. also Kwon Doo-Young, "North Korea's Economy and Foreign Liabilities," *East Asian Review*, Vol.2, no.4 (winter 1975), p.428 (table 1 adds up to almost the same figure).
7. *NKQ*, Vol.2, nos.3–4 (1975), p.1 ("DPRK in Crisis").
8. Institute for International Policy, *International Policy Report*, Vol.1, no.1 (December, 1975, Washington DC), p.1 and *passim*.
9. *Op. cit.*, p.104. (Information on the following discussion on DPRK trade up to 1969 comes from Chung, Ch.4.)
10. *ibid.*, p.142.
11. *ibid.*, p.160.
12. This aphorism is attributed to Joan Robinson, but I do not know its exact source.
13. *ibid.*, p.106 (cf. also Table 29, p.107).
14. *ibid.*, p.141.
15. For example, the *FEER Asia Yearbook (1975)* gives DPRK imports as about $650m. p.a., with a trade deficit of $250m. (implying exports of about $400m. (p.240); while on the previous page a box gives *exports* for 1974 as $640m. and *imports* as $400m.! Even if this is a publishing error, a South Korean source (also for 1974) has $820m. for imports and $570m. for exports (the deficit figure remaining at $250m): see *NKQ*, Vol.1, no.3–4 (1975), p.135.
16. *FEER Asia Yearbook (1975)*, p.239.
17. Chung, *op. cit.*, p.111.
18. Edith Lenart, *loc. cit.*, suggests 'almost half' (p.36); but *FEER Asia Yearbook 1975* gives only 15 per cent (p.239).
19. *NKQ*, Vol.2, no.3–4 (1975), p.111, citing *Korea Herald* (Seoul), September 28, 1975. The same source says that by 1975 of DPRK machinery imports 42 per cent came from the West and 58 per cent from the USSR, as compared with, respectively, 21 per cent and 79 per cent only two years previously (*ibid.* p.110).
20. Lenart, *loc. cit.*
21. *US News and World Report*, March 3, 1975 (reported in *NKQ*, Vol.2 (1975), p.58.
22. *NKQ*, Vol.2, no.3–4 (1975), p.61.
23. *NKQ*, Vol.2, no.1 (1975), p.59.
24. Radio interview with Goeran Engblom, managing director of the Swedish Export Council, Stockholm Home Service February 9, 1975;

extracts in *NKQ*, Vol.2, no.1 (1975), pp.56–58. Despite the debts, Engblom expressed 'great hopes' of the North Korean market, and the interviewer Anders Tunberg referred to the 'strongly expanding Korean industry'. For Japan: Susumu Awanohara in *FEER*, December 19, 1975, p.37.

25. See David Parker, "North Korea: Venturing Into the World," *FEER*, October 24, 1975, p.28.

26. Chung, *op. cit.*, p.104.

27. *NKQ*, Vol.2, no.3–4 (1975), p.135, citing a South Korean source. For South Korea, the figure of 77 per cent is attributed to the Bank of Korea (*FEER Asia Yearbook* (1976), p.284).

APPENDIX B

Koreans in Japan and the DPRK

Perhaps the final judgement on the 'two Koreas' may be left to those who are best placed to judge them; namely, the 600,000-odd Koreans in Japan. A history (by no means concluded) of gross exploitation and discrimination[1] has created strongly radical and nationalistic tendencies among this group; thus as early as 1933, Koreans comprised over half of the communist labour federation *Zenkyo.*[2] With the post-war creation of two states in Korea competing for the loyalty of Koreans, a recent study notes that 'North Korea most effectively courted . . . Japan's Koreans in ethnic education and national identification, in contrast with the South Korean Government, which provided practically no assistance and seemed at times, in alliance with the Japanese Ministry of Education, even opposed to such concerns.'[3]

The education of Koreans in Japan has indeed been a consistent priority for the DPRK, which over the years has channeled large sums (over 20 billion *yen* between 1957 and 1975, or about US $70 million)[4] for this purpose to Chongryun (the General Association of Korean Residents in Japan), the pro-DPRK organisation of Koreans in Japan. Chongryun now maintains 161 schools (including a university) with some 50,000 students, as well as a business network of 14 enterprises and 38 credit associations.[5]

Thus it was that 'in 1960, 445,000 of Japan's Koreans designated North Korea as their mother-country, while only 163,000 opted for South Korea — despite the fact that almost all of Japan's Koreans originated from Korea's South.'[6] With the 'normalisation' of relations between Japan and South Korea after 1965, however, the granting of permanent resident status to Koreans in Japan was made conditional upon their registering as citizens of *South* Korea. Despite such quasi-blackmail ('The Japanese Ministry of Justice reported that the majority of applicants sought permanent residence status in order to be eligible for National Health Insurance benefits and compulsory education privileges'),[7] by the time registration closed in January, 1971, just over 350,000 Koreans had applied for it; or, put another way, some 270,000 or 43 per cent had refused to do so, despite the vulnerable position in which this decision left them under Japan's draconian immigration laws. Subsequently, many who had registered campaigned to have their registration altered from 'South Korea' to plain 'Korea'.[8]

It should also be remembered that between 1959 and 1974 92,000 Koreans left Japan to settle permanently in the DPRK,[9] which no doubt welcomed them for economic reasons (to ease its labour shortage) as well as patriotic ones. Of these, 75,000 or over 80 per cent went in the short period 1959–1962;[10] the relative trickle subsequently (including a complete hiatus 1967–71) is a reflection of the obstacles placed by the Japanese government in the way of Chosen Soren activities, as otherwise more might have gone.

All in all, we can say that — despite many forms of constant harassment — up to two-thirds of the Koreans in Japan have shown some degree of support for the DPRK; and, of these, some quarter of a million are Chosen Soren members[11] and as such hard-line supporters of the DPRK on its own terms. Whatever the significance of 'Kimilsungism' in a monolithic society like the DPRK, its remarkable vitality in the ideologically pluralist (not to say hostile) environment of Japan provides food for thought.

NOTES

1. See Richard H. Mitchell, *The Korean Minority in Japan* (Berkeley: University of California Press, 1967), for a full account.
2. Jonathan Unger, "Foreign Minorities in Japan," *Journal of Contemporary Asia*, Vol.3, no.3, p.307.
3. G. A. DeVos and W. O. Wetherall, *Japan's Minorities* (revised edn.),

London: Minority Rights Group, Report no.3, September, 1974, p.15. (Hereafter 'MRG'.)

4. *Korean Review* (Pyongyang: Foreign Languages Publishing House, 1974), p.174. Chongryun, *This Is Chongryun. Twenty Years of Juche* (Tokyo, 1975), pp.67–68.

5. Figures in *Newsweek*, January 19, 1976. (For an account of Chongryun, see Changsoo Lee, "Chosoren: An Analysis of the Korean Communist Movement in Japan," *Journal of Korean Affairs*, Vol.3, no.2 (July, 1973), pp.3–32) [Chosoren is an abbreviation of the Japanese name for Chongryun].

6. Unger, *op. cit.*, p.308.

7. MRG, *op. cit.*, p.16 (citing Japanese sources).

8. Unger, *op. cit.*, p.311.

9. *Sekai*, no.3, 1975, p.190 (from a Chongryun source).

10. MRG, *loc. cit.* (quoting Mitchell, *op. cit.*).

11. *FEER*, March 29, 1976.

Section IV

Outside Pressures

Chapter 6

The Roots of Intervention

Malcolm Caldwell

Between 1950 and 1953 the largest coalition of imperialist forces ever assembled intervened in the civil war in Korea. Sixteen Western and pro-Western states, including Britain and South Africa, fought overtly alongside the Seoul régime for three years. By late 1977 the only US troops on the mainland of Asia east of Turkey were in Korea — some 40,000 — many in forward positions, accompanied by a nuclear arsenal estimated unofficially at 6–700 weapons.

The questions are inescapable: why Korea? Why did Korea necessitate the intervention of such a multi-national coalition? Why have US troops stayed there, with nuclear weapons, when they have withdrawn elsewhere? And, as well as the specific situation of Korea, what is the overall strategic context which explains this extraordinary US presence?

US interest specifically in Korea dates from 1866, when an armed merchantman, the *General Sherman*, forcefully attempted to open up the peninsula to trade, sailing up the Taedong river as far as Pyongyang, letting off salvoes as it went. It was eventually set alight by Korean resistance fighters, and sank with all hands. However, imperialist pressures were maintained, and in 1876 Korea signed a treaty liberalising trade with Japan; this was followed by similar treaties with the United States (1882), Britain (1883), and Russia (1884).

To appreciate the process by which Korea has come to play so crucial a part in US strategy today, it is best to pick up the story in the inter-war period. As a result largely of protectionist measures by the European colonial powers, the US share of international trade began to shrink dramatically after the Great Depression, provoking alarmist prophecies about being excluded from world commerce. East and South East Asia were particularly important areas for US industry and the prosperity of the US economy in general. By 1939 the US was obtaining nearly a third of its total import requirements from this region — more than from any other single region in the world.[1] Over half of US raw material imports came from Asia. In key commodities such as rubber and tin, dependence upon South East Asia in particular was almost total.[2] Over a quarter of all US trade in the immediately pre-war years was with Asia and Australasia — a volume nearly two-and-a-half times that with Latin America.[3] The US business community therefore needed no prompting to appreciate what was at stake.

Japan's move into southern Indo-China in July 1941 indicated its decision to 'strike south' into South East Asia. Washington at once began preparing to go to war for control over the region's resources. US leaders recognised that Japan's real goal was South East Asia. As Dean Acheson commented: 'the move south was Japan's central purpose and real objective, and the Pearl Harbor attack a diversion to protect it.'[4] Pearl Harbor, of course, had more than a 'diversionary' purpose; it was designed to try to knock out US forces long enough to enable Japan to achieve a *fait accompli* in South East Asia. From the point of view of US leaders, it was extremely important in rallying US public opinion — as opposed to business opinion — in favour of war.

The Second World War succeeded in bringing an abrupt end to the great depression which had so shaken American business confidence. The question, however, remained: how could a recurrence be avoided in the post-war period? This question above all others preoccupied top American thinking throughout the duration of the war.[5]

Much of the responsibility for drawing up the blue-prints was left, characteristically, to a non-governmental body — the Council on Foreign Relations (CFR). As a result of CFR investigations into the availability of industrial raw materials, and into the scale of sales needed to keep an American industrial capacity greatly expanded by war demands fully occupied in peace-time, it was concluded that the US empire (and they did not hesitate — *among themselves* — to use the concept and vocabulary of imperialism)[6] required would have to

embrace *at least* the Americas, Western Europe, all the territories that had fallen within the jurisdiction or influence of
the old colonial powers, and the Pacific rim. (It was hoped,
in addition, that the Soviet Union, and those parts of Eastern
Europe to be ceded to it as a result of war-time bargaining,
could also be integrated, but this was not to be.) Economic
activity within this vast empire under US hegemony would be
lubricated by dollars injected into the system in the form of
economic 'aid', American overseas investments, and American
military expenditure. The wheels of American industry would,
in turn, be kept busy by the purchases of dollar recipients and
by the raw materials delivered up in return for aid and trade.
To complete the complex there would be a series of international agencies with a variety of servicing functions related
to the general design: the IMF and the World Bank, for
instance, and, of course, the United Nations. It was, of course,
recognised that fulfilment of this programme would require
the stifling of social revolution everywhere in the empire —
and thus a world-wide network of US military bases was in-
corporated as an integral part of the plan.

American power was never in practice to prove quite equal
to the demands of this ambitious imperial quest. Contrary to
intentions, discontent in the armed forces at the end of the
war forced Washington into rapid demobilisation, which pre-
cluded any significant intervention — which would, in any
event, merely have postponed the inevitable — in the Chinese
civil war, and long before 1949 it had become clear to the
White House that China was 'lost'.[7] Acceptance of this harsh
reality brought with it an even greater determination to secure
what had from the beginning been recognised as the two
frontier posts where American power received its most vigor-
ous challenge: Korea and Vietnam.

Actually, high though hopes had been of building up an
important market for American goods in China in the post-
war period, its 'loss' was not of any great direct economic
significance. Strategically, though, to have had a vast buffer
like China shielding the heart areas of US concern — Japan
and maritime South East Asia (Malaya, Indonesia and the
Philippines) — would have been invaluable. However, considerable thought had already been given in Washington to

securing the key passes of access constituted by Korea and Vietnam. Traditionally they had formed the routes for transmission of people and ideas from the Asian mainland to the island perimeter. As recently as the 1930s and the early 1940s their importance had been underlined by Japan's concern to hold them and to use them as passageways to China and South East Asia. Post-war protection of Japan, it was argued, demanded retention of Korea, just as protection of Indonesia, it was argued, demanded retention of Vietnam.[8]

Japan and Indonesia, for American policy-makers and businessmen, were in quite a different economic league from China, and *were* perceived as central to successful performance of the entire American empire. Why? Briefly, because a resuscitated Japanese capitalism was seen as an essential component of international capitalism, its revived industrial and commercial dynamism now locked into and contributing to the overall performance and prosperity of the Western powers; contradictions there would be, of course, but it was hoped, with good reason, that the outcome of the Pacific War assured that these would not assume the sharpness and intractability of the inter-war period, at least for the foreseeable future. But Japan certainly could not and would not revive without access both to those South East Asia raw materials and markets for which it had gone to war against the West, and to the territories which had formed the core of its empire for virtually half a century — Korea and Taiwan.

Korea posed special problems, since the former colonial power was for the time being a defeated 'enemy'. There was no alternative, therefore, but for the US directly to occupy the country, or at least the southern part, where it has stayed to this day.

The first decade of the post-war US empire in Asia saw the Korean war of 1950–53 throw bright light — for those able to see — upon Washington's objectives and the methods it was prepared to use in pursuit of them. As other contributions in this volume make clear, US leaders, whatever their public rhetoric, were perfectly well aware that in trying to impose a client régime in South Korea they would have to repress virtually the entire Korean people and try to extinguish the fierce longing of the Korean people for independence, national unity and social revolution. It was a goal whose costs had to be set against its wider, global benefits.

First, quashing the Korean revolution enabled the US to proclaim that the 'loss' of China could not be taken as a signal that it would regard with indifference similar revolutions elsewhere in the 'free world' empire — a totality upon which hinged the economic recovery of international capitalism. The unrestrained savagery of the repression of the Korean people in peace and war was a clear indication of this determination. Truman's Declaration of June 27, 1950, utilising the start of the Korean War to initiate a tougher policy against social change throughout East Asia from Taiwan to Indo-China is pellucid in this respect.

The Korean War and East Asia

The start of the Korean War was the occasion for a codification of a much harder US counter-revolutionary position not only in Korea, but over much of East Asia, including Indo-China. Truman's statement of June 27, 1950, spells this out.

'In Korea, the Government forces . . . were attacked by invading forces from North Korea. . . . In these circumstances, I have ordered United States air and sea forces to give the Korean Government troops cover and support.

The attack upon Korea makes it plain beyond all doubt that communism has passed beyond the use of subversion to conquer independent nations and will now use armed invasion and war. . . . In these circumstances, the occupation of Formosa by Communist forces would be a direct threat to the security of the Pacific area and to United States forces performing their lawful and necessary functions in that area.

Accordingly, I have ordered the Seventh Fleet to prevent any attack on Formosa. . . . The determination of the future of Formosa must await the restoration of security in the Pacific, a peace settlement with Japan, or consideration by the United Nations. I have also directed that the United States forces in the Philippines be strengthened and that military assistance to the Philippine Government be accelerated.

I have similarly directed acceleration in the furnishing of military assistance to the forces of France and the Associated States in Indo-China and the dispatch of a military mission to provide close working relations with those forces. . . .'
Source: Department of State Bulletin, Vol.23 (July 3, 1950), p.5.

Secondly, the war served an important economic function for the United States and its Asian allies. For the US it initiated a major post-war economic boom while providing the rationale for the permanent war economy.[9] In Asia as a whole, including Japan, the economic pulse was sluggish in the early post-Second World War years. The Korean War transformed this picture. The tempo of economic activity picked up at once. Raw material prices soared, filling the coffers of regional exporting countries. US military orders expanded employment and brought booming business to Japan. Everywhere, the boost afforded by the war was felt — just as, later, US escalation in Indo-China was to bring profits to those in Asia, like the Seoul régime, prepared and in a position to cash in on it.

At the end of the war in 1953 Korea was devastated from end to end. It was not immediately a particularly attractive economic prospect for Western capital.[10] However, after 1961, when the present dictator, Pak Chung Hee, a former officer in the Japanese Imperial Army, staged a coup, things began to change. Under intense pressure from Washington and Japanese big capital, Tokyo and Seoul 'normalised' relations in 1965, against widespread popular opposition in both Japan and Korea. This 'normalisation' was not by any means a purely diplomatic operation. It had extremely important economic connotations. Japanese capital began to move back into Korea in a big way and South Korea became one of the main territories, along with Taiwan, Hong Kong and Singapore, for a type of intensive ultra-dependent export-oriented industrialisation. Along with Taiwan and Hong Kong, two similarly dependent political entities, South Korea has become the spearhead of a global operation by imperialism directed against both the Third World as a whole and against the working classes in the advanced industrial countries. (This is discussed in chapter 4 above.)

On the military level, tension in Korea has remained consistently high since 1953. There have been numerous cross-border incidents in and across the Demilitarised Zone (DMZ), with many deaths as a result. Most of the troops which fought under the UN flag have since withdrawn — except the large US contingent, some 20 British soldiers and a unit of Filipino troops.

The incendiary nature of the conflict across the 38th Parallel, graphically revealed in the Pueblo incident of 1968 and the Poplar Tree incident at Panmunjom in 1976, was underlined in Richard Nixon's final TV interview with David Frost. Nixon revealed that in April, 1969, Henry Kissinger had called for the bombing of North Korea in response to the DPRK's shooting down of a US Navy EC-121 plane. 'Kissinger came down hard . . . And he said "We must react strongly". And he advocated taking out two or three North Korean airfields as a result of this.' Nixon added, 'Frankly I tilted toward it,' but eventually went along with senior foreign policy advisers who counseled restraint.[10]

The US débâcle in Indo-China in 1975 again concentrated world attention on Korea. Washington immediately made clear that it was committed *in a special way* to the Seoul régime. As the pro-US régimes in Phnom Penh and Saigon collapsed, US leaders announced that they would launch a nuclear first strike in the event of a new war in Korea. The US presence in Korea currently consists of some 40,000 troops plus an estimated 6–700 nuclear weapons (at a cautious estimate).[11] And when two US officers died in an incident in the demilitarised zone in August, 1976, America at once deployed a naval task force from the Pacific, F-4 jet fighters from Okinawa, B-52s from Guam and F-111 warplanes from Idaho in a show of force, with nuclear implications.

What of the other major powers involved? The position of Japan is detailed elsewhere (Ch. 8). The only two states with which Korea has a land frontier are China and the Soviet Union. Both have a deep concern with Korea, through which both China and Russia have been threatened by an expansionist Japan in the past hundred years. US and Japanese propaganda has obscured the crucial fact that the countries which historically have a real right to be concerned, not about Korea itself, but about the use of Korea by others, are China and Russia. Both had troops in Korea; but, unlike the US, they withdrew them promptly: the Soviet Red Army, which entered Korea in 1945, withdrew in 1948; and the Chinese People's Volunteers, which entered the Korean War in late 1950, withdrew in 1958. Both China and the Soviet Union support the DPRK's stance on withdrawal of all foreign forces and peaceful reunification.

Korea's tragedy is to lie at the point where the real or alleged interests of major powers meet; it lies, too, at the point where capitalism and socialism encounter each other. But it would be quite wrong to present the situation as somehow 'neutral'. It is capitalism and the capitalist states, especially the US and Japan, which have intervened in Korea, divided the country, and distorted the process of social change which the people of Korea so manifestly desired and desire. It is only the West which keeps foreign troops in Korea. While the régime in the North is headed by a former guerrilla fighter against the Japanese, the régime in the South is headed by a man who fought in the Japanese Army against his own fellow-countrymen.

The West has also intervened by distorting history. Far from Korea being a 'threat' to anyone, it is Korea which has been used and abused to attack and/or threaten other countries; but the countries which have been attacked and/or threatened are not Japan, much less the United States; they are China and Russia.

Western intervention in Korea continues, and takes on new forms with international significance. After invading and devastating Korea itself, the US built up a bloated South Korean military force, commanded by former Japanese trainees; this force has functioned not only to oppress the Korean people, but was further sent by the US to fight against the Vietnamese people.

The mercenary role of the Pak régime on the military front

is paralleled by its mercenary role at the economic and social level. The country's labour force has been literally placed at the disposal of foreign capital. Within South Korea itself many of the new industrial enterprises have been located in special enclaves which are, in effect, isolated from the rest of the country and in which foreign capital can exploit local labour at a maximal rate. Meanwhile, labour is exported under KCIA supervision to the Middle East (and South Africa), thus allowing imperialist and sub-imperialist capital to utilise a controlled low-wage work force — and avoid creating a local proletariat. At home and abroad the government promotes the prostitution of Korean women for foreign men. The international significance of foreign intervention in Korea is world wide — it has reached from the Ginza to the handbag of the Governor's wife in Baton Rouge, Louisiana, and from the textile mills of Lancashire to the rice fields of Vietnam. US intervention has simultaneously internationalised South Korea's role and isolated the Korean people. It is crucial to get the history and dynamics of the situation in perspective. It is not Korea which threatens anyone. It is the West which has intervened, distorted and brutalised, and it is this intervention which must be brought to an end so that the Korean people can live united and independent, at peace with themselves and with the rest of the world's peoples.

NOTES

1. Jonathan Marshall, "Southeast Asia and US-Japan Relations: 1940–1941," *Pacific Research & World Empire Telegram*, Vol.4, no.3 (March-April 1973), p.6.
2. Jonathan Marshall, "Pearl Harbor," *Pacific Research*, Vol.5, no.3 (March-April 1974).
3. Marshall, "Southeast Asia and US-Japan Relations," p.14.
4. Dean Acheson, *Present at the Creation* (Norton, 1969), p.37, cited in Marshall, *ibid.*, p.21.
5. Gabriel Kolko, *The Politics of War: Allied Diplomacy and the World Crisis of 1943–45* (London, Weidenfeld & Nicolson, 1969), passim.

6. L. Shoup, "Shaping the Postwar World," *The Insurgent Sociologist,* Vol.5, no.3 (Spring 1975).
7. See J. F. Melby, *The Mandate of Heaven* (London, 1968) and Mary A. Waters, *GI's and the Fight Against War* (New York, 1967).
8. See Peter Dale Scott, "The Vietnam War and the CIA-Financial Establishment," in Mark Selden, ed., *Remaking Asia: Essays on the American Uses of Power* (New York, Pantheon, 1974); also the same author's "Exporting Military-Economic Development — America and the Overthrow of Sukarno, 1965–67," in M. Caldwell, ed., *Ten Years' Military Terror in Indonesia* (Nottingham, Spokesman Books, 1975).
9. Joyce and Gabriel Kolko, *The Limits of Power: The World and United States Foreign Policy, 1945–1954* (New York, Harper & Row, 1972), Book III.
10. *Light,* San Antonio (Texas), September 4, 1977; *The Age* (Melbourne), September 5, 1977.
11. Center for Defense Information. *The Defense Monitor,* Vol.5, no.1 (January 1976), pp.1, 2, 5; *International Herald Tribune,* April 10–11, 1976.

Chapter 7

The United States in Korea

Youngja Yang and Gavan McCormack

American involvement in Korea has been a catastrophe for the Korean people. America first divided the peninsula, then suppressed the democratic, nationalist, communist and socialist forces in the area it controlled, and, when enforced division and repression led to civil war, employed the most sophisticated technology at its disposal to create unprecedented destruction and to kill approximately three million people. Interference in Korea cost the US a staggering $189 billion over the years 1945–1976,[1] much of it war expenses and veterans payments which were simply recycled within the American economy, but about $12 billion was economic and military aid to the client régime in Seoul. As of late 1977 there were still over 40,000 American troops and 600 to 700 nuclear weapons in Korea.[2]

Past rationales for this commitment — such as containment of alleged Soviet and/or Chinese expansionism — are no longer functional, even for a conservative US audience, nor do US policy makers any longer attempt to refer to Pak Chung Hee's dictatorship as a 'threatened bastion of democracy and the free world'. Instead the rationale is given in terms of two related factors — prevention of unification by the north by force of arms, and Japanese interest.

The change in the rationale has not softened the obduracy with which the US continues to block Korean reunification. The US has combined studied blindness to northern initiatives for a gradual, peaceful reunification with unswerving support for the stubborn southern attitude that reunification can be projected into the distant future, typified by Pak Chung Hee's remark that 'It took Silla 120 years to achieve unification.'[3] What is left is a firm American commitment to the *status quo*, to maintaining the Korean peninsula divided.

163

It should be understood that this division, accomplished in 1945, is itself the direct result of American policy, and that the successive purges of the left and the witch-hunts against progressives, communists and independence-minded nationalists in the south by régimes created and supported by the US have been the main factor responsible for the frustration of moves towards reunification. As a January, 1976, study by the Center for Defense Information, a high-level Washington research organisation, puts it, 'Regrettably, the most salient American objective in North-east Asia has become the preservation of the *status quo*.'[4]

US emphasis on preserving the *status quo* in Korea has long been justified, in part because Japan claims a crucial strategic interest in the region. As Defence Secretary Donald Rumsfeld put it, 'US support of South Korea is essential to the security of North-east Asia, as Japan sees the security of South Korea as intimately related to her own security';[5] the point is even more categorically made by a liberal critic of US government policy, E. O. Reischauer: 'The United States has no direct strategic interests in South Korea, nor would a unified Korea under Communist leadership be a hegemonic extension of either Chinese or Russian power but rather a Korea more able to resist both. What is chiefly at stake in South Korea, apart from our concern for the well-being of the Koreans themselves, is the security of Japan.'[6] There are two main points to be made about this: first is that the Japanese interest is not a legitimate defence interest in the real sense of the term but a compound of corrupt and neo-colonial ties running directly counter to the interests of the Japanese as well as of the Korean people; second is that *even if* the Japanese sincerely believed that a united country on the nearby peninsula would constitute a threat to Japan it cannot be legitimate for Japan, or indeed for any power, to deny the right of independent nationhood to its neighbours. Indeed, for the United States to justify its policy by reference to the interests of Japan, whose record towards Korea is a long and dishonourable one of exploitation and aggression, is an affront to the Korean people.

United States support of the Pak Chung Hee régime can be

resumed briefly under three heads — military, economic and diplomatic.

Korea is the only foreign country other than Germany in which a full US division is stationed. It also has installed a panoply of nuclear weapons there — nuclear missiles, nuclear mines, nuclear artillery and nuclear bomb-carrying F-4 Phantom fighter-bombers.[7] There are two things to be noted about this nuclear arsenal: first unlike in Europe, where both confronting forces possess such weapons and both are committed not to use them first, in Korea the US alone possesses such weapons, the north has renounced any intention of developing them and there has never been any intelligence report suggesting that this claim might be untrue. Second, in the wake of the 1975 US collapse in Indo-China a new nuclear doctrine, nuclear first-strike against a non-nuclear enemy, was proclaimed. James Schlesinger, then Secretary of Defense, first announced this doctrine in Seoul in June, 1975. Ron Nessen, the White House spokesman, reiterated it: 'The use of limited strategic nuclear weapons would be one of the options open to the United States in the event of a war (in Korea),'[8] and Schlesinger's successor as Secretary of Defense, Donald Rumsfeld, reaffirmed his predecessor's doctrine on May 28, 1976, saying that he would 'not rule out the use of nuclear weapons' in Korea.[9] As Richard Falk puts it, 'Nothing more profoundly contradicts the basic well-being of the Korean people than for a foreign government to threaten nuclear devastation in the event that the present artificial *status quo* is disturbed.'[10]

US taxpayers pay about $700 million annually to maintain American troops in Korea, and have spent a total of $11 billion on their upkeep since the Korean war ended.[11] Although one of the UN resolutions on Korea passed in the autumn of 1975 called for the dissolution of the UN command and the withdrawal of all foreign troops stationed in Korea under its flag, the US Ambassador to the UN, Daniel Moynihan, had announced in advance that regardless of the passage of any resolution American troops would not be withdrawn.[12] The American response to further pressure on this score will presumably be the switching of the juridical basis of the forces from the UN resolution to the bilateral US-South Korean treaty. With the advent of the Carter administration after the November, 1976, election, the possibility of change in Korea policy has been much debated. The portents are examined in detail in later chapters.

The South Korean military has also been heavily subsidised by American aid. Indeed, until recently, only the food and clothing for that 600,000 man force had to be met from Korean funds. US military grants to the Seoul government since 1950 have amounted to $4 billion and since 1971 have been considerably stepped up.[13] A military modernisation plan was drawn up in 1971 and revised in 1975. Under it the South Korean government was to put in $3 billion and the US government $4 billion by 1980 — of which nearly $2 billion had been put in by mid 1976.[14] The rate of payments was somewhat reduced in 1975, as part of a Congressional attempt to pressure the Pak régime to ease its draconian repression, but the mood had changed in 1976, when $490 million in aid was approved and $838 million worth of arms were set aside for purchase by the Koreans on cash or credit for the 1976 and 1977 fiscal years.[15] The potential of vast arms deals of this kind for destabilising the military situation in the Korean peninsula is obvious. It is striking that the level of military aid to South Korea is far in excess of that given to any other East Asian country, about 8 times as much as goes to Taiwan, $6\frac{1}{2}$ times as much as to Indonesia, and nearly 6 times as much as to Thailand.[16] Moreover, it was only in March, 1976, that Congress discovered an originally $1\frac{1}{2}$ billion commitment made in 1971 to assist in the South Korean arms modernisation programme, since this, along with 33 other secret agreements between the US government and Pak Chung Hee, was only then reported to Congress by the General Accounting Office. This was despite a 1972 law to the effect that the Secretary of State should submit to Congress the text of any international agreement, other than a treaty, within sixty days of its enactment.[17]

Involvement by private American banks and businesses with the Pak régime also runs at extremely high levels, and in the straitened circumstances of the régime's astronomical debt in the past few years that involvement is crucial. The $6 billion or more debt at the end of 1976,[18] and the likelihood of its continuing to increase at a rate of about $2 billion per year has been mentioned. Indebtedness, even on this scale, is not unique to South Korea, but Korea is one of the sharpest examples of the phenomenon common to the oil-poor countries of the Third World. The 'aid' they have been accustomed to receive bilaterally or through institutions like the World Bank proved inadequate to the problem that hit these countries with the sudden trebling of their balance of payments deficits from 1973. Private multi-national banks therefore stepped in, a large percentage of them American-based, and made funds available on strictly commercial terms, i.e., on a short or medium-term basis and at commercial interest rates. By August, 1975, 83·5 per cent of foreign bank loans and credit lines to South Korean banks ($2·3 billion) came from American banks.[19] A group of countries in which South Korea figures large, but which also includes Brazil, Argentina, Peru, Chile, Zaire and a few others, by early 1976 owed $20 billion to a group of 21 US banks.[20] The strength of the US government's political and military commitment to these countries is obviously a major factor in stimulating the banks to act in this way and, as one commentator noted, this involvement, although ostensibly private, greatly increases the imperatives of US government commitment, since countries like Zaire, and South Korea, could not be allowed to drown without 'putting the whole of Wall Street at risk.'[21] The fact that the largest US banks choose to lend to borrowers in South Korea 'amounts that are 14,000 per cent greater than the amounts they lend to people in India' is indicative of their faith in their government's commitment, and of the spurious nature of distinctions between private and public involvement.[22] If US involvement in such multi-national institutions as the World Bank and Asian Development Bank, both of which treat South Korea as a specially favoured case, is taken into account the US role in sustaining the Pak régime becomes even greater.[23]

In diplomatic terms it is clear that US initiatives have been as important to the continued acceptance of the Seoul government in international organisations as they were in the creation of the Republic of Korea in 1948. However, the US commitment is no longer backed by the power and influence it enjoyed then. Throughout the 1950s the US could boast of 70 per cent support in the UN on the Korean question. In the 1960s, when many new members, particularly non-aligned

countries, joined the organisation, support for the US-South
Korean position declined to 50 per cent; this gradually weak-
ened to the point where in 1975 for the first time the General
Assembly passed a resolution sponsored by countries friendly
to DPRK.[24] 1975 thus marked an important turning-point,
but the UN voting was anomalous, for a quite incompatible,
US-sponsored resolution was also passed. As a result the US
use of the UN cover for its military operations in Korea has
not yet ended, but the writing is on the wall.

US government thinking on Korea remains as firmly committed as it was in 1945 to a separate and divided peninsula
and the exclusion from power in the south of liberal or democratic elements that might favour compromise with the north
in the interests of reunification. The latest strategy to perpetuate the division of Korea is Kissinger's proposal for a four-
power (US, South Korea, DPRK, China) conference 'to reduce tension in Korea'.[25] In return for recognition of the Pak
régime by the DPRK and China, the US and the Pak régime
would recognise the DPRK. Such a 'cross-recognition' formula
has been repudiated by both the DPRK and China and their
criticism that by freezing the 38th Parallel such a scheme
would merely preserve intact the greatest single source of
tension and danger in the area seems hard to deny. The deeper
wrong embedded in the Kissinger thinking is that of seeing the
'Korean problem' only in terms of stability and balance of
great power interests. This perspective has been at the root of
the historic injustice that the Korean people have suffered in
modern times — 45 years of colonial subjugation and exploitation, followed by 31 years of imposed division. As Richard
Falk puts it, 'Korea has never been a threat to others, but becomes dangerous because foreign countries vie for its control
or domination.'[26] Today the greatest barrier to unity and independence in Korea is the Pak régime, which in turn owes its
existence to support from Japan, the United States and, more
recently, Europe. Since political life in South Korea itself is
now frozen under Pak it is difficult to expect any new initiatives from that quarter. It is therefore all the more necessary
that the American, Japanese, and European peoples, whose
governments, financial institutions and multi-national corpor-

ations support Pak, should clearly understand the mechanisms and consequences of that support, and should themselves establish strong ties of solidarity with the Korean people.

NOTES

1. *Korea Bulletin* (San Francisco), Vol.3, no.5 (May, 1976), p.3. For background on US involvement in Korea, see Soon Sung Cho, *Korea in World Politics: An evaluation of American Responsibility* (Berkeley and Los Angeles, University of California Press, 1967).
2. Center for Defense Information (Washington, DC), *The Defense Monitor*, Vol.5, no.1 (January, 1976), pp.1, 5.
3. Quoted by Mr Bae Dong-ho at the Emergency International Conference on Korea, Tokyo, August, 1976. Silla was the first unified Korean state (from AD 675).
4. *Defense Monitor*, January, 1976, pp.1–2.
5. Cited in "Dokyumento," *Sekai*, May, 1976, p.258 (re-translated back from Japanese).
6. Reischauer, "Back to Normalcy," *Foreign Policy*, no.20 (Fall 1975), p.207; Reischauer is disputing the validity of the stance; he continues: 'Even for Japan, a defense line in the straits between it and Korea makes more strategic sense than one in the middle of the peninsula.' See also the Brookings Institution study by Ralph Clough, *Deterrence and Defense in Korea* (Washington, 1976), p.44: '. . . the principal justification for the US defense commitment to South Korea . . . is the potential damage to US-Japanese relations that would result from the military conquest of South Korea by North Korea.'
7. Details in the *Defense Monitor*, cit.
8. On June 23. "Dokyumento," *Sekai*, September, 1975, p.221.
9. "Dokyumento," *Sekai*, August, 1976, p.261.
10. Richard Falk, "Prospects for Korea: An American Perspective," (Japanese text), *Sekai*, October, 1976, p.140.
11. *The Defense Monitor*, cit., p.6; *Korea Bulletin*, May, 1976, p.3.
12. On August 12, 1975. *Korean Journal of International Studies* (Seoul), Vol.7, no.1, 1975–6, p.81.
13. *The Defense Monitor*, p.6.
14. *Ibid.*; Richard Falk, *Sekai*, November, 1975, pp.68–9.
15. *Korea Bulletin*, June, 1976, p.3.
16. *Asia Research Bulletin*, March 31, 1976; p.190.
17. "Dokyumento," *Sekai*, May, 1976, p.270; *Japan Times*, March 2, 1976,
18. Harold van B. Cleveland and W. H. Bruce Brittain, "Are the LDC, in over Their Heads?" *Foreign Affairs*, July, 1977, p.734.

19. *Richard Halloran, New York Times*, November 21, 1975, reprinted in "Important Documents on the South Korean Economy," *Korean Studies*, supplement, April, 1976.

20. Peter Wilsher, *The Sunday Times*, June 13, 1976; Emma Rothschild, "Banks: The Politics of Debt," *New York Review of Books*, June 24, 1976.

21. Wilsher, *op. cit.*

22. Rothschild, p.25.

23. South Korea has been the largest borrower from the ADB (see *ADB Quarterly*, January, 1976, p.8). In 1975 it borrowed $898·8 million in loans and received $106·9 million in IDA (International Development Association — the World Bank 'soft loan' affiliate) credits from the World Bank and $101·5 million from the ADB. The US government-funded Export-Import Bank also favoured South Korea with more loans than any other Asian country — $502·5 million. ("Banking in Asia," *FEER* supplement, April 23, 1976, pp.74, 77, 85.

24. *Korea Bulletin*, Vol.2, no.11 (November, 1975).

25. *Korea Bulletin*, Vol.3, no.7 (July, 1976).

26. Richard Falk, *Sekai*, October, 1976, p.142.

Chapter 8

Japan and South Korea, 1965–75: Ten Years of 'Normalisation'

Gavan McCormack

The importance of the Korean issue in Japanese politics in the modern era needs no stressing: in pre-war Asia it was the Korean people who paid dearest for Japan's rise to great power status; independence was restored to Japan at the height of the Korean war and on terms partly dictated by it; the war itself was the occasion of Japan's first great post-1945 economic boom; and subsequently the southern half of the Korean peninsula, under a fiercely anti-communist and, more recently, quasi-fascist régime, has seen the development of a stronger Japanese commitment than any country elsewhere to its continued existence, and thus, implicitly, to continued division of the country. This paper is primarily concerned with the most recent phases of this process, but the significance of recent developments is best understood against a brief statement of the historical context.

The fact that in the Meiji period (1868–1912) Japanese imperialism and aggression took shape and were directed first and foremost against Korea was due to several sets of conditioning circumstances. Within Japan, the consensus on which policy towards Korea was based was wider and deeper than that which existed on any other foreign policy issue, with the single exception of the drive in the nineteenth century to see an end to the unequal treaties. There were differences over the timing or the method by which Korea should be subjected to Japan, as during the *Seikanron* (literally the 'subjugate Korea' debate) in the 1870s, but not over the goal itself. On that liberals were fully in agreement with the government oligarchs. Secondly, in international terms, the process could occur because it won the approval of the major Western powers.

Japanese imperial expansion in Korea was given its formal ratification by Britain in the Anglo-Japanese Alliance (1902) and by the United States in the Taft-Katsura Agreement (1905). Only when Japanese ambition went beyond Korea, to north-east China ('Manchuria'), then to the rest of China and beyond, did the powers object.

The first phase of Japan's imperial expansion reached its peak and entered a period of prolonged crisis in the immediate aftermath of World War One. The Anglo-Japanese Alliance was terminated at the Washington Conference in December, 1921; US rivalry and suspicion of Japan deepened at the same time; and the March 1st, 1919 movement in Korea marked a turning point in mass popular resistance by the subjects of Japanese imperial rule. The external circumstances that had favoured the establishment of Japanese imperial rule in the Meiji period all gradually turned against it thereafter until eventually the empire was itself liquidated in 1945. Significantly, however, the domestic consensus on imperialism, particularly with regard to Korea, remained unchallenged to the end.

For a time after 1945 Japan reverted to introspection and concentration on domestic reconstruction in a way reminiscent of the early decades of Meiji. That period passed at latest by the early 1960s, by which time a definitely reconstituted Japanese imperialism developed in close symbiotic but subordinate relationship with the United States.[1] As part of that process the same basic pattern of inequality and exploitation as characterised Japan's relations with Korea in the pre-war Japanese imperialist system was reconstituted, particularly and with greatly accelerating speed since the 'normalisation' of relations between Japan and South Korea in 1965. As in Meiji Japan, the process has been facilitated by several sets of favourable circumstances. Again, within Japan, the consensus of the main political and economic groups on the importance of the security of the anti-communist régime in South Korea, and on Japanese political and economic ties with it, is almost universal, while internationally the readiness of the main Western powers, in particular, of course, Japan's ally the United States, to accept if not positively encourage that situation, is clear.

In looking at the relationship between Japan and South Korea in the period after 1965 the first obvious question is why it took until 1965 for 'normal' relations to be restored, and why the government of the Democratic People's Republic of Korea (DPRK) in the northern half of the peninsula was excluded from the process of such 'normalisation' when it occurred.

Till the outbreak of the Korean war, Japan's relations with the rest of the world were, of course, conditioned by the fact of occupation. During the Korean war, in the course of which the occupation was ended, Japan enjoyed the first of its remarkable post-war economic booms. To a considerable measure this was due to US procurements and war contracts, for which Japan received about $5 billion in all during the course of the war. The Japanese contribution to the war included the supply of napalm and shells, the repair of planes and tanks, and the services of an important detachment of ex-Japanese army and navy men who were Korea specialists as advisers and consultants to the Americans. The Japanese Navy also took part in combat operations (though this was concealed at the time). It was an inauspicious beginning for any attempt at a new policy of friendliness or neutrality towards Korea. Furthermore, as part of the price of independence the Japanese also accepted, at the time of the negotiation of the San Francisco Treaty of September, 1951, the principle of hostility to North Korea and the sanctity of the 38th Parallel dividing the peninsula.[2] Given their involvement in the Korean war this was hardly surprising.

A preparatory conference between Japan and South Korea was held at US insistence just one month after the San Francisco conference in the Autumn of 1951 in an attempt to restore relations between the newly independent Japanese and the Syngman Rhee régime (1948–1960). All such efforts during the Syngman Rhee period were unsuccessful, however. The Rhee régime claimed at least $2 billion in compensation for war damages from the Japanese, while the Japanese not only refused to consider any obligation at all but even called for the return of Japanese property left behind, as they put it, at the end of the war.[3] This anti-Japanese policy, or rather this demand for compensation from Japan for the past record of imperialist exploitation and war, became the single plank on which the discredited Rhee régime had any support.

The Rhee régime was eventually overthrown after an upsurge of popular protest in the spring of 1960 and the liberal Chang régime which followed it saw a brief period of conciliation in relations with Japan. This, however, was short-lived, as Chang was overthrown by a miltary coup led by Pak Chung Hee in May, 1961. Initially, the Pak régime identified itself with the strong popular opposition to 'normalisation' with Japan, but, once established, Pak revealed a very different aspect. Pak had, after all, as Lieutenant Okamoto Minoru in the Japanese imperial forces, been a favourite of the Japanese during the Second World War. At his class at the Japanese military academy in Manchukuo it was he who had been chosen to give the graduation address, pledging himself to 'fall like cherry blossom in the holy war for the establishment of the Greater East Asia Co-prosperity Sphere and in defence of the ōdō rakudo (realms of righteousness)' before being chosen for the special honour of training at the Cadet Academy in Tokyo.[4] Once in power, eighteen years later, Pak was in a position to do something about his pledges as a young man.

As US aid began to dry up in the early 1960s, Pak's five year plan (1962–7) quickly ran into severe difficulties. It was an alternative source of funds and aid as well as loans, and also of technology, that Pak began to turn to Japan. In doing so, it is significant that he abandoned the long-standing Korean position of demanding *reparation* payments, i.e., payments due as of right because of the long period of colonial exploitation.

On the Japanese side, the ruling *élite* that emerged through and after the US occupation showed a remarkable continuity in thinking, even in personnel, with its pre-war antecedents. The notion of Japan's special mission as leader of Asia, and therefore of the destiny of its neighbours to be subordinated to Japan, was common to all the mainstream post-war Japanese conservative leadership. A few examples should suffice:[5]

'Ultimately, the emphasis of Japanese diplomacy should be

given to close co-operation with America. In order to do this, the Republic of Korea and Formosa will have to be closely related. If feasible, it would be nice to form the United States of Japan with the Republic of Korea and Formosa' (Ono Banboku, Vice-President of the Liberal-Democratic Party, 1958);

'Japan should penetrate into Korea, following the example of Itō Hirobumi' (the Japanese Resident-General who masterminded the annexation of Korea). (Ikeda Hayato, Japanese Prime Minister, 1962);

'Managing Formosa, annexing Korea, and dreaming of co-operation among the five races in Manchuria — if this was Japanese imperialism, it was an honourable imperialism.' (Shiina Etsusaburo, Japanese Foreign Minister, 1962);

'Some say Japan should apologise to Korea for its past government, but Japan is not without excuse. . . . Clearly Japan controlled Korea, but Japan did good. . . . It would be better if Japan had held Korea for another twenty years' (Takasugi Shinichi, Acting Chairman of the Japan-Republic of Korea Conference, January, 1965).

For a final example, one may cite ex-Premier Kishi Nobusuke in June, 1965, at a time of rapidly growing protest against the settlement with Japan and the consequent imposition of strong military controls in South Korea. Kishi's reaction to this situation was to comment that the suspension of free press, parliament and opposition in Korea made circumstances ideal to effect a settlement of long-standing issues. Contempt for democratic processes and the continuance of arrogant imperialistic thinking about Korea in Japanese ruling circles is manifest in all these cases.

Unanimity on the part of the Japanese and Korean leadership on the need for *rapprochement* was powerfully reinforced by American pressure, for the mid-1960s saw the beginning of the so-called *'katagawari'* (literally 'shift (a burden) onto another's shoulder') policies, by which Japan was called upon by a hard-pressed US to assume greater responsibility for a shared empire in North-east Asia.

The advent of 'normalisation' was greeted by widespread riots, protests and demonstrations in Japan as well as in

Korea. The opposition was based on the failure of the settlement to deal with the issues arising from Japanese liability for
the thirty-five years of colonial subjugation, and on the likelihood that a new Japanese relationship with the south would
simply facilitate a new type of Japanese imperialist penetration
and control that would *inter alia* antagonise the north and
make more difficult the eventual settlement of the question of
unification. This was especially so since in Article 3 of
the Treaty Japan endorsed the southern régime's claim to be
the sole legal government in Korea. The economic clauses of
the treaty, by which $800 million of Japanese money was to
be infused into the Korean economy in the form of Japanese
goods and services financed by grants, loans, or credit, were
attacked as a device to open the economy to Japanese capital
and aggravate existing levels of corruption. On the military
level the treaty, formally bilateral, was seen as being actually
a trilateral agreement in which the US was the unspoken
partner, as the crucial military ally of both countries. The
advantages the US derived from the strengthening of the Pak
régime as a result of the new Japanese commitment are obvious. Beginning in 1965 Pak was able to send 312,000 soldiers
to Vietnam, for whose services the United States paid $1·7
billion.[6] The Satō-Nixon Agreement of 1969, affirming that
'the security of the Republic of Korea was essential to Japan's
security' — confirmed in the summer of 1975 — is the most
precise public expression of this joint commitment to the
southern régime, and implicitly to opposing reunification of
the country.[7]

During the years 1965–75 integration and co-ordination
advanced to a high degree. The same years have often been
cited as the years of economic miracle in South Korea. The
Seoul régime has indeed succeeded in boosting exports and
GNP, but only at the cost of an enormous debt and stagnation of the domestic economy. It has followed three main
principles: exports first, dependence on foreign capital, and
low wages and rigid labour discipline, backed by the apparatus of state power.

Since 1973, in particular, there has been a tendency for
Japanese investment to move into the heavy and chemical industry sectors (from light industrial processing), but the struc-

tural dependence on Japanese capital and technology remains unchanged. Indeed, this is precisely in accord with long-term Japanese strategy for the incorporation of South Korea into a single Japanese-run economic system. This strategy has been clearly set out on a number of occasions. In October, 1965, the two sides actually published a joint report setting out their plans for an 'international vertical division of labour', and it was stipulated that Japan would sub-contract out to Korea part of its labour-intensive, export-oriented processing industry.[8] This principle was greatly extended in 1970 in the memorandum prepared by Yatsugi Kazuo for presentation to the second general meeting of the Japan-ROK Co-operation Committee.[9] It is in accordance with the Yatsugi plan that important parts of major Japanese industries such as steel, aluminium, petro-chemicals and even shipbuilding are being transferred to South Korea. These plans assume a permanent division at the 38th Parallel and a permanent patron-client relationship between Tokyo and Seoul.

The attractiveness of shifting labour or pollution-intensive industries to South Korea is obvious when one understands that the hourly wage for labour in manufacturing industry in South Korea is between one-seventh and one-eighth what it is in Japan,[10] that agitation over wages or conditions, or over pollution for that matter, is forbidden or strictly regulated, and also that sites for factory development cost around 70 cents per square foot in Seoul as against $28 in the suburbs of Tokyo.[11] In many of the major sectors of Korean industry Japanese capital is already dominant.[12]

There are, of course, plenty of Third World countries where the pattern of economic development strongly resembles that of South Korea. But there are two unique features in the Korean case: first is that this is in an extremely tense and divided country, bristling with nuclear weapons; second is that the economic dependence of Korea is concentrated to a remarkable degree on Japan, the very country whose direct colonial rule is such a fresh and bitter memory in the minds of so many of its people.

What is the measure of Japanese economic penetration and influence in South Korea today? Till about 1961 most foreign capital inflow was in the form of direct aid, particularly

American aid, but as this source began to dry up the tendency
was to concentrate heavily on loans, either government or
private. These were the essential fuel of the boom years of
1968–69.[13] Up till June, 1975, there was a net intake of $1,461
million Japanese loans.[14] However the Koreans had to an-
nounce in 1971 that no less than 85 per cent of enterprises
dependent on Japanese loans had become insolvent. The main
reasons for this were the system of rebates, bribes and com-
missions within which the loan enterprises functioned, and
the inflated initial prices at which the Japanese plant and
equipment, frequently obsolescent, was supplied to Korea.[15]
The net result, since the repayment burden had to be taken
over by the Korean treasury, was a serious worsening of the
Korean balance of payments. By May, 1973, the outstanding
foreign debt was $3·5 billion, more than 40 per cent of GNP.
By the end of 1975 it was already up to at least $6 billion, and
a high percentage of new loans was going straight to service
the old.[16]

From around 1970 there was, therefore, a shift away from
this strategy of dependence on loans in the direction of encouragement of direct foreign private investment. A series of
remarkable incentives was worked out (including total tax exemption and guaranteed freedom from strikes) and the first
special Export Processing Zone, where the Korean government provided free roads, water, harbours and so on, was set
up at Masan. In the Export Processing Zone over 90 per cent of
all investment is Japanese.[17] In South Korea as a whole between
1965 and 1976 694 Japanese 'joint ventures' were set up.
Japan's total capital involvement over these years was $2,334
million (grants, loans and credits: $1,700; direct investment:
$634 million). In terms of investment, Japan is overwhelmingly
South Korea's main supporter, accounting for 66 per cent of
the total.[18] In terms of the much greater sums involved in loans
and credits the Japanese role is less (19 per cent), although it
is still second in importance only to the US.[19]

In trade, too, the level of dependence on Japan is extremely
high. Japan is South Korea's main trading partner, and the
volume and imbalance of the trade is so great that all the
Japanese aid and investment flowing to South Korea between
1965 and 1975 amounted to less than a third of the Japanese
trade surplus for the same period. For the $2·3 billion capital

flow *to* South Korea, the $7·8 billion extracted by Japan in trade alone was a handsome return.[20] Even in the very difficult year of 1974, when Japan's overall trade figures fell seriously into the red, it was possible for it to keep up its exports, reduce imports, and thus generate a $1·2 billion surplus on trade with South Korea. The advantage was retained at the same level in 1975.[21] Although the Koreans managed to reduce their import dependence on Japan to 34 per cent, the terms were still such that 69·6 per cent of their overall trade deficit stemmed from trade with Japan.[22] It is also important to realise that over 30 per cent of the foreign trade of South Korea is handled by Japanese trading companies.[23]

The pattern here is familiar enough. It is that of control of the commanding levers of the economy passing into foreign hands and wealth being siphoned from the less developed to the more developed countries — in short, of imperialism.

The relationship which has developed, when viewed as a whole, is such that *Business Week* could speak in 1973 of progress towards 'economic hegemony';[24] the *Asahi*, also late in 1973, was warning of the consequences of the unification (*ittaika*) of the two economies;[25] and a recent analysis by a distinguished Japanese economist concluded that South Korea had become 'an overseas branch of the Japanese economy,' its export boom no more than a 'subsidiary Japanese boom.'[26] Japanese representatives even sat in on the drafting of the 3rd Five-Year Plan in 1972,[27] and in May, 1976, agreement was reached on overall Japanese involvement in the 4th Plan, from 1977, to the tune of $4 billion.[28]

However, it is not primarily or simply the economic relationship that should be stressed. The political consequences of mutual reinforcement and symbiosis between the reactionary forces of both sides who are the actual beneficiaries of the process, together with the military possibilities of the situation, deserve equal attention.

The diversion of foreign aid and investment funds into direct funding of the Pak apparatus, particularly at election time in 1967 and 1971, is now well established on the American side. Bob Dorsey, Chairman of Gulf Oil, revealed in testimony to the US Senate Multinationals Subcommittee in May of 1975 that his company had been forced to pay $4 million to Pak's party campaign funds in those years.[29] General Motors revealed separately that it had been levied $¼ million in 1972.[30] On the Japanese side there have been no startling admissions, but the overall stakes are much higher, the connections much closer, and there can be no doubt that the Korean demands are proportionately much greater. The most reputable Japanese journals have reported cases of kickbacks and bribes.[31] Indeed it seems reasonable to assume that there is no need for the payoff to be made as crudely as it was in the case of the Americans since it has been structured into the relationship.[32] The startling fact that 85 per cent of the enterprises set up with Japanese loan funds till 1971 eventually went broke has already been mentioned above. That figure speaks for itself, but there are other examples that have come to light more recently. It was revealed in the Japanese Diet in 1973, for example, that the railway cars for the Seoul subway system, which was being built as a Japanese aid project, had been supplied to the Koreans at ￥63·8 million ($237,175) each when their price in Japan was ￥35·9 million, or just a little over half that sum.[33] The Korea Aluminium Company was the subject of a Japanese Foreign Ministry study in 1972, when it was found that only one half of the $13 million Japanese investment was earmarked for construction purposes and that $6 million had simply disappeared.[34] A leading Japanese automobile manufacturer produced for ￥3 million in South Korea the same vehicle as was on sale for ￥1·7 million in Japan.[35] It is widely believed that the initial $123 million with which the prestigious Pohang steel project was financed ($73 million of them being Japanese taxpayers' funds) also contributed substantially to Pak's re-election in the closely fought contest of 1971,[36] together with the $3 million from Gulf and the ￥4·8 billion ($13·3 million) from the subway car swindle already mentioned. The examples could be multiplied.

The scale of the graft involved may perhaps best be understood from the fact that the Lockheed bribe affair, which from early 1976 shook Japanese society to the foundation, involved a total sum of about $10 million. This is literally 'peanuts' when compared with the amounts involved in Japan-South Korean corruption. If the commonly accepted figure of a 20 per cent kickback in the case of loans to South Korea is used as the basis of an estimate, that would mean that $300 million was appropriated by rightist business and political figures in Japan and Korea in the ten years 1965–1975.[37] To this would have to be added a comparable figure to cover numerous 'fiddles' in the $577 million Japanese investment figure, too. Apart from the personal enrichment for those personally connected with this business, and the burden it imposes on the working people of South Korea who ultimately have to pay for such 'aid', the political role that these vast sums play is clearly great, not only on the Korean side in helping to finance Pak's political apparatus and (in the past) win elections, but on the Japanese side as well. However, the Pak régime will certainly not allow any airing of these matters in Seoul, and because of the grave political implications in Japan, where many leading figures of the Liberal-Democratic Party, as well as the largest Japanese companies — Mitsui, Mitsubishi, and so on — are involved,[38] it may be doubted whether the corruption investigations at present under way will go to — or even near — the bottom of these matters.

As one commentator observed recently, 'To unravel the Japan-South Korea "connection" is to start pulling at the very fabric of Japanese politics.'[39] Various charts have been drawn of the connections, linking Pak personally to Mitsubishi through its president, Fujino Chujiro, still an avowed believer in the old Greater East Asia Co-prosperity Sphere, or to former Prime Minister Kishi and through Kishi to the Japanese oil interests, or through ex-Korean CIA chief Li Hu Rak to Mitsui.[40] The precise truth of these remains difficult to determine. The subject is obviously highly sensitive, and political pressures appear to have been brought to bear in at least one recent case to prevent publication by a major newspaper of a 24,000 word report in which 'personal relationships between Korean and Japanese political, government, and business leaders — including the role played by some notorious gangster leaders — are fully detailed.'[41]

The present Japanese leadership clearly sees it as being in its interest to support its co-operative protégés in Korea, and it is equally in the interest of the Pak régime to do all it can to help perpetuate the rule of its patrons in Tokyo. The best assurance of stability for the South Korean régime would indeed seem to be the consolidation of a single reactionary, even fascist, system dominating South Korea and Japan jointly.

The closeness of the Tokyo and Seoul régimes has meant little improvement in the lot of Korean residents in Japan. The pressures imposed on them as a consequence of the 1965 treaty have already been referred to above (Chapter 5). It should be understood, however, that even the boon of permanent resident status and permission to leave and re-enter the country — which is all that registration as a South Korean citizen ensures — does nothing to alleviate the disabilities Koreans living in Japan have always suffered. Whether one is registered as a northern or a southern Korean one is still automatically disqualified from being a lawyer, or a public employee of any kind, from teacher in a state university or school to municipal bus driver or guard on the national railways. The barriers of legal disability in the public sector are matched by barriers of deeply ingrained prejudice that work just as effectively to exclude Korean residents from employment in the major Japanese companies in the private sector. These Koreans, it should be remembered, are in many cases born in Japan, possibly of parents imported as slave labour to work Japanese mines or factories during the war, to whom Japanese is the first, and perhaps only language.

If there is any lesson to be learnt from Japan's past it should be that growing imperialism and exploitation of other peoples leads directly to the suppression of the freedom and rights of the Japanese people, too. Perhaps the most illuminating historical parallel for the present Japanese relationship with Korea is to be found in Taishō Japan's China relationship, characterised by 'yen diplomacy' to buy over warlords, politicians and businessmen, and to set up dummy joint ventures and try to gain exclusive control over the resources of China.[42] That policy, of course, failed, but as it gradually galvanised the Chinese people into determined nationalistic and eventually revolutionary resistance to imperialism so it led, on the Japanese part, to the attempt at a military solution — the militarism of the early Shōwa (1926–   ) period, and thence to war. It is significant today that all Korean political opinion save that of Pak and his associates is fiercely critical of the present Japanese connection. Thus in 1970 Kim Dae Jung, the opposition political leader who in 1971 almost unseated Pak as President, denounced the 'economic co-operation between Japan and Korea' as having 'aided corruption and built up the wealth of the Government party and a section of the Zaibatsu';[43] in 1974 the National Congress for the Restoration of Korean Democracy, when it functioned briefly in Seoul, was calling, among other things, for an end to foreign aid,[44] and the March, 1976, Declaration for National Democratic Salvation, issued in Seoul's Myong Dong Cathedral by a galaxy of courageous religious and political leaders, denounced the Japan-ROK treaty as having 'resulted in this country's economy becoming entirely controlled by Japan, with all its industries and the labour force becoming the victims of Japan's economic invasion.'[45]

Yet both Pak and the Japanese leadership are intent on strengthening the existing ties — Pak because his survival depends on it, and the Japanese political and business leadership because, in a sense, the movement for the restoration of democracy in South Korea threatens it as much as it does Pak. Not only would the success of that movement lead to a complete restructuring of the present economic relationship — something which in itself they would deplore but could cope with — but it would also lead to exposure of the present corrupt system and the consequences of that would be likely to dwarf those of the Lockheed revelations.

Thus it is with the present régime in Seoul that Japanese government and business has chosen to identify itself more closely than any other elsewhere in the world, while at the same time the Democratic People's Republic of Korea, the other half of a divided country, remains the only country written in the 'forbidden' column in Japanese passports. No country other than South Korea (the Republic of Korea) gets the periodic assurances that its security is regarded as indivisible from that of Japan itself. It is a régime and a state in which torture is endemic; kidnapping is justified (of students and intellectuals from Europe in 1967, and of Kim Dae Jung from Tokyo in 1973); corruption is rife and systematic; the Korean CIA has a network which one American legal scholar reckoned recently to include about 10 per cent of the overall population;[46] and in which liberal opposition leaders have either been murdered, as Chang Jun Ha appears to have been in a clumsily rigged mountaineering accident in 1975,[47] or imprisoned as Kim Dae Jung has been for advocating the restoration of democracy, and in which the country's greatest poet, Kim Chi Ha, having developed chronic tuberculosis during previous spells in prison, has again been sentenced to imprisonment for his outspokenness, this time for life. It is also a country whose people express a greater dislike for Japan than for any other country save the Soviet Union and China.[48] It is, finally, the one country in continental Asia in which US land troops still remain, and in which US tactical nuclear warheads are deployed.

If the analogy already referred to between present-day Japan-Korea relations and Taishō Japan's China relations holds any validity there is at least a considerable difference in the strength of opposition today to the continuance of present trends, although the gap between popular sentiment and ruling class opinion in Japanese political and economic circles is considerable. The consensus on the Korean issue among the latter seems as united as it was 100 years ago, and the principal world powers encourage the process of Japanese domination in Korea as actively as they did then. As in the Meiji period, Japan's future is closely intertwined with that of Korea. The last ten years in particular have seen a remarkable quickening of the process. Yet the outcome, whatever the short-term success of Japanese economic diplomacy in sustaining a viable and compliant anti-communist régime in Seoul, seems likely in the longer run to be either economic insolvency and chaos, as the Institute for International Policy in Washington predicts,[49] or open revolt, bred of conditions of intolerable oppression and tyranny, as authorities like Harvard's E. O. Reischauer now think possible.[50] There is, however, also a less cataclysmic possibility — that the Korean democratic movement may succeed in peacefully casting off the dual incubus of foreign imperialism and domestic tyranny, but this would have to be done in the teeth of many years of Japanese and American planning and commitment to the contrary.

Reversing the Satō-Nixon and Miki-Ford proclamations on

the need to preserve the Seoul régime in the interests of Japanese security, it is clear, rather, that it is Japanese complicity with and support for the Seoul régime which blocks democratisation in South Korea, which makes ever more difficult the reunification which all Koreans desire and deserve, and which is therefore itself a major cause of instability on the Korean peninsula.

NOTES

1. Jon Halliday and Gavan McCormack, *Japanese Imperialism Today*, Penguin and Monthly Review, 1973.
2. See Herbert P. Bix, "Regional Integration: Japan and South Korea in America's Asian Policy," in Frank Baldwin, ed., *Without Parallel: The American-Korean Relationship Since 1945* (New York, Pantheon, 1974), pp.196-8; James Auer; *The Postwar Rearmament of the Japanese Maritime Forces, 1945-71* (New York; Praeger, 1973), pp.63-77.
3. Joungwon A. Kim, *Divided Korea: The Politics of Development, 1945-1972* (Harvard, 1975), p.242.
4. Chung Kyungmo, "Aru minzokushugisha no shōgai" (Life of a certain nationalist), *Sekai*, December, 1975, p.64. Like Marshal Ky of recent Vietnam fame, Pak, too, is an admirer of history's strong men — Bismarck, Hitler, De Gaulle. (According to the Korean commentator, T.K., *Sekai*, May, 1975.)
5. Kwan Bong Kim, *The Korea-Japan Treaty Crisis and the Instability of the Korean Political System* (New York, Washington and London, 1971), p.49; Nakagawa Nobuo, "Nikkan jōjaku taisei jū nen" (10 Years of the Japan-ROK Treaty System), *Sekai*, November, 1975, pp.76-7.
6. The total number of troops at any one time was 47,872, but because of rotation of troops, leave, etc., the overall total was 'approximately 312,000.' Baldwin, *Without Parallel*, p.29. The precise payment total is difficult to compute. The authoritative Washington-based Institute for International Policy's *International Policy Report*, Vol.1, no.1, December, 1975, p.8, gives $1·7 billion for 'Payments to Korean troops in Vietnam war,' but, as Baldwin points out, under the Brown Memorandum of March 4, 1966, the US was also paying vast sums in 'new military equipment, assistance to South Korean businessmen in Vietnam, and employment of South Korean civilian workers in Vietnam.' He estimates the overall total to be about $10 billion (*Without Parallel*, p.30). See also the more recent article by Baldwin: "America's Rented Troops: South Koreans in Vietnam," *Bulletin of Concerned Asian Scholars*, October-December, 1975, pp.33-40.
7. For the 1969 text see Halliday and McCormack, *op. cit.*, pp.241-4. On the reaffirmation, see Nakagawa, *Sekai*, November, 1975, p.101.
8. Nakagawa, *ibid.*, p.86.
9. Halliday and McCormack, pp.155-6; Bix, p.216.
10. Sumiya Mikio, "Kankoku no rōdō ichiba" (The labour market in South Korea), *Ajia Keizai*, Vol.16, no.4 (1975), p.48. The gap between

Korean and Japanese wages has widened considerably since the 1960s, and even since 1970.

11. *Newsweek*, November 19, 1973.
12. Halliday and McCormack, p.153; *Asahi shinbun*, November 4, 1973.
13. "Masan yūshutsu jiyū chiiki no jittai chōsa" (Investigation into the actual condition of the Masan Free Export Zone), *Sekai*, May, 1975, p.26.
14. *Dong-A Ilbo*, September 13, 1975, cited in Nakagawa Nobuo, "Nikkan o tsunagu kuroi kōzu" (the black plots linking Japan and South Korea), *Ekonomisuto*, March 23, 1976, p.41.
15. "Masan yūshutsu . . .," *Sekai*, May, 1975, p.27; Joungwon Kim, p.278.
16. *Asahi shinbun*, September 20, 1973; for 1975 figures see above.
17 "Masan yūshutsu . . .," *Sekai*, May, 1975, p.31.
18. "Zadankai," *Keizai*, August, 1977, pp.37, 45.
19. *Ibid.*; see also table in Chapter 6 above.
20. Between 1966 and 1976 Japan exported $14·8 billion worth of goods to South Korea, importing $7 billion worth in return. (*Korea Review*, Vol. 1, no.1, May, 1977, p.23; see also *FEER*, November 28, 1975.)
21. Sumiya, *Sekai*, November, 1975, p.136; for a table of Japan-ROK imports and exports between 1972 and 1974 see Sumiya, "Oitsumerareta Kankoku keizai" (Korean economy in a corner), *Sekai*, September, 1975, p.41. For 1975 see *FEER*, April 23, 1976, p.129.
22. *Business Asia*, March 19, 1976, p.91.
23. *Korea Newsletter*, no.35 (December 15-January 1, 1976).
24. *Business Week*, cited in *Japan Times*, September 1, 1973.
25. *Asahi Shinbun*, November 4, 1973.
26. Sumiya, *Sekai*, September, 1975, p.42; November, 1975, p.132.
27. Nakazawa Osamu, "Japan-Korea Mutual Corruption Sphere," *Ampo*, Vol.7, no.1 (Winter, 1975), p.46.
28. "Dokyumento," *Sekai*, August, 1976, p.262.
29. $1 million in 1966 and $3 million in 1971. *Newsweek*, May 26, 1975, p.39.
30. "Dokyumento," *Sekai*, October 1975, p.210.
31. See on this Joungwon Kim, p.264.
32. *Asahi shinbun*, May 22, 1975.
33. Bernard Wideman, *FEER*, November 12, 1973.
34. *Ibid.*
35. Halliday and McCormack, p.150.
36. *Ibid*; Nakazawa, p.47.
37. Nakagawa, *Ekonomisuto*, March 23, 1976, pp.41-2.
38. Kwan Bong Kim (*op. cit.*, p.88) notes that Japan's 'Korea lobby' in-cludes 'the fifteen top capitalists in Japan, who finance the key fac-tional bosses in the Liberal-Democratic Party.'
39. Nakazawa, p.47.
40. Kitazawa Yoko, "Kidnapped: the Kim Case and the 'Korean Con-nection'," *Ampo*, no.18 (Autumn, 1973), p.20; Muto Ichiyo and Mark Selden, "Neo-colonialism and Development in Asia," *Ampo*, Vol.6, nos.3-4 (Summer-Autumn, 1974), pp.52-3.
The well informed *Far Eastern Economic Review* correspondent, Koji Nakamura, reported in 1974 (August 30th issue) that 'Political leaders

who are believed to have "strong contact" with South Korean leaders include: Prime Minister Tanaka, former Prime Ministers Nobusuke Kishi and Eisaku Sato, former Finance Minister Takeo Fukuda, Finance Minister Masayoshi Ohira and International Trade and Industry Minister Yasuhiro Nakasone.'

41. Koji Nakamura, *FEER*, October 3, 1975.
42. Chung Kyungmo, *Japan Interpreter*, Vol.9, no.2 (Summer-Autumn, 1974) passim.
43. Cited in Halliday and McCormack, p.163.
44. *Sekai*, March, 1975, p.204.
45. *Ampo*, Vol.8, no.1, March 1976, p.40.
46. Richard Falk, Professor of International Law and Politics at Princeton, "Kankoku no genjō ni kawaru mono" (An alternative for the present Korean situation), *Sekai*, November, 1975, p.41. Other estimates of the number of KCIA operatives range between 20,000 and 40,000. See *Asahi Shinbun*, August 17, 1973.
47. Chang Jun Ha was one of the outstanding liberal opponents of the Pak régime, as he had much earlier been one of the most committed opponents of the Japanese imperialist régime in which Pak had served. (For a chronological contrast of the two lives, see Chung Kyungmo, *Sekai*, December, 1975, pp.61–71.) In the early 1960s Chang had founded the influential journal *Sa Sang Kye* (World of Ideas). More recently he had been organiser of the 'Petition of a million signatures' movement, which had aimed to force Pak to return to the pre-1972 constitution, but which had been suppressed under Pak's martial law measures when it began to snowball. On the very suspicious circumstances of his death: T.K., "Shizuka na sensen" (Quiet front), *Sekai*, November, 1975, p.143. Also Roy Whang, *FEER*, September 12, 1975.
48. "Dokyumento . . .," *Sekai*, October, 1975, p.216.
49. *International Policy Report*, p.1.
50. *International Herald Tribune*, August 17, 1974.

Chapter 9

Britain, Europe and Korea

Gavan McCormack

'Really there isn't a great deal of difference between Seoul and Birmingham. Business practises are very similar.' George Turnbull, Managing Director of Hyundai Motor Corporation, formerly of British Leyland. (*Sunday Times*, October 27, 1974)

Britain played a direct role in the two major interventions that lie at the root of the Korean tragedy. First, Britain provided the political alliance and cover of a then world power for the definitive Japanese seizure of Korea in 1910. In 1902 Britain signed the Anglo-Japanese Alliance with Tokyo, Japan's first formal alliance with a major Western power. In effect, this alliance called for mutual support for each other's imperialism. In 1905 Japan signed a less prominent agreement with the United States, the Taft-Katsura agreement, under which the US supported Japanese colonialism in Korea in return for Tokyo's commitment to respect US rule in the Philippines. It was these two agreements which allowed Japan to enslave Korea.

Second, when Japan surrendered in 1945 and Korea was divided, on US initiative, Whitehall followed the US lead on all key issues concerning Korea — from the original division in 1945, through the imposition of the Syngman Rhee régime and the suppression of the democratic opposition, to the war which followed. In 1950, when full-scale war broke out, the Labour government swiftly despatched troops to support the US. This contingent played its part in causing the deaths of some three million Koreans and Chinese and reducing the Korean peninsula to rubble. 670 British died, with another 2,690 missing or wounded.[1]

Part of the lack of concern in Britain can be attributed to lack of information. René Cutforth has described how two very strong pieces he sent to the BBC about napalm (used only by the US/UN side) were suppressed — part of a virtually blanket suppression of unwelcome information by the British media.[2] Pursued for a sufficient length of time, this censorship created the climate within which the information, when finally published, had almost no effect. Yet, lack of information was not the whole reason. Cutforth also records that, even when the evidence was available, the British troops, unlike the Americans, remained indifferent to the violence and oppression of the régime on whose behalf they were fighting; the corollary of this, of course, was indifference to the sufferings of the Korean people which the British, by their presence were perpetuating.

Since the Armistice in 1953, Britain has continued faithfully to follow the US line, maintaining that the Seoul administration is the 'sole legitimate government in the Korean peninsula' and acting as one of the most powerful members of the Seoul lobby at the UN. This support, moreover, covers diplomatic, military and economic spheres, and appears to be both enthusiastic and unconditional.

Since the Korean War, most of the 16 countries that fought under the UN flag have withdrawn. By the time of the clash at Panmunjom in August, 1976, all that was left of the UN force in Korea, apart from the Americans and the Koreans themselves, was a handful of Filipinos and a British 'Honour Guard'. This support, though flimsy, is nevertheless highly valued by the US and Seoul régimes as symbolic of continuing international commitment. It was not for nothing that the US admiral who negotiated with the North over the Panmunjom affair in August, 1976, presented himself at the Conference room 'flanked by his British, Filipino and Korean colleagues,'[3] and in the case of a new war it is reasonable to assume that symbolic support would give way to something more substantial.

That the Labour government is satisfied with the present situation seems clear. In April, 1976, the British Defence Minister, Roy Mason, announced during a visit to Seoul that Britain was to co-operate in the 5th ROK defence build-up plans, from which it can be assumed that British weapons and weapon technology are to be made available to the Pak régime.[4] So far, not a word of protest has been uttered in Britain about this pledge of military support for a dictatorship as brutal and as corrupt as any. Sensitivity in the Labour government and movement to arms deals with régimes in South Africa and Chile has yet to be matched by recognition of the implication of British intervention in Korea.

The Mason visit is consistent with the attitude Britain has taken in the UN on the Korean issue. Britain is one of the staunchest members of the so-called 'Core Group' of Seoul supporters, made up of itself, the US, Japan, Canada, Belgium, Holland, West Germany, New Zealand and Costa Rica. As the *Far Eastern Economic Review* described this group in mid-1976: 'Their concern is two-fold: to persuade the South Koreans to continue fighting in the UN against growing pressure in support of North Korea and to drum up fresh support from the Third World.'[5]

The British military presence and government commitment might perhaps be defended on the grounds that they enable Britain to exercise some restraint on the Seoul régime, but the record quickly disposes of such sanguine thoughts. Two examples should be sufficient to demonstrate this.

In 1967 the South Korean CIA kidnapped or inveigled back to Seoul under false pretences about 150 students, artists and intellectuals who were studying or resident in Europe and North America.[6] The promotion and manipulation of war scares and spy sensations, punctuated by trials and executions, play an important part in generating the sense of crisis and fear on which the régime depends. Many of this group of 150 were soon released, but 17 were held, tortured, tried, and sentenced to death or long imprisonment in secret trials in Seoul. The governments of West Germany and France, on whose territories the main KCIA operations had taken place, protested vigorously (the West German government threatening to sever all contact and cease all aid). The Seoul government therefore commuted the death sentences and eventually released all these detainees — the last, though, not till 1971.

In 1969, however, a second batch of students was brought back to Seoul and placed under arrest. The main detainee was a Cambridge university student, Pak No Su, known in England as Francis Park. He was induced to return to Seoul by the offer of a government job, arrested and charged with being a northern spy and the alleged mastermind of North-South contacts via Berlin. The evidence against him was thin. A confession was wrung from Pak himself under torture, and witnesses against him in some cases had to have all their toenails extracted before being persuaded to testify. The British Embassy in Seoul and the British government ignored the fact that Pak had been abducted from Britain and took no interest in the affair. The CIA Director in Seoul boasted that he anticipated 'no worries over diplomatic issues' this time, and Pak was hanged in July, 1970. Before he died, 4,000 Cambridge students signed a petition on his behalf, and a few principled individuals made energetic efforts to save him.[7] He could be killed by the régime with impunity for two main reasons: the British government, unlike the French and West German, simply did not care, and the British people were not mobilised in time to take any effective protest action.

The second case was in 1974, at a time when world opinion had been aroused by the passing of sentence of death on the country's leading poet, Kim Chi Ha. Such sentiment reached even to the level of diplomats from many European countries serving in Seoul. The British, however, maintained an attitude of aloof unconcern. A spokesman at the Embassy in Seoul commented: 'We're a commercial embassy, actually. South Korea is a land of golden opportunities for the British businessman.'[8] There is a certain logic in this position, since repression and exploitation are the soil within which South Korea's 'golden opportunities' are nurtured. Yet it is a régime Britain helped to create, fought to defend and to which London has given unwavering diplomatic and military support; this attitude of studied unconcern is clearly a positive encouragement, and some responsibility for the terror that operates in South Korea must attach to it.

Despite the possibilities of commercial success which British representatives on the spot rate so highly, Britain's economic involvement with the Seoul régime is considerably less than that of the United States or Japan. The British (and European) connections with Seoul should not be minimised, however, particularly since resentment in South Korea of the relationship of dual dependency towards the United States and Japan, who between them control the heights and direction of the economy, has become so strong that a diversification of support is politically of increasing importance.

To the end of 1975 European money made up 10·6 per cent of the overall foreign investment total, although much of it (6·2 per cent) was from Holland and presumably represented Shell Oil interests.[9] It is in terms of loans, however, that the European role is very great and has been increasing dramatically in recent years. 21·5 per cent of all loans to South Korea to the end of 1975 came from Europe, the main shares being Britain, 6·2 per cent, France, 5·9 per cent, and West Germany, 5·1 per cent.[10] That figure was up to 28·2 per cent in the first six months of 1976,[11] and leapt again to 40 per cent of the $991 million total induced in government and foreign loans in the first five months of 1977.[12] It is clear that the European rôle in this field of financial support for Seoul has become a key one, and the analysis in Chapter 4 above demonstrates just how important the continued infusion of huge sums of foreign loan money is.

Both government and private institution in Europe are involved. Of the $10 billion in foreign loans needed for the 1977–81 plan, $900 million, or 9 per cent, is expected to come from France alone.[13] When French Finance Minister Barre visited Seoul in July, 1976, shortly before becoming Premier, he indicated that full French official cooperation could be expected. South Korea's first merchant bank, the Korea Merchant Banking Corporation, set up in 1976, is half owned by Lazard's of the UK, who put up $2·5 million of the US $5 million capital.[14] Less than a year after the foundation of this institution it was reported to be 'taking the lead in international fund raising for Korea', and about to be followed into the field by a joint venture involving Hill Samuel.[15] Two other British banks, Barclay's and Lloyd's, were reported in mid 1977 to be about to set up branches in Seoul.[16] Seoul is therefore having considerable success in diversifying sources of financial support, and, no less significantly, in creating a broader spread of commitment to maintenance of the *status quo* in the peninsula. Furthermore, the European financial involvement with Seoul must be seen in context together with the general European support which Seoul has always enjoyed in the United Nations and the general reluctance in Western Europe to develop any substantial links with the Democratic People's Republic in the northern half of the country.

One of the most important British contributions has been in the establishment of a motor car industry, however extraordinary it may seem that British finance and industry should enthusiastically promote the development of a car which is specifically designed not for Korean markets — the Korean masses are certainly not prospective customers — but for the overseas market, in which Britain figures largely.[17] Barclay's Bank has been heavily involved in the financing of this operation. £20 million credit was made available by Barclay's in September, 1974, to Hyundai Motor Co, with full blessings from the UK government which attached its official guarantee to the transaction through the Export Credits Guarantee Department of the Board of Trade. Barclay's has continued to be the main financial backer of the £100 million integrated plant which has been set up at Ulsan; much of the plant equipment was bought from Britain, from British Leyland in particular; and a team of technical experts was despatched from Leyland to help the project get started. One of them, George Turnbull, became General Manager of the new company, and has promised that the company's jauntily named passenger vehicle, the 'Pony', will hit British markets in 1977. This Barclay's/ Leyland/Hyundai venture has the built-in advantages of South Korea's police state labour controls, very low wages, and the high technical proficiency of Korean workers; plus the backing of the British state. The labour component in the cost of production of the 'Pony' is only 10 per cent, about half the European figure.[18] Similar backing from the big UK banks and the British government has also been given to another important competitive industry — steel. These cases represent important political support for the Seoul régime; they also indicate the new ways in which capital moves to seek profit; playing off the low-wage periphery against the

working class of its own country, even at the expense of de-
pressing its 'national' economy.

The extremely important nuclear power sector of the South
Korean economy is also receiving full support. The second
nuclear power plant of the Korean Electric Company at Kori
near Pusan is being financed through a record British government loan of $116 million, supplementing $290 million from
the US EXIM Bank, the remaining $133 million coming from
a group of international banks in which the British giants
Lloyd's, Midland and the commercial banking firm of Lazard's
are tied with leading US and French banks.[19] The plant is to
be constructed by America's Westinghouse in conjunction with
the British General Electric Company.[20]

British business has also been prominent in the latest 'international' scheme to prop up the Seoul régime: the utilisation
of South Korean workers in the Middle East, which is also a
major means for recycling oil money and lessening Seoul's
debt.[21]

As far as trade is concerned, the British market is proving
increasingly important to South Korea, both in absolute
terms, and in view of the fact that the balance of trade has
lately shifted heavily in South Korea's favour, as can be seen
from the following table:[22]

UK imports from South Korea (in £ million)

1969	1970	1971	1972	1973	1975	1976
4·0	6·2	5·6	10·1	27·0	74·5	110·0

UK exports to South Korea

1969	1970	1971	1972	1973	1975	1976
12·0	11·3	22·2	25·1	21·4	52·6	65·5

Britain's imports include both goods from the Export Processing Zones like Masan, particularly electronics equipment,
hi-fi sets and so on, which are only technically Korean, being
assembled from imported Japanese components in Japanese
factories, and clothing, produced under the appalling conditions already described.[23] In whatever sector, the workers
involved are denied the most elementary human rights.

Overall, the pattern of increasing commercial contacts seems to represent a commitment in British government and business circles to reinforce existing diplomatic support and to help the Seoul régime ride out its crisis of indebtedness. It was in response to a plea by the South Korean Deputy Foreign Minister, Tae Wan Son, in March, 1974, that the Korea British Business Promotion Committee was set up with representatives on both sides from the highest levels of government and business.[24] In May, 1976, after talks between British Trade Secretary, Edmund Dell, and the South Korean Deputy Premier and Economic Planning Board Minister, Nam Tok-u (Nam Duck Woo), it was announced in London that Britain had promised to increase its capital co-operation with South Korea in power generation including nuclear power, the iron and steel industry, and the machinery and chemical industries.[25] Britain, in other words, will do all it can to help.

The Seoul régime has employed the services of a parliamentary, business and publicist lobby in Britain which has enjoyed considerable success in concealing from the British public the nature and implications of the connections between the two countries and in whitewashing the repression that is now endemic in South Korea. The British press, with few exceptions, is silent about what is happening in South Korea. In British universities there is only one specialist in Korean.[26] In parliament there is a Seoul lobby which comprises not only well-known Tories but also Labour members, some enjoying strong trade union backing.[27] There is an Anglo-Korean Society, which publishes selective summaries of Korean news. There are also well-funded organisations which promote the image of the DPRK as an international pariah.[28] And, on a (presumably) private level, there are individuals like Sir Robert Thompson, Britain's leading authority on counter-guerrilla warfare, who, despite his close association with US failures in Indo-China, has been consulted by Pak Chung Hee, and has given his endorsement to Pak's military strategy based on prosecution of a 'short, violent war' against the North.[29]

There has also been occasional support for the victims of Pak's Emergency Decrees and sweeping 'Anti-Communist' legislation. And there have been minuscule groups of British supporters of the DPRK. What there has not been is an organised popular movement of support for, and solidarity with, the people of Korea.

Thus the kind of contacts which exist between Britain and Korea, at government, commercial and private levels, serve to reinforce the machinery of repression and exploitation by the Pak régime, and by multi-national corporations and banks. Britain maintains a token military presence at Panmunjom and provides arms and weapons technology to the Pak régime; it continues to refuse recognition to the DPRK, and is an active member of the South Korea lobby in the United Nations. In all these ways Whitehall plays an important role in preventing a Korean solution to the Korean problem.

NOTES

1. *The Times*, August 12, 1974.
2. *The Listener*, November 11, 1969, p.343. In his book, *Korean Reporter* (London, 1952, p.104) Cutforth records an episode which throws a fascinating light on the class issues involved in the war. On one occasion the Chinese attacked a British tank unit and went only for the officers, refusing to kill the British rank-and-file troops, even in the heat of battle.
3. *Time*, September 6, 1976.
4. BBC, *Summary of World Broadcasts (SWB)*, April 23, 1976. The *Rodong Sinmun* (Pyongyang) attacked the visit as 'an unpardonable criminal act, obstructing the independent and peaceful reunification of our country and increasing the danger of war' (*SWB*, April 27, 1976).
5. Russell Spurr, *Far Eastern Economic Review (FEER)*, June 4, 1974, p.12.
6. *Ronin*, Vol.1, no.4–5 (August, 1972), pp.7–8, quotes extensively from a 1969 report issued in Geneva by the International Commission of Jurists in relation to this case. One of those kidnapped, Professor Yun I-Sang, a distinguished composer, reported in detail on the episode in a speech to the Emergency International Conference on Korea, Tokyo, August, 1976, and to the Conference for a New Direction in US-Korea Policy in New York in April, 1977.
7. *Ronin*, cit., pp.9–10. Lord Caradon, former British Ambassador to the United Nations, made representations in Seoul on Pak's behalf on several occasions. On the torture to Pak himself, see also Robert Whymant, *Guardian*, January 4, 1973.

8. Robert Whymant, *Guardian*, August 27, 1974.
9. Kim Fa Hyo, "Minami Chōsen ni okeru 'Keizai kindaika ron' hihan," *Chōsen Shiryō*, August, 1977, p.35, table 3.
10. *Ibid*.
11. *SWB*, July 21, 1976. The US and Japan accounted for 12·2 and 16·7 per cent respectively.
12. Yamakawa Akio, "The Harsher Side of the 'Remarkably Developing' South Korean Economy," *New Asia News*, November 4, 1977.
13. *SWB*, May 26, 1976.
14. *Ibid*. This merchant bank project was strongly criticised by the main South Korean opposition party, the New Democratic Party (NPD) (*Businss Asia*, March 5, 1976).
15. *Financial Times*, January 24, 1977.
16. *Asia Research Bulletin*, May 31, 1977.
17. On British involvement in this operation: Kim Sam-o, *FEER*, September 5, 1975; Robert Whymant, *Guardian*, November 3, 1975; *Korean Economy: Development, Industry, Trade*, published by the Permanent Mission to the ROK to the European Communities (Brussels), no.1, 1975, p.58.
18. *FEER*, August 27, 1976, p.81.
19. *Korea Herald*, January 19, 1977.
20. *Financial Times*, November 18, 1976.
21. *The Times*, September 23 and 24, 1976. Sir William Halcrow & Partners are engineering consultants on the biggest Korean operation in the Middle East, at Jubail in Saudi Arabia.
22. Figures to 1973 from *Korean Economy: Development, Industry, Trade*, op. cit., p.59.
    1975 and 1976 figures from *Financial Times*, March 17, 1976, and January 24, 1977.
23. In the first quarter of 1976 South Korea exported 156,000 suits to Britain at a price of £8.50 each, about half the cost of a comparable British suit (*Guardian*, July 13, 1976). See p.68, n.24.
24. ROK Mission (Brussels), *Korean Economy*, cit., p.59.
25. *SWB*, May 26, 1976.
26. W. E. Skillend of the School of Oriental and African Studies, London University, is a contributing editor of the Seoul-based *Korea Journal*, joint editor of *News in Korea*, published by the Anglo-Korean Society, and principal promoter of a European Association of Korean Studies. This Association, heavily subsidised by funds from Seoul, met in London at the end of March, 1977. (See Martin Walker, "Korean Studies Start a Row," *Guardian*, March 30, 1977).
    For interesting light on Korea studies and those involved in them in North America, see Sugwon Kang, "President Pak and His Learned Friends: Some Observations on Contemporary Korean Statecraft," *Bulletin of Concerned Asian Scholars*, October-December 1975.
27. The Chairman of the Anglo-Korean Parliamentary Group is Albert Roberts, Labour MP for Normanton, sponsored by the NUM (National Union of Mineworkers). In addition there is a British-North Korean Parliamentary Group whose Chairman (in 1976) is James Lamond with William Wilson as Secretary.
28. See, for example, David Rees, *North Korea as a Subversive Centre*,

published by the Institute for the Study of Conflict. On the Institute, see Chris Mullin's enlightening report in the *Guardian*, July 16, 1976.

29. During a 20-day visit to South Korea in early 1976 (*FEER*, March 26, 1976, p.25).

Chapter 10

Korea and the Middle East

Nigel Disney

Capitalism has always implied the movement and migration of labour, beginning with the migration from countryside to town. Labour migration has also been international: Chinese labour was imported into the US and Latin America in the nineteenth century and into South Africa in the early part of this century; there have been massive imports of labour into Europe from North Africa, the Caribbean, India and Pakistan since World War II; imported Mexican labour (legal and illegal) is widespread in the southern states of the US; the development of capitalism in the US, Canada, Australia, New Zealand and South Africa could not have taken place without large-scale emigration from Europe. Now, in step with the global thrust of the multi-nationals, an increasingly important element in the export/import of labour involves transfers *between* Third World countries. This is particularly so in the case of the Middle East oil-producing states.[1] These states are importing workers from both non-oil producing Arab states and from countries in Asia; there are now over 30,000 South Korean workers in the Middle East.

The phenomenal rise in the incomes of the oil-producing states that followed the hike in oil prices subsequent to the 1973 Arab-Israeli War means that these Arab states now have sufficient funds to embark on ambitious development programmes. Saudi Arabia, for example, is allocating $142 billion to its Five Year Plan. Large sums are being spent on the

This is a revised version of an article that first appeared in *MERIP Reports*, no. 61 (October, 1977). *MERIP Reports* is published by the Middle East Research and Information Project, P.O. Box 3122, Washington, D.C., 20010.

construction of roads, harbours, oil-refining projects, steel works, etc. What many of the oil-producing states lack is not money but labour power, both skilled and unskilled. Most of the skilled and managerial personnel comes from Western countries; the unskilled labour comes mainly from other Arab and Third World countries.

In recent years South Korea has become the most important source of Middle East labour. Its trade with the Middle East has expanded dramatically since the 1973 war. In 1977 South Korea expects its exports to the Middle East, in the form of numerous construction contracts, to pay for its $1·7 billion oil bill. The use of South Korean labour is mutually beneficial for the rulers of both the Middle East oil producing states and South Korea. For the rulers of the Middle East oil states it is one way of blocking the emergence of an indigenous working class which could pose a threat to their rule. For South Korea, it is a source of badly needed foreign exchange earnings. It also has a political function. South Korea hopes to find allies in the Middle East among the reactionary oil-producing states for its repressive policies.[2]

South Korean Trade with the Middle East

In 1973 South Korea's exports to the Middle East were $45 million. In 1976 they had risen to $900 million. The South Korean government whose companies won $2·4 billion construction contracts in 1976, expects earnings from exports to the Middle East to rise to $1·7 billion in 1977.[3] Saudi Arabia, where most South Korean construction is concentrated, is now South Korea's fourth most important overseas market.[4] The Middle East has also become a source of loans for the South Korean economy. In 1976 the Korea Development Bank raised $24 million through a bond issue in Kuwait.[5] Recently the first joint Arab-South Korean bank opened in Seoul, the Kuwait-Korea Banking Corporation.[6]

Much of the increase in exports and income from the Middle East is a result of South Korea's success in gaining a large share of construction contracts. In 1966 South Korea won a mere $11 million in such contracts,[7] but between 1973 and March 31, 1977, the total had increased to $4·1 billion. The government is reportedly hoping for another $5 billion worth of contracts in 1977,[8] and the Ministry of Construction has targeted an income of $680 million from Middle East construction in 1979;[9] 90 per cent of all overseas construction by South Korean firms is now in the Middle East.[10]

'We concentrate on oil-producing countries because wealthy men always have a project,' said Construction Minister Kim Jae Kyu. A South Korean construction executive agreed: 'No one else in the world has as much money to spend on industrialisation as the Gulf states. And no one else is burdened with such a lazy labour force. If these countries had to depend on their own workers, they'd never get anything done.'[11] The absence of an indigenous proletariat is doubly advantageous for South Korean companies and the South Korean government. They can bring their own labour from South Korea to the Middle East, which gives them a competitive edge over contractors from high-wage countries such as the US, Great Britain and Japan. It also increases their foreign exchange earnings, since 80 per cent of the workers' pay is remitted to South Korea. Thus for South Korea, projects in the Middle East are far more attractive than in other parts of the world, such as South-east Asia, where there is plenty of cheap local labour.

The absence of an indigenous industry in the oil-producing states means that as much as 85 per cent of the material for a construction project is imported from South Korea. 'We make the steel in our own plant, we put it in our own barge, which was made at our own shipyard. Our own sailors take it to our own construction crews overseas, where we sell the barge as part of a new dock facility,' was how a Hyundai executive described the process.[12]

Hyundai is the major South Korean contractor in the Middle East, with 6 major projects worth $1·912 billion in Saudi Arabia alone, including building the $944 million port of Jubail.[13] It has also won a $180 million contract to expand the naval base there, as well as contracts in Kuwait and Bahrain. It hopes to make a profit of at least 5 per cent of the gross value of the work, in addition to the profits to be made by the various sections of the Hyundai group that will supply materials for the projects.[14]

The South Korean government has played an active rôle in

promoting expansion into the Middle East. The Korea Trade Promotion Corporation, a government agency established in 1962 to promote exports, has eight centres in the Middle East and plans to establish another five in the Gulf. In November, 1975, Pak Chung Hee founded the Korea Foundation for Middle East Studies (KFMES). KFMES has 15 professional staff members and 15 economists from Seoul's leading banks drafted under government orders. Its task is to advise firms on trade opportunities in the Middle East, to run orientation schemes for personnel assigned to the area, and to research trade opportunities.

The South Korean government has also formed the Korean Overseas Construction Corporation, which brings together 28 companies involved in construction in the Middle East. KOCC gives tips on new projects in the area and advice about bidding techniques. The South Korean government also gives substantial financial incentives to overseas contractors: they are eligible for low interest loans, a 50 per cent corporate tax exemption and a five-year tax holiday on exported construction materials. The government steps in if firms fail to meet deadlines, and helps break through the frequent log-jams at Middle East ports.[15]

The Workers

'Our workers are our best selling point. They're tough, they work hard and they never complain.'[16] There is a mythology growing up about the diligence of South Koreans in the Middle East. According to an apocryphal story, King Feisal of Saudi Arabia (or King Khalid, depending on the version) was driving home one night and passed a group of workers labouring under floodlights to complete a project on time. He ordered his car stopped so he could find out who they were; he is then supposed to have issued instructions 'to give more work to the Koreans'.[17]

However, the Saudis were less than pleased with the behaviour of South Korean workers at Jubail when in March, 1977, several thousand of them rioted, decisively shattering the myth of their total passivity.[18] According to one account, the riot 'lasted two and a half days and left parts of the port construction site seriously damaged'.[19] Although the immediate causes of the riot were not reported, low wages and long hours of work were the underlying factors. The Saudis were furious, and threatened to bar Hyundai from any future contracts. The Korean government was alarmed: government officials and Hyundai representatives scurried to Saudi Arabia and managed to placate the Saudis. The Korean government told companies to increase wages and improve leisure facilities. Since the riot, South Korean firms have landed more contracts in Saudi Arabia, so the Saudis have evidently been placated by Korean government assurances that there will be no future trouble.

The reality of the 'diligence' of the Korean workers is very much the product of a semi-militarised labour force. In early 1976 the South Korean government converted several military bases in South Korea into training centres for construction workers financed jointly by the South Korean government and the construction companies. The centres can turn out skilled welders, truck drivers and heavy equipment operators in three months. Much of the recruiting for these centres is done by the government, which offers soldiers an early discharge if they sign up for the Middle East.

Once they get to the Middle East, these ex-soldiers will find life little different from that in the army. They are housed in isolated compounds built by the construction firms, where they are kept supplied with Korean food, tapes of Korean TV shows and cassettes of Korean music. They are isolated from other workers, both from the indigenous population and from other countries, and from any danger of political 'infection'. At one stage, the Korean workers marched to the job sites in military formation, wearing their job uniforms. 'For a while, the Arabs were crabbing to us that the South Koreans were a bunch of automated soldiers, who wore uniforms everywhere and marched in formations of 30. So, as tactfully as we could, we passed on the complaint to the South Koreans,' said a Western diplomat. Now the Koreans do not march to work, and wear their work uniforms on the site.[20]

Estimates of the number of South Korean workers in the Middle East vary from 20,000 to 34,000;[21] most of these are in Saudi Arabia (estimates range from 16,000 to 25,000).[22] 1,600 workers are in Bahrain, building the Arab Shipbuilding and

Repair Yard.[23] Although most South Koreans in the Middle East are engaged on construction projects, there are also some doctors and nurses. Two hundred doctors and nurses have been despatched to Kuwait, despite the fact that typhoid and encephalitis still exist in South Korea. The number of workers is expected to increase: Iranian and Saudi development plans both rely on the increasing use of foreign labour. The Gulf states and Jordan are planning to import as many as 15,000 stevedores who have previously worked with the US Marines.[24]

Korean Air Lines is now running a service between Seoul and Bahrain three times a week, with every flight fully booked; workers headed for Saudi Arabia are then shuttled by ferry from Bahrain. There are also weekly flights from Seoul to the Saudi cities of Dahran, Jeddah and Riyadh.[25]

The average wage for the Korean worker is $300 a month for unskilled workers and $500 for skilled workers.[26] The hours are long: in Bahrain 10 hours a day, with just 2 days off a month.[27] They sign one year contracts, with the possibility of a year's extension. The workers also receive food, accommodation and transportation. 20 per cent of their wages are paid in local currency and the rest in *won* in South Korea. Although more than the average wage in Korea, by Middle East standards for foreign workers the wages are low. *Korea Business* summed up the situation aptly: 'Koreans working abroad have been displaying fine professional skills and a firm dedication to their duties, even if they have not been paid at satisfactory rates.'[28]

Conclusion

The export of South Korean labour power to the Middle East must be seen within a wider context than South Korea's need for foreign exchange and the Middle East's need for cheap labour. It is also another way for the US and Japan to recycle the oil crisis: as these two countries buy oil from the Middle East, Korea uses its earnings from construction projects to pay off its debts to them. This also has the advantage of being a fairly long term solution — the construction boom in the Middle East is likely to go on for at least another 10 or 15 years.

Furthermore, the recent signing of a $150 million contract for electrification in the Asir region of Saudi Arabia suggests that South Korea may be moving from purely intensive labour projects to those that require the sort of technological level usually associated with Japan or the US.[29] Since South Korea's debts to the US and Japan will grow, the export of labour is one way of ensuring that foreign exchange will be available to pay back the loans that keep South Korea tied to imperialism.

Although the export of labour may bring short term advantages to the South Korean economy, it will do nothing to alleviate the plight of the South Korean masses. The outburst of protesting workers in Saudi Arabia, together with the recent surge of the labour movement within South Korea itself suggest that the Korean mercenary state may meet increasing resistance to the super-exploitation of workers at home and abroad.

NOTES

1. See Fred Halliday "Labor Migration in the Middle East," *MERIP Reports*, no.59, August, 1977, for a description and discussion of some of the implications of this phenomenon.
2. And not only the oil-producing states. According to *Newsweek* (April 25, 1977), South Korea has offered to train Moroccan troops — currently bogged down in their war with the Polisario guerrillas in the Sahara — in counter-insurgency tactics.
3. *Financial Times*, August 30, 1977.
4. *Far Eastern Economic Review (FEER)*, May 20, 1977.
5. *Middle East Economic Digest (MEED)*, October 10, 1976; *FEER*, October 15, 1976, gives figure of $20·3 million.
6. *Events*, May 20, 1977.
7. *New York Times*, September 24, 1977.
8. *FEER*, May 6, 1977.
9. *FEER*, October 15, 1976.
10. *MEED*, July 16, 1976.
11. *New York Times*, September 24, 1976; *Asian Wall Street Journal*, October 22, 1976.
12. *New York Times*, September 24, 1976.
13. London *Times*, September 26, 1977.
14. *MEED*, July 16, 1976.
15. *MEED*, July 16, 1976; *Asian Wall Street Journal*, October 22, 1976.
16. Park Moon Young, Director for Overseas Co-operation in the Ministry of Construction, quoted in *ibid.*, October 22, 1976.
17. Different versions of this story are in *MEED*, July 16, 1976; *Newsweek*, June 30, 1975, and *Asian Wall Street Journal*, October 22, 1976.

18. Different accounts of the riot are in *MEED*, April 1, and May 6, 1977; *Korean Daily News*, April 6, 1977; *FEER*, May 6, 1977; *Asian Wall Street Journal*, May 11, 1977; *Economist*, May 14, 1977; and *Business Week*, May 16, 1977.
19. *Economist*, May 14, 1977.
20. *Asian Wall Street Journal*, October 22, 1976.
21. *MEED*, July 16, 1976; *Financial Times*, August 30, 1977.
22. *MEED*, April 1, 1977; *Economist*, May 14, 1977.
23. *MEED*, May 27, 1977; *New York Times*, May 21, 1977.
24. *MEED*, July 16, 1976, and October 8, 1976; *New York Times*, September 24, 1976.
25. *FEER*, May 20, 1977.
26. *MEED*, July 16, 1976; *New York Times*, September 24, 1976, quoting the then Minister of Construction Kim Jae Kyu, gives figures of $500–2,000 a month; *Asian Wall Street Journal*, October 22, 1976, says the figures are $300–2,000 a month, with an average wage of $600 a month.
27. *MEED*, May 27, 1977.
28. *Korea Business*, no.11 (1975).
29. *Financial Times*, August 30, 1977.

Section V
Reunification

Chapter 11

Observations on the Presentation and Perception in the West of the Korean People's Struggles

Jon Halliday

In their long struggle for independence and liberation, the Korean people have had minimal understanding and support from peoples in the West. Ignorance and lack of concern with the history and social structure of distant, middle-sized countries like Korea is common enough in the West; but Korea is a special case: in 1945 it was occupied by the US and the USSR without the Korean people being consulted — and manifestly against the desires of the Korean people; in 1948 it was divided on the initiative of the US, with the support of all the leading Western countries; in 1950 sixteen Western and subordinate countries combined to invade it; and the major Western countries have since then constituted an active bloc of support for successive régimes in South Korea. That support has been given by Western governments partly because Western peoples have failed to understand the aspirations of the Korean people for social justice and to support their inalienable right to national self-determination without outside interference.

The central political fact about Korea in 1945 is that it was one country, with an unchallengeable sense of national identity and a heroic left-wing movement that had the support of the overwhelming majority of the population. Unless this is constantly kept in mind, subsequent issues such as how Korea was divided — and therefore how it can be reunified — can easily be distorted or misunderstood. Korea is just as much one country as Vietnam or China. A people's right to unify their country as they see fit is a central principle which was widely recognised in the case of Vietnam prior to 1975; it must be applied equally in the case of Korea.

What are the obstacles to greater understanding of Korea in the West, and how can they be overcome?

First, there is the obstacle of gross ignorance. Some areas are critical for understanding, and being able to adopt a position of solidarity with, the Korean people.

1. In August-September 1945, the Korea people established a broad national administration which had effective control over the entire country.[1] The US, in effect, invaded Korea in September 1945.

2. Both the division of Korea and the establishment of a separate régime in the south in the years 1945–48, and the specific régime set up in Seoul by the US, headed by Syngman Rhee, were opposed by the overwhelming majority of the Korean people; moreover, the proposals which the North Korean government (and pre-DPRK administration) and the South Korean opposition put forward (or endorsed) for preventing the division of the nation demonstrably had the support of the overwhelming majority of Koreans in both north and south throughout the entire period 1945–1950 (i.e. between the Japanese surrender and the start of the Korean War).

3. The Korean War of 1950–53 was a civil war, both ultimately caused by and complicated by large-scale outside intervention. The war cannot be understood without reference to the extensive popular opposition to the US and the Rhee régime throughout the period prior to June 1950 and following. Not only were there widespread urban and rural uprisings, there was also an extensive guerrilla movement, which continued during the post-June 1950 period. As pointed out elsewhere, the invasion by the Western coalition (which included such stalwart defenders of democracy as South Africa) was accompanied by a heavy campaign of misinformation and secrecy. Unfortunately, this campaign was extremely successful. On a simple level, for example, the US-UN side was able successfully to deny that Japanese forces were taking part in the war; yet, in 1973, a high US official revealed publicly that the Japanese had been involved — *and in combat operations*.[2] It is striking that the experience of the Vietnam War, where US mendacity was widely exposed, has not been extended in any meaningful way to Korea, where the United States itself

engaged in direct aggression against a popular movement for independence and social justice from 1945 on. Not the least of the US's achievements has been its relatively successful disqualification of material and information from Korea which challenges the 'orthodox' position. Yet, as time goes by, it can be more easily seen how many crucial elements in the material produced by the South Korean opposition and by the DPRK (North Korea) were unjustifiably ignored. (There is also a major problem of how this information was presented by the DPRK.)

An important further point is that the division of the country and the polarisation of the two régimes, have tended to lead to concentration on these two régimes. This is especially misleading as regards the South, as it tends to lead to a combination of neglect of the South Korean people and assimilation of them to the existing Seoul régime. The South Korean people have never given their support to the Pak régime, which seized power in a putsch and rules by draconian decrees. The South Korean opposition has broad support among all sectors of the population and has kept alive the Korean people's heroic traditions. It deserves the attention and solidarity of the peoples of the West. One of the direst victories of the White and Blue Houses would be if Pak's skullduggery turned the West to either ignorance or neglect of the interests of the Korean people.

The DPRK

Just as the fundamental principles concerning the Korean nation and specific crucial historical facts have been ignored, so the DPRK (Democratic People's Republic of Korea — North Korea) is very little known and understood in the West — far less known and understood than, say, the DRV (North Vietnam) was before the reunification of Vietnam.

The first thing to be said is that the West has made a major contribution to the relative isolation of the DPRK. For half a century up till 1945 Korea was under Japanese colonial domination — endorsed by the Western powers. Under Japanese colonialism, it was extremely difficult for most Koreans to have any contacts with the outside world; members of the Korean diaspora in China and the USSR had contacts there; some other Koreans were in Japan; and a few, like Syngman Rhee, in the US.

When Japanese colonial rule was brought to an end, it was still difficult for Koreans to travel abroad, or for foreigners to visit Korea. The USSR, which had troops in North Korea between 1945 and 1948, was, of course, partly responsible for this; but the main responsibility — both as regards South Korea and for the isolation of the North — belongs with the West.

The isolation of the DPRK is not a minor matter. It has contributed to the lack of understanding in the West not only of the DPRK, but also of Korea as a whole. Given the history of unflagging Western violence against Korea, the suppression and distortion of information, the unrelenting espionage against the DPRK, it is not surprising that the DPRK is overtly suspicious of the West as a whole. This is wholly understandable. The plain fact is that few even of those organisations, groups and individuals in the West who gave understanding and support to the Vietnamese people have done the same for Korea, and the Koreans know it.

As the governments in the West have worked to isolate the DPRK, so the peoples in the West must find ways to break down this isolation.

It seems appropriate to ask the following question: how do most people in the West find out about the DPRK, and what do they know about it? Most people in the West who know anything at all about the DPRK probably do so through advertisements placed in the Western bourgeois press by the DPRK itself. These are almost all either about the personal rôle of Kim Il Sung, or ascribe most of the achievements of the DPRK in high measure, or entirely, to Kim.

The problem can be divided into two parts: 1) defects in the ability of people in the West to *perceive* what is happening in Korea, and why; 2) political practice in the DPRK itself, including the way the DPRK has chosen to present its revolution, not only abroad but also at home.

The failures of Western audiences are generally known, and there is little fundamental disagreement likely on this aspect.

The unparalleled economic and social achievements of the

DPRK (see Ch. 4) are of such magnitude that they clearly entitle the DPRK to a serious and, *prima facie*, sympathetic hearing abroad. This is precisely what the DPRK has not received. The DPRK's achievements would, if better known, receive recognition for what they are: outstanding accomplishments in the face of extremely heavy odds.

The experience of the DPRK is something new. The DPRK had the first ex-colonial revolution. Furthermore, the DPRK claims to belong to the tradition of scientific socialism founded by Marx and Engels. It specifically ascribes its achievements to socialist practice. It must, therefore, be assessed according to the criteria of socialism.

One of the fundamental principles of socialism is that history is made not by individuals, but by the organised masses. There have clearly been new developments in political life in the DPRK — for example, the development of a very large Communist Party, the Korean Workers' Party (KWP), in which about one quarter of the adult population is estimated to have membership.[3] What is most difficult to comprehend is the real relationship between the party and the masses, and between the masses, the party and the top leadership. Some of the information on this is contradictory.

Most official advertisements and publications both internal and external, as well as official descriptions internally, and 'artistic' productions, place overwhelming emphasis on the rôle of one individual, Kim Il Sung. In doing so, they frequently ignore the hard work and creative contributions of the Korean masses as well as the rôle of the KWP. On the other hand, what Kim himself says has quite a different emphasis: he ascribes the DPRK's achievements to the Workers' Party and the people — not to himself.[4]

However, much of the official presentation of political practice in the DPRK clashes with the basic principle of socialism mentioned above — viz., that history is made by the organised masses. The presentation of the achievements of the Korean people and the KWP largely as attributable to Kim personally raises basic questions about both socialism and democracy in the DPRK. These questions have yet to find answers.

Further, the DPRK's practice demonstrates a lack of understanding of the need for *mediations* between two very different political situations. Solidarity involves *mutual* understanding and information. The DPRK's presentation of its case is counter-productive certainly in Britain, and surely in the West as a whole. This is an observation both about the West, and about the DPRK.

The DPRK's presentation of itself is an integral part of its political practise. This practise affects the Korean people as a whole, and therefore, *inter alia*, the possibilities of rousing the solidarity for the Korean people, especially as regards re-unification. It is a tragic fact that the DPRK's presentation of political life in the DPRK has made many people in the West (and elsewhere) hesitate about supporting or endorsing any of its objectives, even concerning a question such as re-unification. The DPRK's presentation of itself is a disservice to itself and to the Korean people as a whole. The comparison between popular support in the West for the Vietnamese people and the lack of such support for the Korean people is self-evident.

Real solidarity requires stating the facts as they are; this is particularly urgent since the unravelling of the situation would be a major blow against the Pak régime. Until these issues are clarified, it is going to be more difficult to combat the Seoul régime. As stated below, the DPRK's position on reunification is practical and widely supported. The DPRK has stated its willingness to envisage the coexistence of two social systems within a Confederation. This laudable position would be immeasurably strengthened by confronting frankly both the dark as well as the bright aspects of Korea's history and politics. Without this, it will be more difficult to rouse solidarity in the West for the reunification of Korea.

NOTES

1. The US Commander, General Hodge, later told a UN Commission that in September 1945 'we came in and found the communists actually ruling and controlling South Korea' (United Nations General

Assembly, *Official Records*, 3rd Session, Supplement no.9 (A/575, Add.2) — *First Part of the Report of the United Nations Temporary Commission on Korea*, Vol.3, Annex 9, p.34); for what Hodge meant by 'communists' see Gunther, cited in n.3 to Ch.1; on the main points immediately following in this chapter, see references in Ch.1 above.

2. James E. Auer, *The Postwar Rearmament of Japanese Maritime Forces, 1945-71* (New York, Praeger, 1973), pp.63-67.

3. See Gordon White, "North Korean Chuch'e: The Political Economy of Independence," *Bulletin of Concerned Asian Scholars*, April-June 1975, for an excellent survey.

4. Some people in the West have suggested that perhaps the DPRK's external propaganda is an 'abberation'. Unfortunately, this is not the case. The external presentation accurately reflects the internal presentation. Yet, this presentation itself does not seem to accord with the facts. In other words, the external propaganda is both 'true' (accurate) and 'false'.

Chapter 12

Reunification:
Problems and Prospects

Gavan McCormack

Korea is one country. Its people shared a common language, political tradition, culture and economy from the time of its unification over 1,300 years ago till its division in 1945. Since then the country has been divided into northern and southern halves. There is no travel or postal and telegraphic communication between the two halves. Millions of families have been separated — in the south alone there are five million families with relatives in the north.[1]

Economically there is a natural complementarity between the two zones. The south has a population approximately double that of the north (34 million to 16 million), living in a smaller but milder, more fertile and less mountainous territory (38,000 square miles to 47,000 square miles). Traditionally the south was agriculturally rich and what heavy industry there was was concentrated in the north. The north is one of the world's top five producers of tungsten, graphite and magnesite, produces considerable quantities of iron and gold, and is especially well endowed with coal and hydroelectric sources of energy supply, while the south is almost totally dependent on imported oil for its energy and also imports most of the raw materials on which its export industry is based.[2] The division of the two sectors is profoundly illogical.

There is an even more profound and tragic absurdity in the way that both natural and human resources that might be productively employed in developing a high standard of living and culture in a united and independent country are now being drained on both sides of the 38th Parallel into the swamp of military spending. The North is believed to possess a combined total of 495,000 men in its three services.[3] Western and South Korean sources estimated that the DPRK was spending about 30 per cent of its budget on defence in the years 1967–1971, but their estimates for later years of 15–17 per cent (1972–1974) tally with recent DPRK figures.[4] The South has 595,000 in its regular services, reserves of over a million, and a para-military force of another two million in a 'Homeland Defence Reserve',[5] not to mention its protecting occupation force of about 40,000 United States troops. Till recently, it had only to meet the cost of feeding and clothing its army — the rest being met by the US. However, the US has gradually put pressure on the Koreans to pay for themselves, at least to pay a good deal more themselves. Thus the percentage of the South Korean budget devoted to the military increased from 28 per cent in 1973 to 34·6 per cent in 1976.[6] Military spending has increased 4-fold since 1972, with a total of $1·5 billion being appropriated for military purposes in 1976.[7] Military spending is a heavy burden on the economies of both sides, which will continue until the problem of reunification is solved.

Unlike Germany, whose division is clearly related to German responsibility for the European war of 1939–1945, and whose neighbours have reason to fear and oppose reunification, Korea has never committed aggression against any of its neighbours, at least until the southern régime hired out troops to the Americans in Vietnam. Korea's tradition, like that of other smaller East Asian states like the Vietnamese, has been one of diplomatic skill and defensive military genius and courage exercised against recurring threats from more powerful neighbours.[8] The division of Korea has been a gross injustice and the rights and interests of its people too long sacrificed to great power interests. Reunification is not only the just and passionate desire of all Koreans, it is also an essential condition for stability and peace in the area.

The division of 1945 was the outcome not of any international agreement but simply of a unilateral decision by the US. Till the end of the war the Allied leaders had been conspicuously vague about their intentions for Korea. At Cairo, in November, 1943, in the absence of the Soviet Union, the intention was proclaimed that '. . . in due course Korea shall become free and independent'; at Yalta, in February, 1945, Stalin gave his informal consent to the idea of a tripartite trusteeship (under Russia, China and the United States). As far as formal international agreements were concerned the matter rested there until December, 1945, when the Moscow meeting of Foreign Ministers from the Soviet Union, Great Britain and the United States resolved 'to re-establish Korea as an independent state on the basis of democratic principles', and recommended 'the setting up of a provisional democratic government at an early date.' By that time, however, the prospect of actually accomplishing this was minimal.

On August 8–9, 1945, the Soviet Red Army entered the war against Japan and quickly penetrated deep into the Korean peninsula. While the nearest American forces were still only on Okinawa, on August 15, the Japanese surrendered, whereupon two decisive initiatives were taken by the United States. First of all, the Truman declaration known as General Order Number 1 designated the 38th Parallel as the line which would divide Russian and American spheres of operation in taking over from the Japanese.[9] According to one source, the decision was reached in the following way:

'Several one-star generals hurried into the Pentagon with the statement, "We have got to divide Korea. Where can we divide it?"

'A colonel with experience in the Far East protested to his superiors, "You can't do that. Korea is a social and economic unit. There is no place to divide it."

'The generals insisted it had to be done. The colonel replied that it could not be done. Their answer was, "We have got to divide Korea, and it has to be done by four o'clock this afternoon".'[10]

The Division of Korea
Senator Symington We go into this country splitting business. . . . First we split Germany. Then we split China. We stay with billions and billions of dollars and hundreds of thousands of people in the case of Germany, China we stay with billions of dollars and thousands of people. Then we split Korea, and stay there with billions of dollars and tens of thousands of military, all at heavy cost to the American taxpayer. Then we split Vietnam. . . . Now we split Laos. . . .

Do you know of any other country we plan to split pretty soon?

Mr Porter (US Ambassador to Seoul) No, sir.

Senator Symington This has been quite an interesting policy, hasn't it, over the years? . . . Our allies don't do (this), nor do our possible enemies. We do it all over the world.

United States Security Agreements and Commitments Abroad, Republic of Korea, Hearings Before the Subcommittee on US Security Agreements and Commitments Abroad of the Committee on Foreign Relations, US Senate, Ninetyfirst Congress, Second Session, 1970, pp.1579–82.

The Russians, despite their militarily strong position in Korea, complied with this American initiative and withdrew their forces behind the 38th Parallel.

Second, the Americans decided to actively oppose all of the progressive forces, including those who had led the resistance to the Japanese.[11] In these two decisions lay the seeds of the subsequent tragedy.

By the end of August, 1945, there were 145 People's Committees in a network throughout the country; centrally there emerged a Committee for the Preparation of Korean Independence (CPKI). On September 6 a Korean People's Republic was proclaimed. It had a comprehensive programme of reforms, including land reform, and punishment of collaborators. Communists were represented in the Committees and in the Government but it was far from being a Communist administration; as a leading non-Communist Korean scholar comments: 'it seems that a serious effort was made to create a workable coalition of all forces to form a government acceptable to the Communists as well as the Nationalists.'[12]

Before the US Commander, General Hodge, even reached Korea, on September 8, 1945, he 'issued a statement saying he regarded the Koreans as "breeds of the same cat as the Japanese" and would deal with them as conquered enemies.'[13] The Japanese colonial authorities were confirmed in power, and Koreans were ordered not to engage in any political activities — even demonstrating for independence was banned.

When Hodge landed at Inchon a delegation from the People's
Republic was there to greet him with flowers. The Japanese
opened up on the welcoming committee, killing five and
wounding nine. Hodge, far from condemning the Japanese,
commended them, and the Korean welcomers were pushed
roughly out of the way.[14] As has been noted elsewhere: 'To
conceive a parallel to this, one would have to envisage the
Allies landing in Yugoslavia in 1945, refusing to deal with
Tito (or even Mihailović), proceeding straight to Belgrade and
reinstating the Nazis and Pavelić in power, bringing the SS out
of prison and arming them to put down demonstrations. . . .'[15]
This was only the start. Throughout the ensuing years, the US
authorities and their client, Syngman Rhee, systematically
waged an all-out campaign of suppression against the democratic movement. In 1947–48, having failed to get the support
they needed *in* Korea, the US decided to split Korea and
shifted the decision to the UN, where there was a solid pro-
Western majority. Throughout this period, the overwhelming
majority of Koreans, North and South, opposed the US-Rhee
move to divide their country. The DPRK consistently opposed the division of the country. And it is out of this combination of the total failure of American policy in the South
and the extensive popular opposition to it, including widespread guerrilla war, that the Korean war comes. It is important to stress, too, that even after the division of Korea
the opposition in the South, which represented the vast
majority of the population, and the DPRK continued to agree
on the same basic principles concerning reunification.[16]

It is commonly thought, however, that whatever the strength
of shared feeling for unity and democracy that existed throughout the peninsula up until 1950, the holocaust of 1950–1953
created such deep bitterness between North and South that
peaceful reunification could only thereafter be regarded as a
distant dream. Yet a careful look at the record since 1953
does not bear this out. Wide popular support for negotiations
with the North on reunification has been expressed in the
South whenever the surface of repression there has been
cracked. April, 1960 to May, 1961 was one such time. The
Syngman Rhee régime was overthrown by a student-led mass
movement for the restoration of democracy which quickly

generated calls for national reconciliation. In May, 1961, a march to Panmunjom was planned by students from North and South, who were to meet there in a demonstration of national unity. On May 19, the day before this was due to take place, a military coup occurred.[17] Pak Chung Hee, one of its leaders and President to this day, wrote later of the reasons for the coup in terms of, *inter alia*, 'naïve students' who 'rashly advocated the opening of unconditional negotiations between South and North Korea at Panmunjom.'[18] Pak's rule quickly cut short both the democratic and reconciliatory aspects of this brief phase.

Again in 1964–65, however, when Pak moved to obtain large-scale financial backing for his régime through 'normalisation' of relations with Japan, mass popular opposition developed. The Japanese settlement was attacked as a mask for Japan's neo-colonial ambitions in South Korea and also on the grounds that it would make reunification more difficult. Demonstrations and active opposition to this treaty involved a total of 3½ million people.[19] The cementing of the Japanese relationship aggravated the contradiction within South Korea between the political/military/business *élite*, who derived enormous benefit from it, and the masses, to whom increasingly unification appeared not only desirable but urgently necessary — the only way out of a dual dependency on the USA and Japan which brought them a steady worsening of their condition.

By the end of the sixties the goal of reunification had gained even stronger support. In effect, Pak could no longer deal with the upsurge in pro-reunification feelings simply with his traditional methods — just doling out prison and death sentences to anyone advocating, or actually making, contact with the North. Thus in 1970, when the opposition candidate in the Presidential elections, Kim Dae Jung, committed himself to seek reunification if elected, 'popular response was so enthusiastic that President Pak, after threatening for a while to prosecute Kim under the Anti-Communist Law, found it expedient to adopt a "me too" strategy.'[20] Pak responded to the oft-repeated northern overtures for talks by allowing limited exchanges between Red Cross delegates at Panmunjom in 1971. Then, in the summer of the following year, after secret exchanges of official representatives between Pyongyang and Seoul at the highest level, the astonishing announcement was made that agreement had been reached on general principles to be observed in working towards reunification.

This was a major and historic breakthrough, and the Joint Communiqué released on this occasion, July 4, 1972, is therefore the crucial document in any subsequent consideration of the question of reunification.[21] 'Big success in promoting mutual understanding' was reached after 'an open-hearted exchange of opinions with the common desire to achieve the peaceful reunification of the country at the earliest possible date'. Three major principles were agreed upon:

'Firstly, reunification should be achieved independently, without reliance upon outside force or its interference;
Secondly, reunification should be achieved by peaceful means, without recourse to the use of arms against the other side;
Thirdly, great national unity should be promoted first of all as one nation, transcending the differences of ideology, ideal (sic) and system.'

A 'North-South Co-ordinating Committee' was set up under the joint chairmanship of Kim Yong Ju, Director of the Organisational Guidance Department of the North Korean Workers Party, and Lee Hu Rak, Director of the South Korean CIA (KCIA), to promote further steps towards unity based on these principles, and in accordance with what was agreed to be 'the unanimous desire of the whole nation which aspires after national reunification'.

Within weeks of the ink drying on this document two men, Pak No-Su and Kim Kyu-Nam, who were alleged to have had contacts with the North *without* official sanction, though no such contacts were ever proved, were executed in Seoul.[22] Arrests were reported of southern citizens who expressed enthusiasm for *rapprochement* with the North, and within a matter of months remaining political freedoms in South Korea were suspended and the *Yushin* system, described in Chapter 7, was inaugurated. This apparently contradictory behaviour by the South, and its rigid stance in negotiations from 1973 to the present, can only mean that it treated the Communiqué

as a device to attempt to disarm the opposition. Because of
the strength of popular feeling in South Korea it was necessary
for the régime to represent itself as standing for reunification;
but, having appropriated the cause of the people, the régime
then went directly against the plain implication of the Communiqué by insisting on maintaining a rabid anti-communist
stance and reinforcing its military machine. However, even
though the Pak régime signed the Agreement out of self-seek-
ing motives and without any intention of honouring it, the
document itself is of historic importance. The fact that it was
signed and the evident wide support it attracted — no opposition was recorded to it at all — provide the clearest indication to date of the unanimity and depth of the desire for
rapprochement that pervades the society of the South as well
as North Korea.

Apart from the invocation of a false 'threat from the north'
to justify police state controls and the progressive militarisation of South Korean society documented elsewhere in this
volume,[23] the official southern stance on unification is at odds
with the 1972 agreement in at least two important respects:
the insistence on the retention of US forces, whether under
UN or US auspices; and the promotion of the idea of dual
entry of North and South into the UN.[24] The question of the
US troops in South Korea was obviously crucial, and it
would seem reasonable to interpret the South's agreement to
the first of the three 1972 principles to mean they would be
withdrawn. However, the South at once advanced a tortuous
interpretation according to which the UN was a 'universal representative body' and therefore not an 'external power' under
the terms of the agreement. Its assessment of the meaning of
the agreement was merely that a period of 'confrontation with
dialogue' was replacing a period of 'confrontation without
dialogue', and anti-communism was reaffirmed as 'our most
basic policy'.[25] The South Korean Prime Minister, Kim Jong
Pil, even said in June, 1975, that 'We cannot look upon the
northern Communists as of the same race as ourselves,'[26] and
in the spring of 1976 a government spokesman stated that
there was no prospect of progress on reunification until 1981,
by which time, he thought, the 1977–1981 Five Year Plan
would have produced a situation of 'absolute pre-eminence' of

South over North.[27] What the Pak régime is pursuing, he made clear, is not reunification, but the chimera of $50 billion worth of exports and a $1,000 *per capita* GNP.

At this point it is necessary to look at the position that has been taken on the issue by the North.

The North's position rests on the rock-solid foundation of its opposition to the original division of the country in 1945–48, its equally incontestable leading role as regards proposals for reunification,[28] and on the demonstrable widespread support for its proposals.

The North has throughout affirmed as its basic principle that a settlement should be negotiated peacefully between the two Korean parties alone, and it has indicated its readiness to negotiate with virtually any Southern representatives at any time.[29] A paraphrased résumé of the main elements of the DPRK position would have to include the following points.

First, Korea is one country; it was divided against the will of its inhabitants by outside forces.

Second, in 1945 and the years following the vast majority of all Koreans showed their unmistakable desire for radical social and political change. In spite of decades of US interference, the Syngman Rhee and Pak client régimes have not been able to alter the *basic* social and political orientation of the Korean people. The Seoul régime is both illegitimate and unrepresentative.

Thus, the North both has to deal with the *de facto* government in the South, and at the same time ensure that it is not excluded from contacts with the people of the South. It has had to walk a difficult line between pragmatism (dealing with Pak and the KCIA) and its own just concern not to be cut off from the people of the South. The North has a right to be concerned about what happens in the South, it *has* to make this concern clear, and yet, equally, it cannot let Pak and the US simply get away with calling this 'interference in the internal affairs of the South.'[30] These problems come out clearly in the negotiations which opened in 1971 between Pyongyang and Seoul, culminating in the July 4, 1972 Joint Communiqué discussed above.

The record of attempts to implement and go beyond the principles agreed in the Communiqué is unambiguous. On procedural matters the South has concentrated on trying to limit the scope both of the matters for discussion and of representation at the talks. For example, on the problem of separated families the South ruled out an exchange of Red Cross missions to carry out independent investigations and would allow instead only written applications, later attempting further to limit this to 'separated elderly persons'. On the question of representation at the talks, the North proposed broadening these 'by the inclusion of representatives of all political parties and other social organisations in North and South' and that a 'Political Consultative Conference consisting of People's representatives and operating independently from the NSCC (North-South Co-ordinating Committee) should be established.' The South rejected these proposals as a complication.[31]

It is not difficult to see why the North wishes to expand the talks. Not only has the Pak régime been exploiting the talks to tighten repression in the South — about which the North has shown concern; the North also has to try to find some way round the fact that talking to the Director of the KCIA and his aides means talking to representatives of the régime, but *non*-representatives of the people.[32]

As on procedural matters, so too on the fundamental question of a strategy for the achievement of reunification serious proposals based on the 1972 agreement have been made by the DPRK (and separately by the Southern opposition). In March, 1973 the DPRK representatives put forward the following proposals at the 2nd Session of the North-South Coordinating Committee:

1. To cease armament reinforcements and the arms race.
2. To withdraw all foreign troops.
3. To reduce the armed forces in the North and the South to 100,000 men or less each, and to drastically cut their armaments.
4. To stop the introduction of all weapons, combat equipment and war material from abroad.
5. To conclude a peace agreement guaranteeing that the above-mentioned problems shall be solved and that the North and the South shall not use armed force against each other.[33]

These five points were repeated by Kim Il Sung in a speech

in June of the same year.[34] The southern President, Pak Chung Hee, gave his reaction to these proposals in a Press Conference in January, 1974.[35] He summed up the northern proposals as 'directed to withdrawing the US forces from Korea, reducing armed forces, banning the introduction of arms from outside and scrapping the armistice.'[36] Except for the last phrase, this was a reasonably accurate summary, but Pak went on to complain, significantly, that they were therefore 'intending to make the South impotent and disarm it so as to realise the Communists' scheme.' Pak's reaction here reveals perhaps more than he intended — exposing in particular the highly significant difference in the two régimes' thinking on the question of dependence/independence. The one clinging to foreign troops, foreign suppliers of weapons and foreign political backing; the other, with no foreign troops stationed on its soil since 1958 and no significant military aid and, as the southerners recently complained, able to develop its industrial base to the point of independently producing battleships and submarines, and, by 1978, MIG fighters.[37]

Pak's objection that 'the contents of their peace proposal call for withdrawal of foreign troops and reducing to 100,000 or less the military forces of each side', an incomprehensible *objection* at first glance, becomes perfectly understandable once this difference is grasped. The southern régime, in taking this position, is clearly in breach of the commitment it made in the 1972 July Communiqué, and its intransigence on this point has been a key factor in reducing the North-South talks to deadlock. A recent analysis of the talks in the respected academic journal, *Pacific Affairs*, reaches the same conclusion:

'Moreover, President Pak's statements on his "unification" policy, when he has no such policy at all, may be characterized as mere rhetoric; such assertions merely reflect the Seoul régime's acute dilemma, being caught between the growing nationalistic aspiration for unification and Pak's apprehension of its realization. Still more, his emphasis since the Vietnam debacle on self-reliance for South Korea, when its very survival is dependent upon continued even stronger American support, is ludicrous. . . .

The North Korean régime, on the other hand, has been

persistently demanding unification coupled with proposals consistent for its realization. Seemingly, it is confident of the outcome of a negotiated unification.'[38]

Analysis of the respective North/South positions since 1972 on the principle of 'Great National Unity' reinforces this judgement. This principle, if it means anything, must mean tolerance of the different social systems — capitalism in the South[39] and socialism in the North. No spokesman for the southern régime has yet indicated readiness to accept the legitimacy of communism in the North, and indeed, as noted above, the southern régime's hostility goes beyond rejection of the North's ideology to denial that Koreans of the North are of the same race. The North, on the other hand, has repeatedly called for the establishment of democracy in the South, and declared its readiness to coexist with the different social system in the South. Since it argues that full political, economic and social integration of the two separately developed systems must take time, it has also made proposals for transitional forms through which 'Great National Unity' might be expressed during that interim period. One such is the idea of 'Koryo'.

Koryo is the name proposed by the North for a Confederal Republic to be made up of the two sectors of the country. The idea was first enunciated in 1960, the name in 1972.[40] Koryo has rich historical overtones in Korea, since it is the name of the régime which held sway throughout the peninsula between the years 935 to 1392, a period in which foreign conquest was successfully resisted and in which cultural and technical attainments were remarkable. The Koryo idea has been voiced a number of times by Kim Il Sung, but originally in the following way: 'The Confederation we propose means forming a supreme national council with representatives of the governments of North and South Korea mainly for the purpose of jointly consulting about questions for the national interests of Korea and co-ordinating them in a uniform way, while maintaining the present different political systems of North and South Korea as they are for the time being.' Kim also said, 'We have no intention to impose our socialist system on South Korea. If the present rulers of South Korea do not force us to change our socialist system, there can be no reason why we do not achieve national unity. . . . It is possible that a country may have various political systems.'[41]

The 'Supreme National Council' envisaged as the official co-ordinating body would have to be complemented, according to Kim, by a 'Great National Assembly', which would provide a forum for contact between members of 'political parties and social organisations of South and North Korea'.[42] Emphasis on this need for a broadening of the basis of North-South contacts has increased in proportion as the Pak régime has heightened repression and consolidated its Yushin brand of dictatorship.

The 'Koryo' idea might present problems in operation. It is, however, at least a serious proposal for the implementation of the 1972 Agreement, and Kim Il Sung has made it clear that he does not expect northern proposals only to be considered, but would welcome alternative southern proposals based on the principles already agreed.[43] Unfortunately, the counter-proposals from the South are either very difficult to reconcile with the principle of 'Great National Unity' — like separate entry into the UN, for example — or else at odds with the principle of the independent solution to the problem — as, for example, the proposal for a North-South non-aggression pact and Korea-wide elections while existing military alliances, foreign troops and nuclear weapons remain in place.[44] It is difficult to resist the conclusion that such proposals are no more than window-dressing for continuing the South's same rigid anti-communist and anti-reconciliationist policies.

The situation, therefore, is as follows. The southern régime is bent on the elimination of communism in both North and South — the Anti-Communist Law and the constant use of war scares to promote a war-time spirit of national mobilisation are basic to the present structure, while the northern régime calls continuously for the establishment of democracy in Seoul. The northern position on negotiations has hardened perceptibly as political repression has worsened in the South, and in March, 1976, Kim Il Sung declared that the dialogue would only be resumed when 'the South Korean authorities stop suppressing democratic figures, release the arrested and detained student youths and patriotic figures, put an end to fascist rule, take the road of democracy . . .'[45] Yet it is clear that the prospects of the Pak régime simply stepping aside and dismantling the *Yushin* system are minimal. For this reason the North has stepped up its approaches to the US in an attempt to negotiate a bilateral peace treaty and secure the withdrawal of US troops that way.[46] The US, however, is unlikely to simply abandon its protégés in Seoul, and has so far refused direct negotiation with Pyongyang.

Beneath the frozen surface of formal political life in South Korea, however, changes are taking place. The régime is increasingly at odds with its people. The democratic opposition has on countless occasions made clear that it is committed to working towards reunification and that it regards the 1972 Agreement as the basis for doing so. The March 1, 1976, Declaration for Democratic National Salvation signed by the outstanding religious and political figures of South Korean society and issued in Myong Dong cathedral in Seoul proclaimed National Unification to be the supreme task,[47] and the former South Korean Observer at the United Nations, Channing Liem, has written as follows:[48]

'To be sure, there are some among the South Koreans whose yearning for unification is tempered by fear of Communism; yet, in the face of the stark prospect that in a divided Korea they would not only lose their freedom to the Pak tyranny, but also lose their country to alien masters, more and more of them are beginning to realise that unification must take priority over all else.'

The difficulties involved in achieving reunification are obviously considerable. But there are two levels of difficulty that should be distinguished. One is that of removing the barriers preventing the Korean people of North and South being able to sit around a table without outside interference to discuss reunification. The main barriers to this are South Korea's military and economic ties to the United States, Japan and other advanced capitalist countries, not with the Korean people. The second level of difficulty concerns the problems of reunifying two societies that have developed for thirty years along such different lines. But this is a problem which the Korean people alone can solve, and if left alone, surely will.

NOTES

1. Research Center for Peace and Unification (Seoul), *The Challenge of Peaceful Unification* (Seoul, 1976), p.6.
2. Basic data here derived from Gerhard Breidenstein and W. Rosenberg, "Economic Comparison of North and South Korea," *Journal of Contemporary Asia*, Vol.5, no.2 (1975), p.167; AKFIC (American-Korean Friendship and Information Center), *Korea: Uneasy Truce in the Land of the Morning Calm* (New York, 1976), pp.8–9.
3. International Institute for Strategic Studies, *The Military Balance, 1976–77*, (London, 1976), p.57.
4. 1967–1974 figures from Donald S. Zagoria and Young Kun Kim, "North Korea and the Major Powers," in William J. Barnds, ed., *The Two Koreas in East Asian Affairs* (New York University Press, 1976), p.35 (from South Korean sources cited *ibid.*); DPRK figures in April 1976 Report on the Budget to the People's Assembly. Other figures in Center for Defense Information, *The Defense Monitor*, Vol.5, no.1, January, 1976, Washington, p.4; Sumiya Mikio, *Kankoku no keizai (The Economy of South Korea)*, (Tokyo, 1976), p.221.
5. *The Military Balance, 1976–77*, p.57.
6. Sumiya, p.222.
7. Sam Jameson, *Guardian*, November 4, 1975; *The Defense Monitor*, cit., p.4. A 10 per cent income surtax and a whole range of other surtaxes were introduced in South Korea in mid-1975 in order to raise an additional $413 million annually towards this military bill. *FEER*, August 1, 1975.
8. For a fine general account of Korean history: Takashi Hatada, *A History of Korea* (Santa Barbara, California, 1969).
9. Jon Halliday, "The Korean Revolution," *Three Articles on the Korean Revolution 1945–1953* (London, Association for Radical East Asian Studies, 1972), pp.1–3, and *Socialist Revolution* (San Francisco), Vol.1, no.6 (1970), pp.96ff. Gabriel Kolko, *The Politics of War: Allied Diplomacy and the World Crisis of 1943–45* (London, Weidenfeld & Nicolson, 1969), p.600.
10. John Gunther, *The Riddle of MacArthur* (London, 1951), p.163.
11. Halliday, "The Korean Revolution," pp.6–7; Soon Sung Cho, *Korea in World Politics: An Evaluation of American Responsibility* (Berkeley and Los Angeles, University of California Press, 1967).
    World Politics: *An Evaluation of American Responsibility* (Berkeley and Los Angeles, University of California Press, 1967).
12. Dae-Sook Suh, *The Korean Communist Movement 1918–1948* (Princeton University Press, 1967), pp.298–9; Carl Berger, *The Korea Knot* (Philadelphia, 1957), pp.51–52.
13. Robert T. Oliver, *Syngman Rhee: The Man Behind the Myth* (London, Robert Hall, Ltd, 1955), p.202.
14. Oliver, *ibid.*, p.203.
15. Halliday, "The Korean Revolution," p.7.
16. See Ch.1 for the April 1948 Conference in Pyongyang and references there; cf. Joyce and Gabriel Kolko, *The Limits of Power: The World and United States Foreign Policy, 1945–1954* (New York, Harper & Row, 1972), Ch.21, on the extent to which the US-Rhee posture was

undermined by the DPRK's strong position on reunification immediately prior to the outbreak of war.

17. John Kie-chiang Oh, *Korea: Democracy on Trial* (Ithaca, Cornell University Press, 1968), pp.89ff.
18. Pak Chung Hee, *To Build A Nation* (Washington, 1971), p.96.
19. Kwan Bong Kim, *The Korea-Japan Treaty Crisis and the Instability of the Korean Political System* (New York, Praeger, 1971), p.116.
20. Channing Liem, "Kan-bei kankei no shinwa to genjitsu" (Myths and Realities of Relations between the United States and South Korea), *Sekai*, February, 1976, p.69; in English in *Korean Studies* (Tokyo), Vol.1, no.2, (February, 1976), pp.24–39. The author was South Korea's observer at the UN with the rank of Ambassador between 1960 and 1961.
21. The wording of the English text of the agreement varies significantly in different sources. This version is from *Peking Review*, no.28 (July 14, 1972), and is the official North Korean English-language version which, even according to the US government publication, *Problems of Communism* (Vol.22, no.1, January-February, 1973, p.69), 'seems most faithful to the Korean-language original'.
22. *Ronin*, Vol.1, no.4 & 5 (August 1972), pp.9–10; no.6 (September 1972), pp.2–3.
23. See chapter 3.
24. Statement by Pak Chung Hee, June 23, 1973 (*The Challenge of Peaceful Unification*, pp.14–15).
25. Lee Hu Rak, press conference, July 4, 1972, in *Confrontation with Dialogue* (Seoul, 1972).
26. "Dokyumento," *Sekai*, September 1975, p.206.
27. "Dokyumento," *Sekai*, May 1976, p.263.
28. For the major ones to 1972, see *Korea Focus*, Vol.1, no.2 (Spring 1972), pp.20–22.
29. The only exceptions have been notorious collaborators with the Japanese, or corrupt figures like Syngman Rhee who were specifically excluded by the North from discussions proposed on the eve of the Korean War in 1950. The grand total of those excluded came to seven people.
30. For example, the North felt — understandably — that Pak's decision to sell Korean troops to the US for use in Vietnam was something which affected all the Korean people, the question of reunification and the future of the Korean nation. On another level, it is clear that the North has a special political relationship with the Revolutionary Party for Reunification;* set up in the South in 1964. Cf. no.39 on the question of the DPRK's analysis of the social system in the South. * Not to be confused with the alleged 'People's Revolutionary Party' (see chapter 3).
31. Koon Woo Nam, "North-South Korean Relations: From Dialogue to Confrontation," *Pacific Affairs*, Vol.48, no.4 (Winter 1975–76), pp.479, 484, 485.
32. Prior to the 1972 talks, the North had insisted strongly on an end to the repression in the South as a precondition for negotiations. It has been suggested that the democratic forces in the South were uneasy at the welcome given by Kim Il Sung to Lee Hu Rak; it is understandable

that the pictures, released by the DPRK, of Kim smiling broadly with Lee at a time when Lee was responsible for unspeakable atrocities, caused concern among the southern opposition. The North has since returned to a much tougher line on the question of repression in the South (cf. below).

33. Quoted in *Memorandum on the Question of the Independent and Peaceful Reunification of Korea*, document prepared by the Delegation of Inquiry of the International Association of Democratic Lawyers, September 1974, p.11.

34. On June 23, 1973 — i.e. on the same day as the statement by Pak Chung Hee cited in note 24 above. Text of Kim's speech in *Korea Focus*, Vol.2, no.2 (September 1973), pp.8–10.

35. *The Challenge of Peaceful Reunification*, p.29.

36. The North does not want to 'scrap' the Armistice; it wants to convert it into a lasting peace agreement. The key point here, which Western sources tend to obscure, is that when the Armistice was signed in 1953, *South Korea refused to sign it.* The US (backed by Britain) is now trying to use this as an argument *against* renegotiating the Armistice — on the grounds that if the US/UN left, there would be no force in South Korea which had signed the Armistice. (The same argument was used in Vietnam.) The DPRK argues that it wants to reach an agreement with the US for the withdrawal of US forces, and will then negotiate autonomously with Seoul. Cf. below.

37. According to an announcement from the South Korean authorities on October 16, 1975 ("Dokyumento," *Sekai*, January 1976, p.29).

38. Nam, "North-South Korean Relations," p.498.

39. The analysis of the class structure of the South is a crucial issue in considering reunification, and the possibility of a Confederation. In his interview with Harrison Salisbury in 1972, Kim Il Sung stated that: 'We do not see South Korea as a complete capitalist society. . . . We can say South Korean society is no more than a society which is just starting to take the road of capitalism or worshipping capitalism or something like that.' (*Korea Focus*, Vol.1, no.3, p.16.)

40. For the 1960 proposals, see Kwan Bong Kim, *The Korea-Japan Treaty Crisis*, p.232; Rinn-sup Shinn, "Changing Perspectives in North Korea: Foreign and Reunification Policies," *Problems of Communism*, January-February 1973, p.58.

41. Kim Il Sung interview with Harrison Salisbury of the *New York Times*, May 26, 1972. *New York Times*, May 31, 1972. Also *Korea Focus*, Vol.1, no.3.

42. Speech of June 23, 1973, cited above, note 34. Another description of this body, substantially the same, in *New York Times* 1972 interview (see note 41).

43. Interview with Yasue Ryosuke, Editor of the Japanese magazine *Sekai*, March 28, 1976, *Sekai*, June, 1976, p.132.

44. Pak Chung Hee proposals of August 15, 1974, *The Challenge of Peaceful Unification*, pp.32–3; essentially the same terms repeated in interview with an Egyptian newspaper on January 22, 1976, "Dokyumento," *Sekai*, May, 1976, p.253.

45. In interview cited in note 44, above.

46. From March, 1974. See Shapiro, p.347.
47. English text in *Ampo*, Vol.8, no.1, 1976, pp.40–41.
48. *Sekai*, February, 1976, p.69.

Bibliography

1. Selected Books

Frank Baldwin, ed., *Without Parallel: The American-Korean Relationship Since 1945* (New York: Pantheon, 1973).

William J. Barnds, ed., *The Two Koreas in East Asian Affairs* (New York: NY University Press, 1976).

Ellen Brun & Jacques Hersh, *Socialist Korea* (New York: Monthly Review, 1977).

Wilfred Burchett, *Again Korea* (New York: International Publ. Co., 1968).

Joseph Chung, *The North Korean Economy* (Stanford: Stanford University Press, 1974).

Gregory Henderson, *Korea: The Politics of the Vortex* (Cambridge, Mass: Harvard Univ. Press, 1968).

Journal of Contemporary Asia (Stockholm: Box 49010, Sweden), Vol.5, no.2, 1975), special issue on Korea.

T.K., *Letters from South Korea*, edited by Sekai and translated by D. Swain (Tokyo: Iwanami Shoten, 1976).

Kim Il Sung, *Selected Works* (Pyongyang: Foreign Languages Publishing House, 1971–), Vols.1–5.

Kim Byong Sik, *Modern Korea: The Socialist North, Revolutionary Perspectives in the South, and Unification* (New York, 1970).

Chung Kyung Mo, *The People vs. Park Chung Hee* (Tokyo: 1976). (Available from National Times, 3-6-8 Kanda Ogawamachi, Chiyoda-Ku, Tokyo, Japan.)

Koon Woo Nam, *The North Korean Communist Leadership, 1945–65* (Alabama Univ. Press, 1974).

Robert Scalapino & Chong-Sik Lee, *Communism in Korea* (Berkeley: Univ. of California Press, 1972), 2 Vols.

Robert Simmons, *The Strained Alliance* (Glencoe: Free Press, 1975).

I. F. Stone, *The Hidden History of the Korean War* (New York: *Monthly Review*, 1952, 1970).

Dae-Sook Suh, *The Korean Communist Movement, 1918–48* (Princeton: Princeton Univ. Press, 1967).

Cho Soon Sung, *Korea in World Politics 1940–50: An Evaluation of American Responsibility* (Berkeley: Univ. of Calif. Press, 1967).

Nam, Koon Woo, *The North Korean Communist Leadership, 1945–65* (Alabama Univ. Press, 1974).

2. Selected Journals

Ampo: Japan-Asia Quarterly Review (1969–), PO Box 5250 Tokyo International. This has regularly published incisive critical analyses of contemporary Asian affairs and has been particularly good on Korea and US-Japan-Korea relations.

Journal of Korean Affairs, Research Institute on Korean Affairs, 9555 16th St., Silver Spring, Maryland 20910, USA. The principal US establishment journal.

Korea Commentary (1977–), the bi-monthly successor to *Korea Bulletin* and *Korea Link* (1974–76), available from US-Korea Research and Action Committee, PO Box 24175, Oakland, CA 94101, USA. Reportage on US-Korea relations and on developments in the North and South.

Korea Communique (1976–), C/O NCC-Japan, No.24, 2–3–18 Nishi Waseda, Shinjuku-ku, Tokyo 160, Japan. Monthly reportage and documentation highlighting the resistance in South Korea, particularly the Christian anti-Pak resistance.

Korean Review (1977–), International Society for Korean Studies, Post Restante Item Toshima Post Office, Tokyo 170, Japan; bi-monthly documentation on both the North and South and on US-Japan-Korea relations.

Korean Studies (1976–), International Affairs Bureau, Central Standing Committee of Chongryun (the pro-DPRK General Association of Korean Residents in Japan). Irregular. Predominantly reprints of press accounts and speeches relating to Korea.

North Korea Quarterly (1975–), Institute of Asian Affairs,

Rothenbaumchaussee 32, D–2000 Hamburg 13, West Germany. Comprehensive documentary record in English with articles on the DPRK, some translated from Japanese. Other basic periodical sources include: *Far Eastern Economic Review*, a Hong Kong-based weekly news magazine; *Asia Research Bulletin* of Singapore, a monthly; *Journal of Contemporary Asia* (see list of books); *Bulletin of Concerned Asian Scholars*, a quarterly (PO Box W, Charlemont, MA. 01339, USA).

Contributors

MALCOLM CALDWELL: Lecturer in the Economic History of East and South-east Asia, School of Oriental & African Studies, University of London; Editor, *Journal of Contemporary Asia*.

WALTER EASEY: Secretary of the Hong Kong Research Project, London; Fellow of Transnational Institute.

AIDAN FOSTER-CARTER: Lecturer in Sociology, University of Leeds; author of several articles on Marxist theories of development.

JOHN GITTINGS: Senior Lecturer in Chinese, School of Languages, Polytechnic of Central London; regular contributor to the *Guardian*, author of *The World and China 1922-1972* (1975).

JON HALLIDAY: Author of *A Political History of Japanese Capitalism* (1975) and co-author of *Japanese Imperialism Today* (1973); articles on Korea in *Bulletin of Concerned Asian Scholars, Socialist Revolution* etc.

GAVAN McCORMACK: Lecturer in History, Latrobe University, Australia; Secretary-General, Korea Committee of Great Britain; author of *Chang Tso-lin in Northeast China, 1911-1928* (1977), and co-author of *Japanese Imperialism Today* (1973).

MARK SELDEN: Associate Professor of History, Washington University (St Louis); author of *The Yenan Way in Revolutionary China, Remaking Asia: Essays on the American Uses of Power* and the forthcoming Monthly Review Press book, *The People's Republic of China. Documentary History.*

YOUNGJA YANG: Member of Korea Committee of Great Britain; research student in politics.